# START YOUR OWN

# WHOLESALE DISTRIBUTION BUSINESS

**Entrepreneur**
MAGAZINE'S

**STARTUP**

# START YOUR OWN

# WHOLESALE DISTRIBUTION BUSINESS

Fourth Edition

## YOUR STEP-BY-STEP GUIDE TO SUCCESS

The Staff of Entrepreneur Media, Inc. & Christopher Matthew Spencer

Entrepreneur Press®

Publisher: Entrepreneur Press
Cover Design: Andrew Welyczko
Production and Composition: Eliot House Productions

This publication is designed to provide accurate and authoritative information in regard to the subject matter covered. It is sold with the understanding that the publisher is not engaged in rendering legal, accounting, or other professional services. If legal advice or other expert assistance is required, the services of a competent professional person should be sought.

Entrepreneur Press® is a registered trademark of Entrepreneur Media, Inc.

An application to register this book for cataloging has been submitted to the Library of Congress.

ISBN 978-1-59918-671-9 (paperback) | ISBN 978-1-61308-428-1 (ebook)

Printed in the United States of America

25  24  23  22  21                                             10 9 8 7 6 5 4 3 2 1

# Contents

Chapter 4

# Raising Money . . . . . . . . . . . . . . . . . . . . . . . . . . . . . . 63

Chapter 5

# Setting Up Shop. . . . . . . . . . . . . . . . . . . . . . . . . . . . . . . 81

## Chapter 10
# Getting the Word Out. . . . . . . . . . . . . . . . . . . . . . . . . . . 159

## Chapter 11
# Interviews with the Experts. . . . . . . . . . . . . . . . . . . . 175

# Preface

Thank you for taking the time to read this book. I am delighted that you have made a commitment to explore the world of wholesale distribution. If you're new to wholesale distribution, let me briefly explain. A true wholesale distributor acquires products from factories and ships them to retailers at wholesale prices. Factories are masters of product manufacturing, while wholesale distributors are sales and distribution experts. Factories can work with internal salespeople and handle their own wholesaling. Some factories prefer to deal with third-party wholesalers, which allows them to move product out of their facility quickly and assign the sales and logistics work to someone else. Other product makers have both internal teams and work with distributors.

I know these relationships and this field well. Starting in 1988, I owned a company that managed a busy warehouse with over 6,000 stock-keeping units. From 2001 to 2008, I traveled the world while educating businesses of all sizes on the use of eBay as a wholesale distribution platform (yes, you can sell pallets and truckloads on eBay). I later worked for Freeman, one of the largest logistics companies in the world, helping wholesale distribution companies. For many years now, I have had the honor and privilege of supporting licensed product development for Kathy Ireland and her company *kathy ireland®* *Worldwide*. Kathy went from "the beach to the boardroom" and her brainchild *kathy ireland®* *Worldwide* now designs and develops consumer products that are distributed to an incredible number of retail stores, reaching over 60,000 storefronts. For over 30 years, I have been involved in every facet of wholesale distribution. I've seen operations as small as a bedroom and warehouses as large as Hangar 51 (the endlessly massive fictional storage facility seen at the end of *Raiders of the Lost Ark).*

Not only have I been fortunate in business, but I have also sent the elevator down to educate thousands of eager learners who sought out my business expertise. This (and every business) requires focus, patience, and discipline. As a Navy veteran, I developed these three skills to the level of mastery.

So, why get into wholesale? Becoming a wholesaler is a great way to make money. Wholesalers with solid sales and business skills will score the best deals from manufacturers and good prices from buyers—but these skills are not innate in the average person and can be learned.

## Why Now?

Things have changed a lot since I typed up my first wholesale invoice back in 1988. I used computers back then, but they didn't connect to the internet. People did a lot of work over the phone, and long-distance calls were very expensive. Now, it's easier and cheaper to start a company than it was in the past. Work is untethered, and people meet digitally. The ubiquitous use of email gradually sent millions of fax machines to landfills. Entrepreneurs have learned to do way more with far less. A wholesaler can work in their *Iron Man* slippers while a warehouse worker at Amazon palletizes and ships their customers' orders by truck. Shared resources have become the norm. Fewer companies own their own vehicles. More companies seek out shipping discounts using apps and sites. Alibaba, Amazon, and other massive companies make product sourcing and price transparency instantaneous.

In addition, there's an endless number of product categories that open up the opportunity for you to start a wholesale distribution sales business. While having working capital can never hurt, strong relationships with factories will allow you credit terms to score sales before the bill comes due. Manufacturers struggle without strong distribution networks, so being in the wholesale business isn't brain surgery. Learning this trade and working hard will bring you to the front door of success.

The companies that buy from distributors depend on the expertise of those distributors. Factories are busy and typically can't give the proper focus to every retailer. When territories are divided and covered by multiple wholesale distributors, expanding into global markets becomes a reality. Wholesaling or distributing isn't limited to bulk sales to retailers. The array of customers includes professional business users (large companies) and commercial, institutional (such as hospitals), and industrial buyers.

## Opportunities Are Everywhere

There has never been a better day than *today* to start a wholesale distribution business. You're never too young (I formed my first corporation when I was 18 years old), and you are never too old to become an entrepreneur. You do need grit—courage, resolve, and strength of character. You'll also need to conduct yourself with integrity so that people will trust you and want to work with you over and over again. So, what are you waiting for?

While you may elect to work directly with cross-border factories, most of your buyers will be within trucking (or train) distance from you. You might fly things to your buyers if they are light and really expensive—or perishable (such as baked goods or live lobsters), but it is likely that most of what you will do will occur on your own continent. There are millions of dollars to be earned in just your local trading area and billions of dollars' worth of commerce awaiting you in your own country. The future looks very bright. In the time I've been in business, America added 78 million more people. That's 78 million more buyers of cars and car accessories, food, sporting goods, fashion, books, movies, collectibles, art, toys, health and beauty products, electronics, business and industrial equipment, and so much more.

Imagine the business opportunities that unfold for just one product. A single car has about 30,000 individual parts, considering everything that it takes to make a car, down to the very smallest fastener. The bestselling American car is the Toyota Camry. You read that right—the Camry is an American-made car that's assembled in Georgetown, Kentucky. The Camry is the most "American-made" vehicle. The American-made index factors the percentage of domestic parts content in a vehicle, where it's built, and how many are sold.

That means a plethora of factories in the good ol' U.S. of A. are designing Camry parts, tooling their factories to make those parts, and pumping out the very components needed to put these Camry vehicles together. What if a new player wants to break into the business of selling to the Camry assembly line? That company will need a wholesale distributor to break the ice, wine and dine the purchasing agent, and manage the paperwork after scoring a big purchase order.

Profits must be top-of-mind for every businessperson. When you start a new business, focus on a few things and do them well in order to become profitable as quickly as possible. Profit is necessary to avoid bankrupting your business. You need not be the best—in truth, you do not need to even be *great* at all—just consistently good at what you are doing in order to maintain a business from inception to long-term profitability. I achieved this by being consistent and sticking with my plan and my process. If you're panicking about the riptide of competition that will pull you underwater, nothing could be further from the truth. As the population continues to grow at a stellar clip, your opportunities are increasing at a phenomenal pace. Sleep soundly tonight because the role of the wholesale distributor is assured now and far into the future. We will not see obsolescence set in, and extinction will not occur for this business species. Factories flourish at making products and will continue to rely on the expertise of distributors to act on their behalf in handling the rest of the product journey after it leaves their facility. While the Camry has thousands of parts, you could start a profitable business selling something as focused as O-rings—a gasket that seals two parts (such as hoses) together.

## What to Expect in This Book

This book is a primer—a nitty-gritty blueprint for running a wholesale distribution business. It takes you step by step through the entire process of setting up your business and making it a fantastic success. If you think you're already an expert on what's covered in any particular chapter, feel free to skip that chapter. It's all here—the nuts and bolts of starting and running your own successful company. So have a seat, whether it be at your kitchen table or the desk in your 100,000-square-foot warehouse, and read on.

In this book, you will find:

► An introduction to the wholesale business and tips on structuring your company
► My recommended methods for researching your market and bringing your plan into focus
► Proven ideas for raising startup capital and managing your money
► Ways to approach sourcing and inventory management

- ▶ Time-tested blueprints for optimizing operations and staffing
- ▶ Marketing methods that accelerate your business and propel sales forward
- ▶ And some sage wisdom from wholesale and industry experts

This book is a wellspring of knowledge that's been distilled down from my three decades of wholesale experience as well as ideas shared with me from other wholesale distributors (as well as manufacturers and other people in business) along the way.

In my long business career, I've enjoyed excellent fortune in trading wholesale and have bought and sold enough goods to fill a container ship several times over. I have also consulted to wholesalers large and small, helping to elevate their success in this flourishing industry.

I welcome you into my circle of friends. Please feel free to write to me with your very own tips, ideas, and personal success stories. Know that I am accessible, and I welcome interaction with you. Not only can you find me on social media @borntodeal, but you are always welcome to email me at borntodeal@gmail.com.

You have begun a unique and fascinating journey, and I'm honored to be your guide through this valuable educational experience. We'll have plenty of fun working together as I show you the ropes. With your enthusiasm and a bit of patience and determination, you too will be operating your very own wholesale distribution empire. You will become your own boss. It is time to claim your piece of this growing opportunity.

# Introduction to Wholesale Distribution

Commerce has been around since antiquity, and at that time, people traded surplus livestock and products in barter transactions to acquire animals and goods they lacked. Barter was first recorded in ancient Egypt. Later, money became the primary medium for trade. Today, many folks still barter (in an effort to dodge the tax bite from the government), but most wholesaling involves currency. Wholesalers have a unique position in the markets they serve and engage more intimately with retailer customers than the factories they serve.

A factory has a limited number of products it produces. It takes time to design and build products. Some factories have internal sales teams. For other producers of goods, dealing with the sales cycle is a distraction for the core business of design and fabrication.

Wholesale distributors, on the other hand, are nimble, immune to the costs associated with trying out new product lines, and can amortize their sales costs across more products than factories. This is the reason manufacturers prefer to delegate the financing and distribution processes to wholesalers.

So, that's good news for anyone who wants to start a new wholesale business. While the five-year survival rate for startups is just over 50 percent on average, do not be alarmed by that figure. I see the cup as *half full*. I have been in business since 1988, and based on my observations, most business failures are preventable by applying success models and common sense. Undue expectations and lack of grit account for a notable number of quitters. For example, if you're stubbornly insistent about facing off against big-box retailers, stop now and move on to another book—that will not work. A niche business and a novel approach is what you need.

In fact, you'll discover that finding a niche is the best way to make a name for yourself in wholesale. You can't be all things to all people, so specializing will be essential to making your mark on the industry. What *could* be the ideal niche opportunity? Think of products that are purchased by people who have disposable income to spend on *stuff*. For example, horse owners will pay top-dollar for unique equestrian-related items such as apparel, accessories, and tack. Hunters spend huge money on decoys, supplies, and gear. The car enthusiast is always tinkering with their classic vehicle and needs replacement parts.

The National Association of Wholesale-Distributors (NAW) boasts that the wholesaler-distributor business activity represents 29 percent of GDP. That's a compelling reason to venture into your own business and I'm going to help you elevate your understanding of this opportunity. Whether you want to dabble or are ready for big-time wheeling and dealing, there's room for you in wholesaling. Whatever your individual situation, whether wholesale freshman or longtime veteran, you read this far because you are looking for something—a revelation of some sort. While it is impossible to write a book that consistently delivers a steady stream of knowledge previously unknown to you, I hope that you find value here and that you feel your investment of time in reading is well-spent. In this chapter, I will walk you through the landscape of the wholesale industry and introduce you to some of the major players you'll meet along the way. Let's dig into how the system works, and learn what it means to become a distributor (that's you!).

## Envisioning Your Business

Start putting on a different thinking cap when you venture into wholesale. The customer experience and expectations must be aligned well with the nature of the work. High-margin retail transactions at scale warrant technical and customer support. Retailers cope with defects and buyer's remorse returns. When trading in the lower-margin wholesale world, the factory needs to be responsible for technical and customer support unless they contract with you to handle these interactions (as an additional concession, and hopefully for an additional fee).

Manufacturer's wholesale pricing will reflect the level of support they offer. A high-pressure processing plant (HPP) that cold pasteurizes will offer little or no return options for their goods since they are nondurable, perishable food products. If the retailer can't sell the HPP baby food, they may want to return it to you for credit or refund, but you'll have no recourse to send it back to where it came from. While moldy cheese can be resold (the blue kind), moldy lettuce cannot! Your terms of sale must be relevant to the goods sold. A defective microwave oven will need to be managed by the factory under a published warranty, but who deals with cosmetic problems such as a misprinted product label? It can become murky, and you have to consider all these possibilities when striking deals with producers of goods and your customers.

While you must serve your customers honestly and fairly, you cannot offer razor-thin margins, liberal returns, interest-free financing, and free delivery. Where newbies fail is when they offer low prices and terms (financing of the order). When the payment doesn't arrive in the promised 30 days, you're scrambling to cope with the lack of working capital. Worse yet, the customer takes 45 to 90 days to pay and you find yourself cash-starved and at the cliff's edge, on the brink of going out of business.

## Deciding What to Sell and How to Sell It

You need to address the approach to picking winning industries—where you'll trade—which can and should be a constantly evolving topic. Wealth-producing ideas require a simple approach, which is a focus on transparent industries that are easy-to-understand and that have durable competitive advantages. For example, I would be highly allergic to the idea of trading in tablet computers that work on open-source operating systems because the marketplace is saturated with them, the margins are extremely low, and customer tastes lean toward known brands. The tablets themselves may not attract me as a business opportunity; however, I would be open-minded about large-scale purchases of tablet accessories. Cases wear out, chargers are left in rideshares, and cords fray—the demand for accessories is always steady, and I do not predict any dramatic change in this demand anytime in the future.

I love business. My passion is making deals. Deciding what you're going to sell is a million-dollar topic. Let's talk about something I know a little about. California is a leader in agriculture, dairy, and meat production. The world's appetite for dairy and meat (especially beef) generates a lot of . . . well, you know . . . manure. Someone has to wholesale tons of the stuff to farmers who use it as fertilizer. Not everyone loves to deal with manure. I'm doubtful anyone even *likes* the idea of handling the stinky stuff, to be candid. My point is you may find an opportunity in undesirable industries.

I'm naturally a curious person, so I find joy in all kinds of businesses. I've successfully wholesaled many products including office supplies, baked goods, vehicle parts, and sundries.

Humble conviction and an open mind will lead you toward the answer to the question, "What should I sell?"

When determining what you'll sell, you also have to decide how you'll reach your customers. If you plan to deliver products regionally using your own vehicle, then you'll be trading with stores—many that don't do business online. According to Amazon's 2018 annual report, nearly 90 percent of retail remains offline in brick and mortar stores. I have

spoken with many retailers young and old, and there is a thirst for the "old ways" of doing business. Some people just prefer to deal with a person and not a computer. I know many people, (a few I consider good friends) who rarely touch a computer or phone. I know a 92-year-old computer expert and a 27-year-old who dislikes anything with a microchip. There's ample opportunity to trade with independent retailers, and this will be one sweet spot for trading. People skills will always remain a competitive advantage for you.

Items that don't do well online may present bigger opportunities for a startup, e.g., gourmet ice cream, craft beer, and local produce.

**tip**

If you're not comfortable talking with people, then consider joining the local chapter of Toastmasters. They will help you gain the courage to speak one-on-one or in front of a thousand people.

There is no question that ecommerce sales are growing; however, unless you have nerves of steel, you'll find the margins painfully low and the volume required to make profits extremely high. I speak to you about this having been involved in ecommerce since 1999. If you are able to pick, pack, and ship individual retail orders for your ecommerce buyers, it may become profitable; however, the landscape is highly competitive, that competition grows by the hour, and it will only get worse. I use the word *worse* because I see the cutthroat world of ecommerce wholesale firsthand, and it's bloody out there. Factories are selling directly to consumers—either themselves or through wholly owned subsidiaries. This is an additional headwind that will challenge someone like you standing in the middle between a producer of something and the ultimate user of that something.

Here are some ways to uncover what you could sell:

▶ Get inspired by products you admire and count on in your daily life.

▶ Look around you—are there unique opportunities in your community?

▶ Talk with people you know—do people in your orbit have wholesale trading ideas?

▶ Ask older, more seasoned *successful* wholesalers to guide and mentor you.

▶ Become a social media voyeur and study what people are *talking about*—what products are they bragging about and loving?

▶ Check out the headlines—what's the latest and greatest?

▶ Subscribe to popular magazines and see what the stars are wearing, drinking and eating—look for trends and for what fans may be buying.

▶ Read the Form 10-K for the top public companies and see what's working for them.

▶ Engage in business scuttlebutt—speaking with retailers, looking at their shelves and asking what's in-demand and what's not selling, and talk with others in the industry to feel the pulse of what's going on.

Deciding what to sell requires intuition, fact-finding, and heart. You can achieve success by identifying the goods that are sold in department, high-volume, and specialty stores—all of which could make up your customer base once you open the doors of your wholesale distribution firm. Walk the floor of these stores, and speak with managers and store employees. Have a list of questions ready. "What is your process for considering new vendors?" should be included among them.

## The Distributor's Role

Do you ever wonder what gave rise to the person in the middle between the manufacturer of goods and the ultimate end user—the person we know as a distributor? Let's explore that by discussing a product as ubiquitous as lubricating motor oil. Oil for use in vehicles is refined from crude oil, formulated (sort of like a chemical soup), quality-tested, and then packaged. Retail and bulk motor oil are then wholesaled to stores and repair shops—and the motorist purchases the oil as part of an oil change service or in the form of retail packaging. Larger repair shops buy 55-gallon drums of the stuff and independent service stations purchase cases of quarts or five-quart jugs. In between, there are wholesale distributors who support the needs of the refiner (a factory of sorts) in placing their oil in the hands of customers.

In some industries the situation can be more complicated—take toys as an example. Some toy manufacturers may only sell directly to retailers. Others sell using a wholesaler to bring products to smaller, independent retailers while selling directly to big chain stores. In the world of discount toys, off-price distributors acquire toys that didn't hit big in chains but that would do well at flea markets and in independent retail shops.

Let's take a look at some of the most common types of wholesale distributors.

*Merchant wholesalers* buy large quantities of products and store them. These companies then resell smaller quantities to retail, industrial, commercial, institutional, and other (smaller) wholesale buyers. Merchant wholesalers can be known by different names depending on the flavor of their services. Industry terms for merchant wholesalers include:

- ▶ Assembler
- ▶ Distributor
- ▶ Exporter
- ▶ Industrial distributor
- ▶ Jobber
- ▶ Supply house
- ▶ Wholesaler

*Agents, brokers, and commission merchants* work out deals on behalf of their clients but rarely (or never) take possession of the goods. Because there are often tax consequences to possessing inventory, wholesale distributors may work out the paperwork in such a way as to be viewed as one of these "non-title" product sellers, but many have warehouses where goods are stored and then sold, with the factory being the seller of record. Compensation comes in the form of commissions, and risk is lower because someone else has a substantial investment in the inventory.

Some are *retail distributors*, who sell directly to consumers (end users). Others are known as merchant wholesale distributors; they buy products from the manufacturer (or another source) then move them from their warehouses to companies that either want to resell the products to end users or use them in their own operations. In years past, it used to be divisive for a wholesaler to also trade directly with consumers because it would stir up resentment with the retailers who felt that the wholesaler could retail for less and cannibalize the retailer's opportunity for sales.

*Manufacturers' sales branches and offices* are wholly owned by the maker of the goods. Sometimes these are legally separate entities for tax and liability purposes. These outfits focus on selling their own product, but it is not unheard of for them to operate just like any other wholesale distributor—selling goods from other, noncompeting manufacturers.

No matter what type of distributor role interests you, there are good indicators that the growth potential is strong and steady even in light of how the changing political landscape affects the industry. The NAW reported $6.01 trillion in wholesale business took place in the U.S. in 2018, with 7.5 percent year-over-year growth. Each of these high-level product categories is ripe for business opportunities and profit. Certain industries will expand faster than others. Consider the growing need for something as essential as disposable hypodermic syringes and injection needs for medical applications. As the population ages (and more people engage in routine vaccination), medical supplies manufacturers and their wholesale distributors are looking forward to growth. Which of the millions of product lines interests you? You can see in Figure 1–1 the product categories that are flourishing— and clues to help you choose which industries to consider as your starting point in your journey to become a wholesaler.

| Description | 12-Month Moving Total in Billions of Dollars |
|---|---|
| Petroleum and petroleum products | $734.43 |
| Drugs and druggists' sundries | 711.54 |
| Machinery, equipment, and supplies | 474.00 |
| Grocery and related products | 640.33 |
| Electrical and electronic goods | 623.08 |
| Professional and commercial equipment | 510.08 |
| Motor vehicles, parts, and supplies | 492.97 |
| Paper and paper products | 99.22 |
| Metals and minerals (excluding petroleum) | 189.25 |
| Beer, wine, and distilled alcoholic beverages | 156.03 |
| Hardware, plumbing, and heating equipment and supplies | 143.58 |
| Lumber and other construction materials | 144.01 |
| Chemicals and allied products | 133.27 |

FIGURE 1–1: **The 2018 12-Month Moving Wholesale Goods Totals Reported by NAW**

McKesson is among the largest California wholesalers of pharmaceutical and medical supplies. "How in the world can I compete against someone that big?" you ask. There is beauty in *smallness*. Even in spite of the growth of HMOs and big hospitals, the individual medical practitioner is alive and well. These small medical offices need personalized service for everything from exam gloves to recovery beds. These are ideal customers for smaller, nimble wholesale medical supplies distributors that offer high-touch concierge service. At this level, the distributor is an extension of the medical office, acting as the de facto purchasing agent—a job title a huge hospital can afford to fill but that a smaller medical office cannot.

Wholesale purveyors blur the lines between retailers and wholesalers. Club stores are a good example, as they permit the end user to shop their aisles but also engage in a brisk trade with wholesale customers (restaurants, convenience stores, etc.). Commerce, California-based Smart & Final is a chain of warehouse-style food and dry goods stores founded in 1871 that does a ton of wholesale business and is equally successful within the same locations selling to retail customers. If you can trade profitably, why not?

The type of wholesale company you ultimately become will depend on your appetite for a particular path. You may decide to operate a:

▶ Business-to-business wholesale distribution company that buys in large quantities and sells to retailers.

▶ Business-to-business brokerage that works on commission and represents one or more factories or larger distributors—known as a manufacturer's representative or business broker.

▶ Business-to-business wholesale distribution company that consigns, takes possession (but not title) of goods, and pays for them at the moment of sale or shortly thereafter.

▶ Business-to-business wholesale distribution company that also operates a hybrid operation selling directly to the end-use customer.

## What to Expect

Where do you want to start? Please do not throw caution to the wind. Let's mitigate risk with some sage advice: I'd recommend that you broker some deals before investing your own money (or that of a bank or investor). There are several ways you can test the wholesale waters before signing a warehouse lease. For example, you can work on commission a few times doing wholesale work for someone else and see where that leads you. Or you can try consignment—i.e., the selling of goods without actually paying for them until they are sold. There is a blurry line between consignment and drop-shipping. There are some legal and tax nuances to consignment. Consignment is not an additional type of wholesaling, but rather a way to avoid getting stuck with goods while being afforded the opportunity to make a sale. You'll receive different explanations of consignment, depending on whom you ask. A consignor lets you take physical possession of their product but retains legal title and the right to take it back within a specified timeframe if unsold. I favor consignment. I've sold tons of goods by consignment. While not a hard-and-fast rule, someone willing to consign has tried other means of selling their product and was unsuccessful. Consigned goods will tend to lean toward closeout and discount categories; however, there are billions of dollars to be made in closeouts. With nearly 400 locations and over $2 billion in sales, 99 Cents Only Stores are just one potential buyer of extremely low-priced wholesale merchandise. Like every savvy retailer, they are looking for wholesale deals to fill shelves.

Drop-shipping, however, is more akin to brokering. You order the product and have it sent directly to your customer. That's not ideal because then the customer list is revealed and even the largest, most accountable company can spring a leak and your valuable accounts are stolen. I love consignment but do not love drop-shipping for that very reason. Consignment arrangements always permit the return of unsold goods, but a drop-ship order may be nonreturnable or a restocking fee may apply.

As for what to wholesale, I recommend nondurable goods over durable ones. Durable goods are things like machinery, furniture, office equipment, industrial supplies, and other products that can be used repeatedly. Nondurable goods are consumable items such as paper, cosmetics, groceries, chemicals, medication, and *oh let's not forget one of my favorites* . . . beer!

# Choosing Your Startup Model

You can approach the *starting out* phase in one of three ways: buy an existing business, start your own company, or buy into a business opportunity.

## Buy an Existing Business

Your success in acquiring a *going concern* (aka an existing company) depends on the historical success of the company you're buying. Many good businesses are sold due to illness, divorce, retirement (the kids don't want to jump in and take over), injury, and a litany of other possible reasons. An ethical business seller will faithfully pass along the knowledge required to succeed along with the coveted customer list.

Buying into an existing business is popular. Companies add partners as a means to inject working capital without the expense of bank interest and to assimilate the skills that the new partner brings to the table. People like new partners to have skin in the game. You should purchase a business or an interest in a business that has a proven track record of being profitable, reputable, and durable. When you join a team of executives, you need to align well with their DNA. Study and get to know the team before approaching them. Anyone looking to sell you something will be on their best behavior. Check out their operation in a covert way (e.g., become a customer and evaluate the experience).

It's a mistake to believe that founders sell their businesses because there is something *wrong* with the company. Often companies are sold for personal reasons—people are going through a stage in their life where they no longer have the desire to be an owner, or they have gotten burned out. Their lack of drive and passion doesn't necessarily mean the business lacks future potential. If, after doing some research, you haven't discovered a company that you are interested in buying, consider working with a broker that specializes in prescreening and selling existing businesses.

## Start Your Own Business

Starting from scratch requires you to do the heavy lifting of the initial setup. You'll need some time to build a reputation, a strong appetite to adopt current trends, and accelerated decision making. You'll be invested and burning through cash until sales start rolling in. Sufficient financing is required to inoculate you against failure. It may take years to build a steady stream of loyal customers.

When you start from zero, you'll be making tons of mistakes along the way and learning through trial and error. I will do my best to help you avert disaster with my personal experiences, anecdotes, and tips that you'll find in the rest of this book.

When you start your own business, you'll be abandoning a steady paycheck, sacrificing your personal capital, throwing caution to the wind, and relying more on other people for your financial well-being; however, the emotional reward that you'll receive for being your own boss is priceless.

## Buy Into an Existing Business Opportunity

Before you buy into an existing business opportunity, you should have already developed a clear sense of how the business operates. Before you purchase a partnership investment, get to know the potential business partner(s) and take a good amount of time for the honeymoon phase of the process. Identify your strengths and their strengths; also identify your weaknesses and their weaknesses. What are *you* good at doing? Will your strengths complement the business? Do you fill a gap that they need, or do they simply need your money? Simply needing your money is not a good reason to buy into a partnership. It's important to communicate clearly and define roles explicitly. Jot down notes during meetings with your prospective new business partners. Respect one another and take time to get to know each other in depth.

Be sure that you share the same values as your prospective new partner. Choose partners who have complementary skills and make sure that they have a track record of success. You cannot simply bail someone out of a bad situation—that never works. It's important to have clear roles and responsibilities defined *in writing*. When buying into a partnership, a written contract is an absolute necessity. Drawing up legal documents can be expensive, but it will also save you a tremendous amount of money in the long run by ensuring there are no misunderstandings. It's much more expensive to get a partnership divorce than it is to simply do everything right in the first place. Be honest with each other and don't pull any punches. A match made in heaven is very hard to find, so be patient in your journey.

## Thinking about Needs and Opportunities

If all you've got is staunch determination and an idle basement, then you can start your company right at home. In our untethered world, working at home is not only for the self-employed. If you're gainfully employed today *at home* (i.e., your employer allows you to telecommute), you could start your own wholesale gig and retain your current job. Home-based management jobs fall into the zone of receiving payment for productivity, not being paid an hourly rate. Heather Nezich at the American Society of Employers concludes from her research that the average American worker is productive for less than three hours out of an eight-hour workday. When I scooped ice cream at Frusen Glädjé in the Beverly Center in Beverly Hills in 1985 for $3.35 an hour, I was well within that level of productivity (or lack thereof). I was a teenager, and I was having fun working at the mall. I didn't have the work ethic that I possess today. Now, I get a whole lot done in a day. Any manager working from home can conduct a wholesale business and keep their day job. In this industry, you're paid for skill, not by the hour. Closing big deals can be accomplished in minutes.

**tip** ⓘ

Check with the appropriate licensing agency before starting a homebased business and adhere to the rules. Your neighbors might not take kindly to a semi-truck filled with plush toys arriving in the neighborhood on a weekly basis and are likely to report you. Be sure your licenses are in order.

When it comes time to set up shop, your needs will vary according to what you decide to trade.

That said, starting small at home may not be your ideal situation. If you want to go big or go home, then you will need to think about what you need in a warehouse. Finding the ideal warehouse location requires you to consider many factors, including:

- ▶ Proximity to your home (think about the daily commute!)
- ▶ Storage needs (now and years from now as your business grows)
- ▶ Access to shipping carrier services
- ▶ Work force availability
- ▶ Costs

## ▶ Building Type Matters as Much as Location

Here's a cautionary tale. Consider the sharp, ambitious neophyte in business who found a wonderful old brick warehouse in a very cheap part of town, close to a freeway (where traffic is fortunately always jammed on the opposite of the daily commute—how lucky!). This too-good-to-be-true warehouse was offered at the perfect price with ample room for expansion. A little warm in the summer but not intolerable. As circumstances would have it, our neophyte set sights on apparel and landed a lucrative opportunity with several top designers. In addition to fashion clothing, one of these iconic brands required our neophyte to carry fragrances with the condition that the merchandise be maintained at a storage temperature never to exceed 75 degrees Fahrenheit. This big contract required our neophyte to invest in equipment to monitor and digitally log the ambient temperature. After all, the neophyte's warehouse would house millions of dollars' worth of temperature-sensitive fragrances. There was just one catch—this nice old brick building wasn't equipped with climate control and lacked insulation. Already at home in these affordable digs, our neophyte bit the bullet and installed central cooling at a substantial cost. Owing to the lack of insulation and the high cost of retrofitting such a large space, the summer utility bills rose to stratospheric levels. To add insult to injury, the city imposes a gross-receipts tax on wholesalers, and all originally perceived advantages to this location became a nullity. While location matters, so does the kind of building you choose. Would-be entrepreneurs often start out making critical business decisions in a silo when what they should do is ask lots of questions. Mentors and others in business—within the trading area—are invaluable sources of wisdom. Engage in business scuttlebutt with these folks before committing to a particular business location or opportunity.

If you're considering competing with your current boss in the same industry, consider asking about a formal partnership. You may be turned down, but then again, you may be surprised to learn that the door is open for a new and different relationship with your employer. If the answer is "no," at least you tried, and it will come as no surprise when you hang up your shingle to start your own company. Do your best to leave on good terms. Don't scorch the earth behind you. If you maintain a class act, you might even receive support or referrals from your former company. Another idea? Offer to buy out your current boss if you've got the funds or financing to do so.

I have always advised businesspeople to live and work in the same community. Time is our most precious commodity. Making the most of travel time is at the very core of why big-time CEOs have drivers and fly in private jets—this enables them to focus on and accomplish work during their travels. If your commute to work is a lengthy one, then rent out your current home and rent or buy a place near your new business. It would be genius if your warehouse had legally permitted living quarters.

A location must be evaluated from multiple angles. Compare the low cost of leasing or purchasing a building off the beaten path against all other factors. Let's explore the biggest considerations about choosing a location a bit further.

## Startup Costs

You can conceivably begin with very little investment. Broker or consign goods working at home and use contract warehouses or ship from the factory to your customer. As your business grows, roll profits into expansion efforts. In 2020, the average warehouse business costs between $10,000 and $50,000 to set up. These figures rise dramatically for bigger operations. The initial outlay may include:

▶ Security deposit and first (and possibly last) month's rent, if you're leasing
▶ Business formation costs (for example, incorporation fees)
▶ Licensing fees
▶ Exterior building signage
▶ Furniture and fixtures
▶ Office supplies
▶ Warehouse equipment (shelving, forklift, etc.)
▶ Insurance
▶ Website setup
▶ Computers and software (or cloud licenses)
▶ Marketing expenses

> ► Payroll funds sufficient for launch
> ► Inventory

Once you get past the anxiety and self-doubt, you'll journey through "analysis paralysis." After a few sleepless nights, you'll gain resolve (or run to the comforting arms of your dearest loved one). Financial concerns will turn even the most courageous person into a puddle of perspiration. You will have to think over startup costs and long-term working capital as you develop your new business. Talk with other wholesalers in unrelated product lines and seek mentorship. You should never seek the advice of anyone who isn't already in the position you'd like to be in or who has not achieved the level of success in business you would consider admirable. Asking the gardener for their opinion would offer the same benefit as asking your distant cousin, the dentist.

## Operating and Scaling Costs

I hypothesize that labor will be your second largest cost of doing business, with the cost of goods being number one. While this is not a book on finance per se—and certainly not a book on banking—I further speculate that at some point you'll need to borrow money in order to grow. The cost of carrying loans on inventory can be substantial because unlike fully secured loans (e.g., mortgages), inventory loans are very risky and have high rates of interest. Companies fold, owners abscond with the cash, mother nature intrudes, food expires, rodents may invade the sacks of grain, etc. Your rent or mortgage might be small or significant, depending on geography.

Let's brush some broad strokes and examine the numbers of the publicly traded company ADDvantage Technologies Group, Inc. (NASDAQ ticker AEY) as an example. ADDvantage Technologies Group, Inc. is a wholesale distributor of new and used equipment and supplies for the cable TV and telecom industries. Their trade includes factory-fresh as well as refurbished and surplus goods. They are relatively small with 141 employees. You and I have the benefit of examining their books because, as with all public companies, they are required to make them publicly available.

I grabbed their 2017 annual report and performed a few basic mathematical calculations. While their figures are in the millions and that is less relevant to you, what *is* pertinent are the percentages. Rounded faithfully, AEY's cost of sales comes to 70 percent. The cost of sales, as I understood it, includes the cost of the products they sell layered in with the freight, refurbishing costs, and all other expenses associated with bringing the goods into inventory. The operating, selling, general, and administrative expenses amount to 30 percent.

While your numbers will be different, at least you can see how another wholesale distributor operates. The cost of goods in this example is roughly 70 percent of the sale. You must not forget that this purveyor sells new and used goods, and the margins for used products are historically better than new ones. If you do not partake in secondhand merchandise, you can expect margins to be lower. As a smaller company, you will suffer the disability of lower buying power, which in itself is a form of expense. My simple advice to you and everyone in business relates to costs. It is far easier to improve your profit margins by leveraging better buying power than by hunting inefficiencies. Most small companies are highly efficient because owners act like . . . well, *owners*. Larger companies employ a bevy of "friends of friends" and family members who may or may not be the hardest workers. Find your success in watching costs and hunting down better prices. The latter can be achieved by cooperative buying where multiple companies engage in purchasing the same products. Companies can work together and buy big quantities and achieve major discounts. How these firms cooperate even more elegantly is by entering into co-op contracts where they divvy up sales territories so that they aren't stepping on each other's toes. It is a hive mentality without a legal partnership. The Japanese *keiretsu* is a model for a set of companies with interlocking business relationships and alliances and the cooperation between companies with mutual interests was a force that helped Japan grow economically for multiple decades after World War II. Many firms form *de facto keiretsu* structures through the cross-pollination of corporate boards and the purchase of stock in other companies. On any scale, cooperation with other strong wholesale firms can propel you forward.

Whatever your approach as you enter into a new business venture, you must be sure to determine your startup costs and amortize these expenses as your operation begins. Setup costs should never be forgotten. If you finance these expenses, you'll feel their impact as you pay down the loan. If you paid cash to open your doors, figure on repaying yourself in the same way you might pay a bank loan and treat your loan to the company as a real loan with interest (and write yourself a check every month to cover the principal and interest on the terms you might have secured from a business bank). This way, you'll factor in the recoupment of these startup costs when pricing your goods.

## Proximity to Your Home

Mike Cunningham was the man who first leased me a Burbank, California, office in 1989 and later sold me the Burbank home I live in today. He was as down-to-earth as they come— may he rest in peace. Mike was a former-welder-turned-realtor who actually accrued most of his wealth developing real estate and leasing or renting it, not selling it on commission.

I bought my current home in fall 1991. I was 21, and Mike made the transaction seem effortless. It wasn't until years later I realized that he was cutting a kid a break and he had finagled deals for me with the seller and the bank. When I spoke with Mike about my goals in business, one thing he said stuck in my head and affected my decisions for years to come. He said, "I never invest in any business or property farther than five miles from my home. Managing these things requires you to have eyes and hands on them. You can make millions of dollars right around the neighborhood where you live, so don't stick your neck out."

It was good advice. Evaluate your appetite for the daily commute. I prefer to work and live in the same city. I would rather pay a little more to have my place of work close to my home. In the '80s and early '90s, I dealt with a long daily drive to and from work, and it became tiresome very quickly. Set a limit. Will your new business open within five miles of your residence? Ten? If you live in a rural area, the options near you may be few and the cars sharing the road to work even fewer—you may even enjoy the smooth ride. In the big city, get as close to home as possible or suffer the wrath of bumper-to-bumper traffic. I'll dive deeper into setting up shop in Chapter 5.

## Storage Needs and Access to Shipping Carrier Services

Storage and shipping logistics are expansive topics. Wholesalers of diamonds will ship using fast, insured services such as FedEx, UPS, or registered mail with USPS. Sellers of mass quantities of consumer electronics will truck their goods or move them via intermodal transportation—the latter involving multiple means of transportation such as rail, ship, and truck—using a shipping container. This occurs without any handling of what's inside the container when it moves between different modes of transport. The shipping container can travel on a container ship, move to a train, then end up on a truck and be off-loaded at your dock—retaining the padlock or seal placed on the shipment by the original sender (unless customs officials open the container for inspection).

Let's get back to the diamond wholesaler. This elite purveyor of exquisite gems might sleep soundly at night knowing their precious inventory is snugly tucked into the safe in the office of a secure building in the best part of town with a 24-hour armed guard controlling the entrance. Being close to the shipping carrier won't matter because the goods are tiny and light—and all the carriers will pick up from the wholesaler. But dealers of large, case goods such as furniture will benefit from being near a border (if the goods are produced in another country), and the warehouse should be situated as close as possible to both the port of entry and a selection of trucking and intermodal transportation carriers.

The larger the goods, the more thought must go into the logistics. Savings of even fractions of a percentage can advance your competitive advantage. A central location or multiple locations distributed across the country will cut delivery times. One of my longtime business associates is the CEO of an iconic perfume brand. Her fragrances have graced the world's most renowned magazine covers and her perfumes are retailed in stores from Beverly Hills to Qatar. While I will not mention the name of her company for reasons of confidentiality, I can mention that her firm works entirely with contract warehouses and neither owns nor leases any storage space. The product is relatively small, and the rent she pays to be in an à la carte warehouse program is low—a fee to cover only the pallets actually being stored. She reviews the *heat map* (the locations of her biggest retailers and wholesale distributors) and periodically adds or removes a contract warehouse based on customer demographics. This strategy allows her to maintain a gorgeous corporate HQ location in a high-rent district while cutting logistics costs and staying nimble. Arguably one of the most successful business-to-consumer retailers, Sears, Roebuck & Co. selected centrally located Chicago for their mail-order fulfillment center, and wholesale distributors delivered their wares by train. Figure 1–2 is a clipping from one of Sears' retail catalogs showing the sheer magnitude of their mercantile plant.

I'll cover expert ways to optimize your operations in Chapter 8.

## The Technological Edge

Startup wholesalers have an edge with technology. Nielsen and the International Telecommunication Union report that at the end of 2018 nearly 60 percent of the 7.7 billion people in the world were among the internet-connected. This connectivity is the medium through which you may cheaply find customers. Large, mature businesses depend on legacy systems and are less nimble than you. Grab this technological advantage and discover new

FIGURE 1–2: **Sears' Chicago Mercantile Plant Circa 1887**

markets everywhere. Independent retailers are selling online. Even thrift stores depend on internet sales to even out the seasonality of foot traffic.

Look at the example of Goodwill Industries, an iconic nonprofit that has been providing job training, employment placement, and community support since 1902. This wonderful cause generates billions of dollars in retail sales through hundreds of Goodwill thrift stores in communities throughout 17 countries. Goodwill stores sell donated merchandise, both new and used, retail and wholesale. Are you skeptical? Simply type the word "wholesale" into the search box at http://shopgoodwill.com. Unfortunately for pickers, Goodwill observed that donations sold through their stores were ending up on other trading platforms, so they simply built their own retail *and* wholesale auction site.

Internet-savvy wholesalers market to customers by phone, through email, on their website, and on social media platforms. The great news about this is that you, too, can benefit from the internet to find unlimited opportunities for locating sources and customers.

In the interest of providing evergreen content, I shy away from mentioning specific sites and elaborating with case studies because the technology that's avant-garde today becomes derelict tomorrow. I cannot prognosticate what will be relevant in the years to come. One thing is certain—your wholesale business will be operated using the latest technology: selecting products with connected devices and marketing deals through customer research, posting ads, and digital marketing campaigns.

Here is a short list of easy ways to weave tech into your wholesale business:

▶ Use Salesforce customer relationship management (CRM) tools to track thousands of prospects, record sales, and manage documents.

▶ Leverage free, open-source WordPress software to build incredible, responsive websites.

▶ Rather than use expensive dedicated computer servers (something I did in years past), use on-demand virtual servers. I use Debian servers provided by Amazon Elastic Compute Cloud (way more reliable than DIY server options). Let the vendor worry about the latest hardware upgrades and software patches—stay focused on your business.

▶ Maintain transparent, online inventory information and pricing—technology makes this a reality. Being messy and disorganized is a customer deterrent.

**tip** ⓘ

Travel the information superhighway to explore the competition, seek out opportunities, and spark new ideas. Type the phrase "wholesale distributor" into your favorite search engine, or bring local focus by adding your city or state.

▶ Leverage call center innovations such as Amazon Connect omnichannel cloud contact center to provide rapid customer service at any hour—a tool for the smallest business or the largest corporation.

Wholesale distributors are using athe following technological methods for elevating their sales:

▶ Socializing on social media (social media sites are providing more business opportunities for me today than in the past)
▶ Contributing industry content (articles, videos, etc.) on popular sites
▶ Online contests and giveaways
▶ Online advertising
▶ Running online auctions and setting up online wholesale stores
▶ Email marketing
▶ Direct mail with a call-to-action to call, email, or visit a website

Most people despise spam email, and most unsolicited email ends up deleted. Businesspeople are a different breed. We don't mind spam as long as it's relevant to us. You'll require a steady stream of prospects, and email marketing is time-tested. Buyers are willing to receive price lists and welcome email as long as it's professional and relevant—not intrusive or overly repetitive. You'll want to reach out to the appropriate trade association (or mailing list broker) for leads. Work only with reputable vendors that have secured opt-in permission from the recipients on their lists, and be sure to follow the rules. Scan the QR code in Figure 1–3 to read the Federal Trade Commission's article regarding the use of commercial email and compliance requirements.

FIGURE 1–3: **CAN-SPAM Act: A Compliance Guide for Business Published by the Federal Trade Commission**

Making the customer experience breezy by way of tech solutions will turbocharge your sales. Older firms still require complicated credit applications and wire transfer payments (to avoid card processing fees). Innovative companies work with free electronic payment services. I use PayPal, Venmo, and Zelle because customers love easy ways to pay. PayPal is only free when moving money between friends and family. How does PayPal know? It's an honor system, and merchants take advantage of this fact. The downside to cheating? You have zero protection in the event a dispute occurs.

## Work Force Availability

The availability of labor is the engine that drives many businesses to move to a specific city. Quality of life is another. Factories and wholesalers often pop up in less desirable, industrial areas where the locals are less likely to complain about loud trucks and other noises or where the city needs the tax revenue these factories and their distribution partners offer. Governments in low-income cities scramble for sources of revenue and often welcome these types of firms.

You will also improve your business if you're willing to hire nontraditional workers. I've hired seniors, individuals with physical disabilities, and mentally and developmentally disabled workers—all with great results. The demand for unskilled and semi-skilled level jobs is typically greater than the supply, which causes managers more pounding headaches than just about any other concern. Faithful employees are even harder to identify, and a manager of a team of ten workers may end up hiring 100 people in the course of a year to keep up with the turnover. YouTube has a plethora of videos that extol the virtues of reducing labor costs through the use of technological marvels. Automation is not causing lesser-skilled positions to vanish, and while inventory-ferrying robots might scurry about the warehouses of megacompanies, your business will depend on real flesh-and-blood hands.

Connect with city officials and speak with successful people in business in the cities in which you intend to hang up your shingle. Of course, government workers will paint a rosy picture, so the steak they provide you with should be consumed with a grain of salt. If you ask enough local businesspeople, you'll receive a fair and honest account of your prospects in the community for success. The growing trend toward hybrid companies that offer true wholesale distribution and pick-pack-ship services (drop-shipping) is a trend to be noticed.

In the next chapter, I'll cover some of the nuts and bolts topics you'll want to think about before opening your doors.

# Structuring Your Business

The nuts and bolts of getting going will rarely be simple. Making your mark requires a unique business name that resonates along with developing positioning and mission statements to fully engage employees, investors, lenders, suppliers, and others with whom you conduct business. Is the business you'd like to start legal? Are there unique insurance considerations such as those that may be required handling flammable or potentially toxic substances? You'll need to conduct your due diligence to ensure compliance. And what legal structure is best for you to keep costs reasonable while still affording adequate protection from lawsuits? You may even wish to hunt down experts to hold your hand along the way.

In this chapter, I'll explore ideas for business planning, branding, legal business structures, regulations (such as licensing), business liability, and more.

## Choosing a Name That Fits

Some firm names leave an impression while others leave people wondering "What the heck does that company do?" I was driving along one sunny day in Los Angeles and saw a place that was simply called *Tommy's*. "Tommy's what?" I asked myself. Tommy's burger? Tommy's vegan food? Tommy's gourmet ice cream? The windows were sufficiently difficult to see through that I simply could not figure out what kind of business Tommy's was engaged in. Now *just down the street* from me is a firm called V&K Distributing Company. A nondescript white building with nothing more than a simple sign with the company name on it. As underwhelming as the business looks from the outside, I understood immediately that V&K Distributing Company is some manner of wholesale business, so I stepped inside. Indeed, I was correct! They are a "wholesale to the public" business. V&K Distributing Company sells bulk dried fruits, canned food, massive bags of nuts, fine tea, gourmet Arabica coffee, exotic cheeses, and confectionery items—with a focus on the local Armenian community. You're in wholesale, so *sound* like a wholesale company. Don't make it too hard for people to "get it." Genuine Parts Company sounds like a car parts distribution company—and that's exactly what they are.

It's critical to brand your new company for today and for its future success. The tactics of *yesterday* are "dumb" today. Way back in 1886, when the covered wagon was pretty much the only way to get from Los Angeles to New York, a guy named Reuben H. Donnelley masterminded the *yellow pages*. Apparently, he ran out of white paper that day, and the idea stuck. Folks would discover brands by picking up one of these huge books with super tiny print in order to find a haberdashery or a farrier. Entrepreneurs knew to make sure their company's name started with an "A" so that their establishment would appear on the first page of the book. As the years rolled by, so many companies used this A-game trick that the names became nonsensical. You look pretty desperate

**tip**

*The Naming Book* by Brad Flowers (Entrepreneur Press, 2020) has some great brainstorming exercises you can try.

when your business name is AAAA Car Detailing. There was even a notorious company in the '80s called ZZZZ Best, which appeared as the very last yellow pages entry.

A company name must be memorable. A fantastic business name is a step towards building your brand and growing it. A great name connects with customers and produces a stickiness with them. The most memorable company names are unique words, such as eBay, Lego, Google, IKEA, Skype . . . you get the picture. Genuine Parts Company certainly picked a meaningful and descriptive name for their auto parts wholesale business—and they've survived *nine decades* in business. Few companies can afford to hire pricey branding consultants. For most, engaging the services of a business naming firm or branding company isn't possible. You'd have to be an Einstein-level business name consultant to be worth hiring, and you'd be better off asking a drunk person sitting at a bar for company name ideas than paying $5 on Fiverr to help you score your brand name. Do it yourself, and avoid the large hole in your wallet. Let me show you an example of one business name that was *changed* by the will of its customers: FedEx. Their name is crowdsourced. Founded in 1972, this massive brand decided to fill a void for a service that was needed in the pre-fax business community—overnight document delivery. Originally named Federal Express, customers eventually found it easier to simply call them FedEx, and the name stuck. In 2000, the company took a tip from their customers and changed their name. It was a smart move for FedEx, which did nearly $70 billion in their 2019 fiscal year and has 239,000 employees. Do you think they would have dominated the market with a name like AAA Shippers?

**tip** ⓘ

Use https://namechk.com as a free, time-saving, and convenient resource to research available domain names and social media usernames. It's quicker than searching one-by-one and generates a report so you can make an informed decision when finalizing your company name to see if anyone is using it online.

Develop and establish your brand identity as a leader, and avoid the hubris of naming your company after yourself. Before falling in love with a company name, write down at least *two dozen* potential names for your company.

Generally, business names fall into two categories: names that describe what the company does and memorable names that don't have a specific meaning to the customer and aren't descriptive of the product being sold. Pick a name that's good now and well into the future (especially online) as your business and your product(s) evolves. Really focus on thinking of the future growth of your company and where you expect your brand to be in the coming years. If you can't secure the internet domain for your brand name, or something darn close to it, then pick from one of the other names you selected and move on.

## Make Your Mark

Far too often, you will want a name that is already registered as a trademark. Don't even consider it. You can easily conduct your own U.S. Patent and Trademark Office search at https://www.uspto.gov for any brand name and ensure it has not been taken. I find that registering federal trademarks is super easy and can be accomplished online. If registering your trademark nationally feels too complex, or hiring an IP attorney is too expensive for your small business, then I'd suggest you secure state trademark protection for a nominal fee. In California, a simple online form is all that's required. State-level trademark protection is strong and is the entry to stronger, national trademarking, which you can secure at a later time once your business has grown. You should also check with the secretary of state and confirm the business name isn't already registered in your state.

Be cognizant that searching the U.S. Patent and Trademark Office website will not reveal state-level registered marks and does not uncover the marks of other rights-holders who may have trademark rights but no federal registration. These rights are referred to as *common law* rights. Common law rights are based on the use of the mark in commerce within a certain geographic area. Common law trademark and service mark rights may be superior to a registered mark if the owner of the common law rights can demonstrate earlier use in a particular geographic area.

For example, Budweiser Budvar Brewery in the Czech city of České Budějovice and the American brewer Anheuser-Busch have been duking it out since the start of the 20th century. Today, Budweiser Budvar is the fourth largest beer producer in the Czech Republic and the second-largest cross-border exporter of the sudsy stuff. In 1939, the two rivals came to a peace accord relating to the trademark Budweiser, which allowed Anheuser-Busch the exclusive use of the trademark in the U.S. Budweiser Budvar beer is imported as Czechvar in Brazil, Canada, Mexico, Panama, Peru, Philippines, and the U.S.; Anheuser-Busch sells its beer as Bud in most of the European Union.

Not every brand name has to be unique. The "Delta" mark has been federally registered for multiple classes of goods and services including airline, faucet producers, 3-D printers, noise suppressors for firearms, antioxidant dietary

**tip** ⓘ

A *trademark* is generally a word, phrase, symbol, design, or a combination thereof, that identifies and distinguishes the source of the goods of one party from those of others. A *service mark* is the same as a trademark, except that it identifies and distinguishes the source of a service rather than goods. The term "mark" in the intellectual property field refers to both trademarks and service marks. Copyrights and patents cover different types of intellectual property and are not the same as a trademark.

supplements, pet kennels, and many more. The registration of similar or identical marks is not necessarily infringing and is also not uncommon. Marks are frequently used by small businesses within a petite geographic area and have the same or similar names. I lost count trying to figure out how many Joe's Pizzas exist in Los Angeles alone! *Trademark coexistence* occurs when two different businesses use the same mark without interfering with each other's businesses. Sometimes overlapping interests and disputes over those overlaps are settled with formal coexistence agreements. As businesses with identical marks grow and expand into other trading areas, the once-peaceful coexistence may turn into divisiveness and conflict. Prevention is always better and less expensive than cures. Engage in a comprehensive online search as a vaccine against a future dispute over your mark. Sometimes the juice isn't worth the squeeze—if a dispute arises and your adversary is a big company with an army of attorneys, seriously consider just changing your company name and moving on rather than footing a hefty legal bill by battling it out in court.

# Business Planning

You can develop a business plan to help you become incredible at running your business. Does a business plan sound too formal for you? Not at all! A business plan can be as simple as a mental plan for making things happen or as precise as a well-developed documental roadmap for guiding your company from startup to ongoing management. There's no right way to write a business plan and you don't need to spend a wheelbarrow full of money hiring a business plan guru. Business plans can take on many different forms. A business plan is a helpful tool for starting a new business or applying for loans, but a superior business plan also provides direction and clarity for operating an existing business. It can be as short as a single page or as long as your heart desires. When researching business plans, you'll discover terms like "traditional" and "lean startup." A traditional business plan is robust and dives deep, while a lean startup plan is sharply focused and only contains summary key points. The perfect business plan is the one that works best for you. The U.S. Small Business Administration recommends that a traditional business plan include these nine sections:

1. An executive summary
2. A description of the company
3. A market analysis
4. An explanation of the company's legal and management structure
5. A description of the product (or service), the customer value proposition, planned intellectual property and product development, and research and development strategies

6. The company's marketing and sales plan
7. Funding requirements (if the business plan will be shared with investors or banks)
8. Financial projections
9. An appendix (for supporting data and documents, credit histories, resumes, product images, reference letters, or other matters that don't fit elsewhere)

The U.S. Small Business Administration provides online guides to assist people with every aspect of starting and operating a business, including developing a business plan. Scan the QR code in Figure 2–1 for their business plan development guide.

FIGURE 2–1: **The U.S. Small Business Administration's** *Write Your Business Plan*

# Developing Positioning and Mission Statements

Positioning is one aspect of marketing strategy and is a concept that evolves over time. Brand positioning is the conceptual place that your company wants to imprint in the customer's mind. Large brands develop precisely worded positioning statements to establish how their merchandise is to be packaged and promoted. A positioning strategy is a part of what is sometimes referred to as the S-T-P approach in marketing—Segmentation-Targeting-Positioning. No company is in a position to satisfy all their customers, every time—people have diverse preferences. Many wholesalers therefore adopt a business strategy known as target marketing. Brand positioning helps a company identify the most profitable market segments. Broadly, positioning can be functional, symbolic, or experiential. Functional positioning addresses and resolves problems and awards benefits to customers. Symbolic positioning engages ego identification, social meaningfulness, and effective fulfillment. Experiential positioning ventures into sensory and mental stimulation.

A *mission statement* is the kissing cousin of a positioning statement; it describes a company's function and competitive advantages—including the business's goals and axioms. The reason we stay loyal to brands is directed by their values. A mission statement can be as simple as "TED is a nonpartisan nonprofit devoted to spreading ideas, usually in the form of short, powerful talks." Some business owners keep them in their heads, while others write them down on scraps of paper, and still others put them in formal documents like business plans.

A company mission statement tells the world why you're in business, while a positioning statement is an expression of how your product fills a consumer need. What makes your company and products distinct and superior? If you cannot find a way to differentiate yourself in the market, you won't survive long. You must live up to your strategic position. If you don't, then customers will call you out by posting unfavorable online reviews and denouncing you on social media. As your company grows, such statements of purpose circulate throughout your ranks and are like the rudder on a ship. With them, your employees can develop strategies that elevate your mission and vision—and build a phenomenal base of cheerleading fans. In my opinion, it does not matter which of the statements comes first as long as you have written them both out. SCORE, the nation's largest volunteer network of expert business mentors, can help you find someone to discover and develop your positioning and mission statements. You can reach out to them at https://www.score.org.

Here are some examples of positioning and mission statements:

*Positioning Statements (for my fictional products and companies):*

▶ Spencer's Meal Replacements—We promise you'll stay slim.

▶ Spencer's Vegan Hot Dogs—Even animals love them.

▶ Spencer's Elevators—Taking you higher than anyone else.

*Mission Statements:*

▶ Spencer's Heavy Equipment—Working hard to provide construction equipment quickly and at revolutionary prices.

▶ Spencer's Snacks—Something savory for everyone . . . and the greatest selection on Earth—creating and promoting great-tasting, healthy, organic snacks.

▶ Spencer's Ice Cream—Fat-free or all-in, offering creamy frozen delights for slimming or sinning. Every taste is ethically sourced and sustainable for our environment and the futures of our children.

I am a customer of HD Supply and love their service, products and corporate culture. Their business focuses on the Maintenance, Repair and Operations (MRO) and Specialty

Construction industry. They are one of the largest in their industry. Here is their mission statement:

> *We aspire to be the First Choice of our customers, associates, suppliers, and the communities in which we operate. This aspiration drives our relentless focus and is reflected in the customer and market centricity, speed and precision, intense teamwork, process excellence, and trusted relationships that define our culture. We believe this aspiration distinguishes us from other distributors and has created value for our shareholders, driven above-market growth, and delivered attractive returns on invested capital.*

A mission statement helps you and others understand what your company does and why you're in business. This can be as simple as a brief written statement of who your customers are, what you sell, and whether you conduct business locally, nationally, or across borders. For example, there are wholesalers who only offer local pickup and who sell big items where the cost of shipping would be so expensive that most buyers wouldn't want to pay the freight. The company that sells commercial kitchen ranges focuses on local and regional trading areas and skips the hassle of dealing with complicated and expensive shipping. Many wholesalers sell to retailers across the nation because what they sell is practical to ship. More experienced sellers ship globally. A clear mission statement becomes more valuable when you add employees—it is important that your team's mission statement is ever-present in the way you conduct business. It embodies the essence of your goals and the reasoning behind them. Your mission statement helps to share your vision not only with employees, but also with customers, vendors, and the community.

The easiest way to develop a mission statement is to study other companies' to inspire ideas for yours.

Here are some of the questions to ask yourself while you sit down to write your mission statement:

▶ Why are you in business?
▶ Who are your customers?
▶ What differentiates you from your competition?
▶ What is your public image?

Avoid the hype of a meaningless mission statement that could describe any company. Vague, high-sounding ideas do not propel you forward. Focus on realistic and meaningful goals that genuinely relate to you and your business.

I've prepared a sample mission statement for the fictional wholesaler of fine canned foods "Farouk's Fancy Foods Distributing."

*At Farouk's Fancy Foods Distributing, we offer a unique selection of hard-to-find delicious foods canned fresh. Everything we sell is ethically sourced and sustainably managed. We gladly ship to anyone on the planet and our prices are fair as are the wages we pay our employees. A percentage of every sale we make goes to help with global environmental causes. We are extremely loyal to our employees and we obsess about our customers.*

Use the KISS method when developing these statements (Keep It Simple, Silly!). While a positioning statement describes an element of a marketing plan (i.e., how you elevate a product), the mission statement focuses on the entire company's core purpose.

As you develop your business plan, and as you're starting your own business, you'll also want to give thought to what sets you apart from competitors in your industry. Your unique value proposition or *UVP* (also called a unique selling proposition or *USP*) articulates what sets your business apart from the competition. This UVP explains the specific ways that you solve customers' problems, the benefits of buying from and working with you, and why someone should pick you over your competition. You can market effectively to a market that you don't know by using your UVP to capture the attention of prospects.

# Business Structure

Considering your legal structure can be a conundrum. For some reason, the government has the ability to make even the most law-abiding citizen feel like they're in an interrogation room. **I am neither an attorney nor a tax professional, so verify all legal and tax decisions with a licensed professional.**

Let's take a look at various legal structures that businesspeople use to operate a company. If your aunt is a CPA or brother-in-law is a tax attorney, you can skip this section and bend their ear over lunch . . . be sure to pick up the tab!

SCORE volunteers can also help you identify the legal structure that's ideal for your situation, or you can reach out to the U.S. Small Business Administration (SBA), which you will find at https://www.sba.gov. From the SBA website, navigate to *Business Guide* and select *Choose a business structure*.

## Sole Proprietorship

A *sole proprietorship* is the most common business structure for someone who is starting a small business. You'll be considered a sole proprietorship if you don't register any other form of business entity. You can use your existing bank account; however, consider keeping a separate bank account for your wholesale business if you voyage beyond being a casual seller (this helps keep the business books separate from your personal finances).

If you read enough books, blogs, and memes, you'll read conflicting opinions about what legal structure to use when starting your business. While it is true that a sole proprietorship exposes the business owner to legal liability, it is also *extremely simple* and easy to manage for a solopreneur. Income is easily reported on the Internal Revenue Service form Schedule C—attached to your 1040 personal tax return. Any other business structure will mandate separate (and often complex) tax forms. My corporation's tax returns involve dozens of pages!

These are all the *really good* reasons to operate a sole proprietorship:

▶ It's easy, streamlined, and low cost.

▶ There are no public disclosure requirements, and therefore, it's extremely private.

▶ Tax returns are easy, and there is no "double taxation."

▶ While multiple people can operate the business, it has a sole owner (you!).

▶ There are minimal licenses to obtain.

▶ As long as you purchase high-quality comprehensive business insurance (and workers' compensation insurance for any employees hired), you'll be protected against most liabilities.

There are endless warnings in the business community about personal liability and the perceived disadvantages of operating a sole proprietorship. It is accurate to say that the proprietor is *personally* liable for the debts and obligations of the business. This means if you get sued or file for bankruptcy, any lawsuit claimants or creditors may have access to your personal accounts, assets, or property. The clear path forward is: Don't get into litigation or stick your neck out so far that you can't pay your bills.

Unless you have a sophisticated grasp of lending *and* borrowing, leave the banking to bankers. The largest potential liability facing wholesalers is poorly performing accounts receivables or accounts that don't pay at all. Companies sometimes use a *factor*, which is a business that buys accounts receivable invoices. Factoring helps even out cash flow and is a form of asset-based lending using the invoice as collateral.

Here are some ways to mitigate exposure to liability, which makes operating a sole proprietorship a logical solution for a single-owner operated business:

▶ Sell existing and well-known brand products where any product liability claims are highly unlikely to end up in your lap.

▶ Provide credit only to the credit-worthy and never extend credit unless you can afford to lose the entire balance owed and still remain in business.

▶ Avoid borrowing money like the plague unless you work with a factor that manages the lending and invoice collection on your behalf.

▶ Only work with top insurance companies, and verify that your insurance company will defend you in the event of a lawsuit.

▶ Require your customers to sign an agreement when opening an account with you that defines clear limitations of liability relating to the goods you sell (an attorney should help here).

If you do right by people, trade ethically, and sell products that are not likely to spark liability claims, a sole proprietorship makes great sense in my humble opinion. If you sell anything that the human body consumes or touches, e.g., drugs, supplements, food, beverages, cosmetics, personal care, and grooming products, you'll want to give serious consideration to a business structure that shields you in the event of a product liability lawsuit.

## Partnership

A *partnership* is the simplest way for two or more people to own a business together. Partnerships are a good way to manage a business when you aren't the only owner and you'd like to test things out before advancing to a more formal business structure. *Entrepreneur* contributor Michael Spadaccini reminds us, "Partnerships can be formed with a handshake—and often they are. In fact, partnerships are the only business entities that can be formed by oral agreement." Visit this link to read Michael's entire partnership article: https://www.entrepreneur.com/article/77980.

In a partnership, each partner has unlimited personal liability, and it is the duty of all partners to pay off liabilities incurred by the partnership. Partners are fully exposed to lawsuits (e.g., product liability suits). Partnerships are easy to form and low cost to maintain. When working with partners, define each partner's roles and responsibilities both through discussion and in a written agreement. Engage the services of an attorney to ensure the agreement is well-considered and legally binding.

## LLC

A *limited liability company* (LLC) protects you from liability in most situations in the event of lawsuits or business failures. You should have liability insurance in place as your primary means of liability protection. Talk with your preferred seller of business insurance about this.

An LLC enjoys much less administrative paperwork than a corporation, owners have a flexible choice of tax regime, and this structure bypasses double taxation. An LLC is not as simple as a partnership and some states impose minimum taxes (e.g., California charges an $800 minimum annual tax on LLCs).

## Corporation

*Corporations* are legal entities that are separate from their owners. Owners have limited liability. Most corporations issue stock, are taxed separately, and can be held legally liable for the corporation's actions while shielding the stockholders and management from lawsuits (in most situations). There are different flavors of corporations. Here is the list:

- ► *Publicly traded corporation*—where shares are bought and sold on a public stock exchange (e.g., NASDAQ).
- ► *C corporation*—a corporation that may have unlimited shares and it taxed on its profits.
- ► *S corporation*—a corporation that elects to pass corporate income, losses, deductions, and credits to its shareholders for tax purposes, and the owners avoid double taxation while benefitting from the same liability protections as a C corporation.
- ► *Nonprofit corporation*—a nonprofit corporation carries out a charitable, educational, religious, literary, or scientific purpose, and doesn't pay federal or state income taxes.

Many gigantic wholesalers operate as publicly traded corporations and some day you could be that large. A wholesaler can operate as a nonprofit provided that the IRS is satisfied that it meets the requisite qualifications. If what you do benefits the public, you can form a tax-exempt corporation to avoid business income tax because you are helping with a cause. If your company distributes hospital supplies exclusively to nonprofit facilities, your business may qualify to be recognized as a 501(c)(3) tax-exempt organization. Ask a legal professional for their input when the timing seems correct.

I run an S corporation, so that I can avoid double taxation while still affording me protection against liability.

Many successful wholesale distributors supported by loyal customers are passed on from generation to generation. While a sole proprietorship dissolves when a person passes away, an "entity" such as a corporation can

**tip**

If you have a simple legal question, post your query at http://www.avvo.com and a licensed attorney will respond with a legal opinion. Seek out professional opinions about the proper legal structure for your business. If you click with a particular attorney, you can consider hiring them.

live on forever. If you can't afford the cost of incorporation and don't want to deal with the added paperwork and additional tax returns, you can address forming a legal structure after your business has become more established. I recommend consulting with a business tax professional to prepare yourself for this timing. The tax preparer should know when the income and tax picture crosses into the zone where it would be appropriate to transition away from being a sole proprietor.

# Choosing the Right Amount of Insurance

Once you have decided on a structure, one of the big-ticket items to knock off your to-do list is to buy insurance. Insurance cannot be purchased *after* liability occurs. While dealing with insurance can become mind-numbing, everyone in business has to cope with this often unpopular subject (and expense). Take my word for it—after any liability claim occurs in your business, you'll be grateful to have a solid partner watching your back and taking care of the fallout while you focus on your business. Being a wholesale distributor usually does not involve a lot of dangerous activities or unusual risks, but it only takes one employee injury or a product liability lawsuit for your thriving, new enterprise to become derailed.

If you send an employee to deliver an order and they are responsible for causing a vehicular accident while on the job, you'll be potentially on the hook for the damage they caused to others, to the vehicle involved, and any injuries sustained by anyone involved in the accident.

## Protecting Workers

Your liability insurance will cover nonemployee injuries at your place of business. Before hiring *anyone*, speak to your insurance broker about the required workers' compensation insurance, which covers your employees in the event of an on-the-job injury. A handy resource for information about workers' compensation laws for your state is located at https://www.workerscompensation.com.

## Business Insurers—Bigger Is Better

While I am all about helping out the "little guy," when it comes to business insurance, *bigger is better.* You want an insurance company propping you up that's *huge* in the event that you have a claim. Your insurance company needs to be friendly and available both at the time they take your money *and* when they are facing a situation where they have to *pay* out money. Financial strength is paramount. Smaller insurance underwriters could easily fold and vanish in the event of civil unrest or a major catastrophe, such as an earthquake. My business was affected by both—the 1992 Los Angeles riots and the 1994 Northridge earthquake. The Northridge earthquake was the fourth costliest U.S. disaster based on insured property losses. Fiddling with one of the "lesser" insurance companies means risking challenges obtaining much-needed support to recover from a business loss. Financial behemoths in the insurance business can cope with the flood of claims that result from major hurricanes and massive temblors. You'll need superb service in the event you have to cope with a less dramatic incident, such as a delivery vehicle accident, damaged inventory from a leaking water pipe, or a roof that's compromised by hail. Indeed I have experienced *all* those situations in my decades in business and every one of them was covered by insurance. Good insurance is not cheap, yet saves you money because bad insurance gets expensive very quickly when it fails to afford the proper coverage.

## Where and What to Buy

Where should you buy insurance? Independent insurance brokers are everywhere. You can talk to your auto, homeowners, or renters insurance company and see if they also offer business insurance. You will get better service (and perhaps a better price) from a company when you have multiple policies with them. You can also reach out to friends, family, and your chamber of commerce for referrals to a great insurance broker. If someone close to you sells insurance, give them a shot at the opportunity. Later I'll state my preferred provider; however, please explore and draw your own conclusions.

Most of the liability you may experience will concern your inventory, equipment, employee activities, and business records. Also, if you own your business's building, you may have to buy separate coverage for it. Because your insurance rates will be determined by the amount of coverage, your location, and the policies of the insurance company, it is important for you to be classified as the correct business type. Insurance companies' rates are based on the severity of the risk they are insuring.

If you don't know anyone who sells business policies, you should reach out directly to the top carriers, and they will help you. Starting a business from home still requires the right insurance to "catch" you if you fall. While some high-quality homeowners policies have coverage for cottage trades, others do not. Risk must be examined to ensure you aren't *over- or under-insured*. While a plush toy wholesaler will likely never need $5 million in product liability coverage, a medical supply distributor that deals with health-care products could potentially need *more*. Ask your insurance broker or company to carefully examine your wholesale business and evaluate the type of policy that will afford you the appropriate coverage.

Consider these factors:

- ▶ What is the probability that the products being sold may cause tort liability? A tort occurs where one person causes damage, injury, or harm to another person. It doesn't have to be intentional and liability occurs at higher frequency when the product is ingested or potentially harmful if not handled carefully. Are food and beverages being sold? Does the business trade in *dangerous goods* such as flammable merchandise (e.g., liquor, perfume, solvents, etc.)?
- ▶ Are there employees?
- ▶ Do customers, vendors, and nonemployees enter the place of business?
- ▶ Does the company use its own vehicles or those owned by employees in the course of business?
- ▶ Is sensitive customer information received and stored in the course of business (card numbers, social security numbers, etc.)?

You can insure damage to your business property and you can insure the liability that may occur when people come in contact with your business, e.g., customers, suppliers, and employees. Business property and liability insurance for a homebased company can be purchased as an added "endorsement" to your homeowners policy, as a stand-alone homebased business insurance policy, or as a business owner's policy which has more comprehensive forms of coverage. The latter would be what you would buy when starting a business that's not in your residence. The smart insurance professional will ask questions relevant to the type of business and will offer a policy that is "just right" based on their expertise. It pays to read the *fine print*, though. Even veteran insurance brokers will add unnecessary coverage that, if removed, will reduce the policy premium. For example, a business that doesn't extend credit will never need or use accounts receivable insurance. The wholesale company that only uses third-party delivery and shipping companies will never need non-owned automobile insurance. Nickels and dimes add up, so save money whenever possible.

Hiring employees and contractors will mandate other types of insurance. Disability insurance benefits are offered to employees in many states and are administered by the appropriate state agency—paid for as an involuntary payroll deduction. Workers' compensation insurance coverage is not taken as a payroll deduction and can be purchased privately or through the "public enterprise fund" when one is available. There are 21 states with a competitive state fund in the workers' compensation insurance market. In my view, the right insurance is that which requires the *least* amount of thought and virtually no time. I find the payroll and workers' compensation rules exceedingly complex, so I simply delegate the entire process to Patriot Software. Patriot Software has a *full-service* payroll solution that is entirely online and extremely easy to use. I added workers' compensation insurance to my account using their pay-as-you-go concession, which was a breeze to set up. My employees are fully covered, and everything is simply handled for me. The monthly time commitment to process payroll is counted in minutes. Insurance premiums and tax returns are dealt with automatically—payment is deducted from my company's checking account. While I prefer using Patriot Software, your tax professional may recommend their preferred payroll partner. Scan the QR code in Figure 2–2 to evaluate Patriot Software's solutions for payroll processing and workers' compensation insurance.

FIGURE 2–2: **Patriot Software's Payroll and Workers' Compensation Options**

I remain a lifelong cheerleader for Berkshire Hathaway, Inc., the company whose genius chairman and CEO is Warren Buffett. Mr. Buffett is among the most successful investors who ever lived and happens to be incredibly clever in the management and operation of insurance. My personal car is insured by GEICO, and my business owner's policy is underwritten by Berkshire Hathaway GUARD—both business units of the "mothership" that is Berkshire Hathaway, Inc. At the end of 2018, Berkshire Hathaway, Inc. employed 389,373 people and held assets of more than $369 billion. They aren't just a huge company; they also charge less. Even daily driving exposes my business to liability, so I carry $1 million in bodily injury liability insurance for my car plus $2 million in additional coverage through an umbrella policy. California only requires drivers to carry $15,000 of bodily injury liability coverage, and I carry $3 million in total! I have to protect my assets and my business *just in case* something does happen. All this extraordinary coverage is truly affordable through Berkshire Hathaway, Inc.'s insurance offerings. I'm not a paid spokesperson . . . *yet.*

There is no one-size-fits-all approach to handling insurance, and a lot will depend on how big your wholesale business grows over time. Large companies often *self-insure*— they pay claims from their cash on hand rather than buying insurance. These large firms can simply absorb financial losses without having to pay premiums—and they, themselves become the insurance company of sorts! Some states, such as California, will certify qualified businesses to self-insure workers' compensation coverage. This makes excellent sense if they've had good claims experience and feel their workers' compensation insurance is higher than it should be. But for you, the small wholesale distributor that operates a busy warehouse or deals in hazardous goods, it may not be quite what you need, so consider self-insurance very carefully. If a forklift driver drops the fork on a coworker's foot or someone forgets their hard hat and something drops on their head from a high shelf, you could be financially done for. Inadequate insurance is also a disservice to those who have a legitimate claim and should receive appropriate compensation for their injuries.

A distributor who wishes to conduct business with well-known retailers, such as mass-market and "big box" stores, will typically face stiff insurance requirements. Walmart has the following vendor insurance requirements (published online):

- ▶ *Commercial General Liability*. Covering personal and advertising injury, products/completed operations, medical payments, bodily injury, and property damage with minimum limits of $1 million per occurrence and $2 million aggregate.
- ▶ *Workers' Compensation/Employer's Liability*. For any supplier whose employees enter their premises—of $1 million.
- ▶ *Automobile Liability*. For any supplier whose employees will be driving on their premises—of $1 million per occurrence.
- ▶ *Product Liability*. $1 million (minimum) up to $10 million per occurrence and $2 million (minimum) up to $20 million aggregate with an exemption if the vendor is considered a very small business (defined by them as a supplier with sales that do not exceed $1 million per year).

While the aforementioned is seemingly daunting and potentially hair-pulling, a petite wholesale distributor selling at or below the $1 million-per-year mark will likely have sufficient insurance to meet all these requirements by simply purchasing an affordable policy custom-tailored by a seasoned, qualified insurance professional. Most insurance companies sell their policies through authorized agents or brokers. Some sell insurance directly by telephone without using brokers. With so many insurance companies providing all types of business insurance, it may be confusing, so it's helpful to shop around to learn about the various companies and their offerings.

Ask an insurance broker if they specialize in insuring businesses and if they have a variety of carriers to choose from. You may do better working with a broker who is an independent agent and can shop your policy to more than one company. Ask the broker to shop your policy only to companies with a strong financial rating. You want an insurance company with a solid financial base that can make prompt payment on claims. You also want to avoid any companies that may have government regulatory actions pending. Don't be seduced by the lowest price quote—it may be from a financially unstable insurance carrier, and you need to be sure that your claim will be paid, promptly, in the event you need to use your insurance policy.

Your insurance broker, just like a real estate broker, is paid by incentives (commissions), and they will want you to be a customer for a very long time. It is in their interest to sell you good insurance and offer you coverage that will protect you both personally and in business—not just sell you cut-rate insurance.

The price of your insurance depends upon a variety of factors, including:

► Your deductible (the amount you have to pay on each claim before your insurance kicks in and starts paying)
► The number of policies you have with the insurance company
► The insurance company's financial strength (rating)
► The amounts and types of coverage
► Your location
► The type of building and its construction
► Your security system
► Your claims history

Insurance is truly designed to cover you in the event of a catastrophic situation. If your delivery truck driver inadvertently runs the company vehicle over a deep pothole, blows a tire, and dents the wheel rim into uselessness, you will pay for it out of your own pocket—not file a claim against your insurance. Most likely, the deductible would be higher than the value of the damage, and the insurance company wouldn't pay anyway, leaving you with a claim on your policy record (not a good thing). You will want your insurance to cover something big, like a runaway truck smashing into your warehouse, a tornado moving the building to a new ZIP code, or an earthquake leveling the business—this is what insurance is for. Don't file claims if you can resolve the issue by paying out-of-pocket for the damage. Consider paying even in a situation where the sum exceeds the deductible

**tip**

Before selecting an attorney, accountant, insurance broker, or any professional to support the launch of your new business, take a look at your own circle of family, trusted friends, and colleagues. Ask for meaningful referrals to stack the deck in your favor. Tap your inner circle for MVPs in the fields of expertise you'll need to hit home runs in your business every time.

and you may face higher premiums by filing a claim. Talk with your agent or broker "off the record" first.

You will find that the rate you pay will drop substantially as your deductible goes up. I suggest you go for a high deductible, such as $1,000 or more if possible. I have one policy with a $5,000 deductible because it saves me boatloads of money. You want your business insurance to be affordable, so in the event of a loss, you want your deductible to be the largest amount you can reasonably pay out of your own pocket without putting a strain on your finances. Ask your broker to give you a variety of quotes based on different deductible amounts so that you can compare the rates and see what makes sense for you. When buying insurance, explore discounts for American Automobile Association members (AAA), seniors, veterans, and the disabled if any of these situations apply. My GEICO premiums reflect a military discount.

## Obtaining the Right Licenses, Permits, and Certifications

The government loves you. Usually, they love you so much that they not only want to keep tabs on your daily business activities, but they also like to get paid to do so. Typically, this is done through a wonderful thing called a business license. There are all kinds of licenses out there for virtually every imaginable occupation, and it is important that you stay in compliance with local, state, and federal laws.

Different states view businesses differently. Some states are quite aggressive about attracting business startups and therefore are equally proactive in giving small businesses lots of breaks. Relaxed regulations and lower (or no) taxes are ways in which some states encourage business development. Some local authorities and states may have laws and/or regulations that affect what you can sell and how you must conduct your business. It is entirely your responsibility to determine not only the tax laws, but also the licensing requirements for your business. I recently shared lunch with a friend and colleague who owns a local father-and-son market. He's the son. The shop doesn't sell tobacco; however, for many years they retailed hookah pipes (but not the hookah). His trade in hookah pipes amounted to only a few hundred dollars per year. These ancient pipes are once again garnering the attention of the public, and customers are asking for them. California continues their war on smoking, and the sale of these pipes is highly regulated. As a result, my friend simply stopped selling them because the juice wasn't worth the squeeze. Don't get caught in the same pickle. Make sure you have the proper licenses or permits, and that they are really worth your money. Let's take a look at some of the most common regulatory paperwork you might run across.

## Licenses

Every state and local jurisdiction will vary. Laws may be very relaxed, or they may be quite strict. Get the whole story before you spend a lot of money opening a business. If you live in a city with restrictive licensing rules, it might be prudent to consider a nearby city in which to hang your shingle. If you're near the border of another state that has more relaxed and business-friendly regulations, the same suggestion applies. Be tactful and careful how you present your business to the government. Some agencies may misclassify what you do, therefore placing draconian restrictions on your business. Reach out to other wholesale distributors and collect tips before you apply for your license(s).

It's completely natural for you to be apprehensive of anything even vaguely resembling a legal matter. But being in compliance with the laws of your city and state is routine and a must.

Before you pay for legal help, you might want to reach out to SCORE, the nation's largest network of experienced, volunteer business mentors (https://score.org). And you will definitely want to give your state and local governments a chance to help you, too. In most cases, your local business license will be sufficient, but some states do require additional licenses.

If you have anxiety about all of this and don't mind paying for the help, you can engage the services of an attorney. Most attorneys are specialists, and you will want an expert in the field of business licensing. Try to obtain a referral from a colleague in business or by contacting your state's bar association, which handles the licensing of attorneys. You can locate the appropriate bar association at http://www.findlegalhelp.org.

That said, it is very rare for an entrepreneur to hire an attorney simply to handle a routine matter such as obtaining a license. I would suggest this only as a last resort. Generally, you will want to work directly with your state and local government and ask them for help in understanding their requirements. If you're friendly and professional, you will no doubt succeed here and save yourself a bundle by doing it yourself. You can post a legal question and receive (limited) complimentary legal advice at https://avvo.com.

## Permits

All states have special permits for businesses that buy products wholesale. When buying this way, most companies don't pay sales tax on purchases made for resale, but they do charge their retail customers sales tax on the final sale. The sales tax is collected by the businesses to be paid to a state agency that will then distribute these taxes to the state treasury and possibly the treasuries of the county and local governments. A permit is required if you're doing business this way. If you sell both wholesale and retail, you will be collecting sales tax from retail customers and then paying it to the state's coffers. You will need to get a *sales tax permit* to do so. Even if you *only* buy and resell to non-retail (or B2B) customers, you'll need to maintain audit-proof records.

States call these sales tax permits by various names, but they all allow the collection and payment of sales taxes. Some of the names used for such permits are:

- ▶ Resale permit
- ▶ Resale license
- ▶ Resale certificate
- ▶ Seller's permit
- ▶ Certificate of authority
- ▶ Use and sales tax license
- ▶ Use and sales tax permit
- ▶ Application to collect and report tax
- ▶ Transaction privilege tax

If your state does not have a sales tax, this is a moot point. As of this writing, only five states do not have sales tax: Alaska, Delaware, Montana, New Hampshire, and Oregon. These permits are also known by other names, depending on your state. States may have different rules regarding the collection and payment of sales tax, as well as other taxes. It would be a good idea to give your state officials a call and ask for details about the rules of the road where you live.

The "locals" may also want a slice of your pie. It's important to contact your local city licensing office and discuss your business. I suggest calling for an appointment with the appropriate employee and speaking to them in person about your proposed enterprise. Don't be afraid to deal with these folks. They are usually quite willing to help any new business and want to assist in making your new business a successful one. Remember that you will be generating new sources of tax revenue for your local community with your payment of a business license and the creation of new jobs for any employees you need, so local governments have a vested interest in seeing your business flourish.

Even if you're planning on working from home, a business permit or license may be required. Be sure to get one and stay in compliance. You might be able to stay under the radar for a while, but as you become successful, someone may let the cat out of the bag. A nosy neighbor might turn you in, and you don't want to deal with the stress of possible fines for operating an unlicensed business. If you're a previous business owner or have worked in a small business, this will all seem routine and quite simple. If you're new to the business world, the mere thought of dealing with government types might cause you to break out in a cold sweat. Don't stress yourself out. It really is a routine matter, and you will take great pride—and be able to sleep well at night—in knowing you're running a completely legit business enterprise.

## Seeking Expert Advice

Among my greatest mistakes getting started in business was spending *too much money* hiring professionals. I incorporated my business at the tender young age of 18, and wanting to be "big time," I felt that I needed to lean on expensive attorneys and high-powered accountants. Ego and fear of getting things wrong drove my boneheaded decisions. Today, I have tremendous respect for a very limited number of attorneys and accountants. I am now far more careful whom I lean on for advice. Not everyone with a bar card understands federal courts, and not everyone with a CPA license can manage an audit. I look to professionals with proven *core competencies* and hire them after substantial vetting, research, and interviewing (yes, I interview professionals!). An entrepreneur will, at some time or another, require professional help. Like a lot of people, I have trusted friends for referrals with mixed results. I have overpaid for professional services recommended by friends who swore by the providers. A wholesale distributor should look for professionals within the industry. Why would you use the same lawyer, accountant, marketing consultant, or social media "guru" as your auto mechanic or hairdresser?

In 1988, I spent a lot of money hiring an attorney to incorporate my business, but you can easily do it yourself. The secretary of state will gladly provide you with the necessary forms and samples to help you get it right the first time. While many companies prefer to hire a bookkeeping service, my accounting is handled in-house. I send reports to my accountant for tax preparation.

Lawyers, accountants, and insurance agents can serve a valuable purpose throughout the life of your company. By answering a few simple questions, sophisticated tax software will accurately prepare and electronically file your Schedule C along with your IRS form 1040, but if you feel like the government has become an insatiable business partner, hire a tax MVP to tackle the alligator. Truly knowledgeable professionals bring exceptional value *at the right time.*

Other professionals such as marketing gurus and business consultants can also come in handy. You can explore the local Rotary Club, the chamber of commerce, or attend a Toastmasters meeting to identify business and professional leaders within your community. Volunteering for local churches and nonprofits can provide networking opportunities as well where you can connect with experts who can give you advice. You may also want to tap into retired executives (remember SCORE) to impart their wisdom in the areas of sales, sourcing, negotiation, pricing, and managing your business.

# Defining and Researching Your Market

Mergers and acquisitions have been occurring since the start of recorded business history. David was petrified at the very prospect of facing Goliath but was able to put his fears aside. David summoned the courage to defeat the mammoth ogre. As businesses evolve from nimble, scrappy startups and become mature mammoths, they lose some facets of their competitive advantage, leaving opportunity in their wake. Not everyone wants to deal with the "big guys," and conversely, petite retailers are unattractive to national distributors because of small order size and low volume.

The wholesale distribution industry evolves persistently, providing new opportunities while dislodging others. The yesteryear predictions of strategists and futurists are coming true as producers are increasingly selling directly to end users, cutting out distributors and other intermediaries, including retailers. The threat enlarges as manufacturers and end users find one another directly. Smart wholesale distributors will always find a way to adapt to the needs of their particular market.

If you're still pondering what you'd like to sell and what market you want to serve— gravitate toward industries where what you offer is consumed over and over again in a short period of time. At this juncture, you should be thinking keenly about what product lines will represent your *core* business activities, and look to your customer base for clues about adding additional product lines.

Becoming an expert in your industry will *supercharge* your results. A person cannot become an expert working in a silo. No successful wholesale distributor succeeds by luck alone. Serendipity can occur, and so can winning a $1.586 billion Powerball prize. The more likely answer to "Why is XYZ company so successful?" is that the company has developed a model for doing business that rewards them in the market with *predictable* and *consistent* results.

In this chapter, I'll explain how to explore and discover the right customers, deploying market research and intel collecting methods, examining the competition and analyzing your industry.

# Gathering and Analyzing Data

A vital operations task is conducting regular industry research and analyzing and applying your findings to how you run your wholesale business. Manufacturers that historically sold exclusively in a business-to-business model are shifting to also add direct-to-consumer sales either under their own name or by acquiring retailers (or setting up their own retail operations). This represents a real threat to wholesalers looking to profit within specific industries where the factory-direct sales trend is likely to grow. While I am always willing to try something—test and explore business opportunities—the number of failed experiments in your journey should be limited by intelligent SWOT analysis. *SWOT analysis* (or SWOT matrix) is a strategic planning technique used to help a person or organization identify strengths, weaknesses, opportunities, and threats related to business competition or project planning. Never imagine you can throw some spaghetti on the wall and hope it will stick. Success requires thoughtful analysis of the industry of interest. See Figure 3–1 for an example of a SWOT analysis matrix.

| S<br>Strengths | W<br>Weaknesses | O<br>Opportunities | T<br>Threats |
|---|---|---|---|
| Swift delivery<br><br>Quality products<br><br>Well-trained employees<br><br>Great working conditions and excellent employee benefits | New to the industry<br><br>A large number of competitors in the same industry<br><br>Limited social media presence<br><br>No CRM tools in place | Expansion into more online sales<br><br>Fast-growing community that is increasing demand for products<br><br>Solid track record in attracting new Investors<br><br>Development of house brands and proprietary products | Changes in regulations are frequent within the industry<br><br>The cost of raw materials is volatile<br><br>Industry consolidation is intensifying competition<br><br>End-user tastes change rapidly |

FIGURE 3–1: **A Hypothetical SWOT Analysis Matrix**

I conduct industry research on a daily basis. For example, while I am a nonsmoker and have zero intention of smoking *anything*, I now examine the cigar industry. Tobacco and related products are often referred to as part of the "vice" industry. Vice industries are so-named because they involve the trade of highly regulated products such as firearms, tobacco (and now legal cannabis), military-industrial complex goods, and products related to gambling. While the Centers for Disease Control (CDC) reports that cigarette smoking has fallen to its lowest point in American history, business information research firm IBISWorld declared that cigar consumption is on the rise with cigar lounges generating $971 million in 2018. With more than 4,700 cigar smoking lounges in the U.S. in an expanding industry, the wholesale distributor of fancy humidors, quality cigar cutters, fine sterling and leather cigar cases, premium lighters, and handmade ashtrays will see a real opportunity to score double-digit margins. I wouldn't have known this if I hadn't opted to research the industry and apply the findings to my own business model.

# Identifying and Connecting with Your Customer Base

Think very hard about how most retailers seduce their customers. The baker entices passers-by with the wonderful aroma of freshly made bread, cookies, and cakes, *and* the smart baker hands out free samples to hook customers. Just as with the retailer, a wholesale distribution company must find the tactical advantage to reach their market. In most cases, it is a zero-sum game, i.e., there are only x dollars of business in your industry, and that industry grows at the rate of y percentage per year (or declines in some industries). Please don't be discouraged by this—it is *very* difficult (but never impossible) to steal market share from your competitors. When I operated a very large-scale wholesale and retail mail-order computer printer ribbon business in the late 1980s to early 1990s, my sales team consisted of 65 employees. We found that our ally in the mission to conquer the industry was customer employee turnover. Whenever the purchasing agent quit or was fired, a door of opportunity would open up; we would get in with the new purchasing agent with friendly talk and reasonable prices. We called on every lead card (indeed, they were 4" by 6" paper cards sold to us by Dun & Bradstreet Corporation) at least four times a year. It was a statistical certainty that with a high enough volume of outreach, we'd score new accounts. The cost of acquiring an account was substantial, but the customer lifetime value was also substantial. Customer retention and reorders is where profits are made.

Identifying the *who* and *what* is incredibly easy to do if your heart leads you to help other people. Doing good and making a difference in people's lives will return financial dividends many times over because you've been making "deposits."

So, who are your customers? Look for them everywhere! They may include:

- ▶ Retail businesses like:
  - Food and drug stores
  - Big-box retailers
  - Department stores
  - Better off-price stores
  - Discount and dollar stores
  - Warehouse stores
  - Independent retailers
  - Etailers
  - Specialty retailers
  - Convenience and liquor stores

▶ Retail distributors and other wholesalers

▶ Exporters

▶ Government agencies

Most of the potential customers on this list probably won't surprise you, but one might—Uncle Sam. The rest of the possibilities on the list are straightforward to approach—you call on or email the prospect and engage in further discussions if there is an interest to do business with you. The government presents an oft-overlooked and interesting opportunity because government agencies are both potential customers and suppliers. Governments at the federal, state, county, and local (city, township, borough, etc.) levels all need IT equipment, alarm and security systems, health-care products and supplies (oh my, can you imagine how many disposable exam gloves the government buys—just look at post office employees), construction and repair materials, janitorial and cleaning equipment and supplies, grounds and landscaping equipment and supplies, and the list goes on. While technically an end user, the government tends to buy so much of one thing, a wholesale distributor would be wise to secure their business whenever the opportunity arises.

Most government agencies have a procurement procedure and often require vendors to go through a bidding process. The bad news is that this red tape can be slow and at times perhaps painful. The good news is that the requirements are usually written and understandable.

These agencies most often use something called a *p-card*, a company or government charge card that employees can use to charge goods and services on behalf of their employers. Many workers can use their p-card to buy wholesale without having to go through an approval or bidding process. These are also referred to as *purchase cards* or *procurement cards*. Wholesale distributors experience less friction in selling to purchasing agents who have p-cards because the buyer can place their orders by phone and the wholesaler can then charge the card using a credit card terminal or mobile payments company.

Whether you want to sell to schools or shipyards, most government agencies have a protocol for bidding on their business. Buyers have p-cards, and their purchase limit will

**tip**

The U.S. Small Business Administration (SBA) Office of Government Contracting is an excellent place to acquire specialized knowledge required to trade with the federal government. Check out the SBA's selection of digital courses for small business executives at: https://www.sba.gov and click on the Learning Center menu.

determine how much they can buy from you before you have to start filling out forms and getting on bid lists. If the single purchase the buyer needs to make exceeds their p-card limit, you can always generate multiple invoices with staggered due dates. Each year, the federal government alone purchases hundreds of billions of dollars' worth of goods and services from pencil erasers to rocket engines. Small wholesale distributors can capture their fair share of the more than $100 billion in federal contracts for goods granted to small businesses.

## Market Research Tactics

You've selected what *you* believe to be a great line of products and identified a customer base, but you must master the method of reaching and engaging them. This requires real, live customers (not just an idea of who they are)—actually, it requires customer *prospects*. If you've already opened your doors and now started thinking about researching your market,

it's too late. Unless you've got really deep pockets and can survive for an extended period of time without sales, you'll need to research your market before you sign a lease or hire the first employee. Essential market research is required, along with a humble conviction.

There are some products that are so incredible and revolutionary that their sales are driven almost exclusively by their reputation for quality and innovation. In my work, I have always focused my attention on manufacturers that are the most emblematic brands in their respective industries. I have noted that business performance— profitability and growth—are most stellar in the area of high-quality brands. Tesla and iPhone are anomalies but not happenstance by any stretch of the imagination. As a wholesale distributor, however, you must not chase after unicorns in the forest. Your desire must be for attainable

**tip**

Anyone who suffers from sweaty palms when facing an audience of one person or a thousand should explore their nearest Toastmasters club. Since 1924, the nonprofit organization Toastmasters International has been promoting communication and public speaking skills— with a membership as of 2018 of 357,000 members.

brands that you can secure at a low enough price that you can wholesale them with predictable success. So, let's talk tactics.

Market research can involve simple phone calls to prospective customers or can become deeply involved studies. Business owners should be in as much direct contact with their customers as often as possible in order to check their customers' pulse and remain intimately aware of their evolving needs. People are very time-starved, and long surveys are less effective than multiple brief ones collected over a period of time. You need to ask yourself "What is my unique offering?" and work on your ability to deliver amazing results. Market research and connecting with customers require excellent communication skills.

Most startups have to cut expenses to the bone in order to ensure success through "lean times." Before "reinventing the wheel" and expending precious time and money on market surveys and research, see what intel you can curate from existing sources such as trade organizations in your industry. Almost *always* someone else has already conducted the research you hope to capture and understand. Juxtapose the cost of doing your own market research against potentially purchasing existing studies from reliable sources. Knowing your customer one human being to another is *really knowing* them. This can only be accomplished with the hard work required to engage with them personally and on a meaningful level. That is what market research is really about—both online and off.

When conducting market research, it helps to look at really big companies and examine their operations and look at where they've been and how they became successful. I'm fond of the auto parts industry. When I lived in Hollywood with my second-oldest brother Erich, I earned a little money working on cars, and I have a great fondness for all things mechanical. Genuine Parts Company is a distributor of automotive replacement parts, industrial replacement parts, and other equipment and supplies. Genuine Parts Company sold a whopping $18.7 billion dollars in goods in 2018. They have been around since 1928 and are a model of steady sales growth. It is also interesting to note that 10 percent of the company's 2018 revenue was derived from the sale of general office products, technology supplies, facility and breakroom solutions, disposable food service products, office furniture, health-care products, and safety and security items. The business products are wholesaled under the S.P. Richards Company, a wholly owned subsidiary of Genuine Parts Company. If I were to venture into either car parts or office products, I'd be particularly concerned about studying the operations of a company that captures such a huge percentage of the market share of these industries. I cannot compete in the areas of buying power or logistics. *What in the world could I sell against such a Goliath?* With a passion for vintage cars, I could specialize in hard-to-find replacement parts for one of my favorite cars, the Datsun (Nissan) Z-car. Now in the sixth generation, the oldest Z-car parts are scarce and expensive. Specialty car parts retailers all over the world would gladly special order these rarities for their collector car customers. What about handmade personal stationery? High-end stationery addicts will pay incredible sums for paper that looks and feels extraordinary and that is only available in the finest stores. In the exotic landlocked South Asian country known as the Kingdom of Bhutan, small factories produce traditional Bhutanese paper that is made entirely by hand from the bark of the daphne bush. After soaking and boiling the bark, the paper masters crush, pulp, press, and dry it to make fabulous cards, notebooks, lampshades, and calendars. I wasn't able to find Bhutanese paper among the 69,000 products offered by the folks at S.P. Richards Company. Market research uncovers untapped opportunities and helps you gain insight or support decision making. It isn't enough to simply draw conclusions from a review of what other companies are or are not offering (or doing), it is also important to talk with customers about their beliefs, needs, and wants to make solid decisions relating to what product lines to carry.

## Gather Intel from Existing Customers

Advanced market research will retard mistakes, increase initial sales velocity, and reveal customers' needs. Customer retention warrants a substantial amount of time spent talking with existing customers, and that means engaging in business scuttlebutt. Did you just quit your corporate cubicle because you absolutely loathed your boss? Did you want to fire him because he kept asking you to give presentations at the company's all-hands meetings? Does the very idea of talking to people make your stomach turn inside-out? There are successful company owners who don't speak directly to their customers, but I think that they should. You must accomplish the mission of securing the intel necessary to move your new business forward. Either you'll need to dive into learning the fine art of small talk, or hire someone willing to pound the pavement and secure faithfully acquired information that you can use to make marketing decisions now and in the future.

It is a mistake to lean on technology as a main source of contact. Email and telephone calls are convenient, but face-to-face interactions are better. Developing deeper connections opens up communication and that's when customers share what's working and what's not working. If your customers are happy, they will stay with you and let you know what they require to continue buying from you. Even big company executives should ride along with delivery drivers and chat with their customers.

## Put Yourself in the Customer's Shoes

Never forget your roots and what made your scrappy, ambitious startup successful. Reaching full potential requires placing a priority on organic growth with your employees being the "secret sauce" to a carefully controlled image. In conducting market research before you launch, determine if there is a general lack of customer service in the marketplace. I find that there often is. Successful companies can lose sight of the ingredients that made them successful in the beginning, and as time marches on, they become complacent and so do their employees. Has this happened with your competitors? It never ceases to amaze me the number of times I cross paths with dour, crabby frontline staff when working with wholesalers. Not too long ago, I needed to purchase a vast quantity of real wood cyma recta molding, and while I didn't mind the long wait time to be served, the wholesale service desk employee came across as indifferent and I then felt rushed after having waited patiently for everyone else before me to be served. The experience was mediocre. This turned on a light bulb for me, and I realized that one of the most accurate, low-cost market research campaigns available to any businessperson is being able to place themselves in the role of a customer of their competitor. Any type of company can obtain unlimited and valuable market research by becoming a customer of its competitor. The dramatic thinkers refer to this as "corporate espionage," but I prefer to call it *good business sense*. Researching your market includes determining the strengths and weaknesses of your competition; or finding out where the white space is, i.e., the products that your competitors aren't carrying and that you should.

Let's talk about food. Who doesn't like talking about food, after all? Every savvy, nonfranchise fast-food restaurateur will insist on the tastiest, crispiest french fries for their customers, and they will try out many wholesale distributors' fries before settling on the supplier who can ensure their vision for fries is fully met. Every frozen french fry wholesaler must reduce the friction for their customer by doing this legwork for them—trying every imaginable potato processing plants' products until only the best-tasting and crunchiest product has been discovered.

Before you giggle and proclaim this to be "nonsense," think about the resort industry. Remember the last time you stayed at a *luxury* hotel? Do you recollect all the fine details? After checking in and heading to the room, think about the specific wonderful smell you experienced when opening the door. Recall the quality of the thick Turkish cotton towels and the dreamy comfort of the bedding. Think about the quality of solid-wood furniture. Do you remember the intense flavor of the in-room coffee? What about the color temperature of the lights—relaxing and not too bright? Reminisce about the appealing wall decor. Was every detail flawless? Hoteliers may have a clear vision for what they demand on behalf of their even more demanding clientele, but they certainly do not have the time to curate the finest of *everything* from a hundred different sources. The wholesale distributor that specializes in couture hotel experiences has worked tirelessly to find the best of everything to offer to these lodging managers—offering everything from case goods furniture to individually wrapped, spa-quality soap. You must always start with the customer and work backward. Maintain intense focus, remain vigilant, and sustain a sense of urgency. You don't want someone else taking care of *your* customers.

## ► What's in a Name?

The name given to distributors will vary by industry. A small food-service distributor is called a "wagon-jobber" or simply a "jobber" and they buy in bulk and deliver small quantities to convenience stores, niche grocers, and bodegas. Jobbers take pallets of product, break them down, and sell them by the case and occasionally unit quantities. While a bakery goods jobber will deliver their delicious goods every morning, canned and packaged goods stay fresh much longer and customer visits will occur weekly or even less frequently.

## Conducting Online Surveys

Internet pioneers first turned to online surveys and encouraged participation with financial rewards, such as guarantees of gift cards for popular retail websites and coffeehouses, or the lure of being entered into a "mega" jackpot giveaway contest. Spam then threatened to suffocate inboxes. As spam emails became easier to detect using artificial intelligence with machine learning, surveys started ending up in the junk email folder, never to be seen again. Please don't think you will outsmart these computers. In 1997, IBM's Deep Blue computer defeated a human chess grandmaster, which I assure you is no small feat. More than two decades later, a cheap mobile phone has more computing power than was used to accomplish the first lunar landing on July 20, 1969 (which required a room filled with computers).

It is tempting (but a mistake) to think that rented email lists and mass email campaigns are effective for conducting market research. I have been there, done that, and failed at it. Even if a survey should survive the advanced computer intelligence of spam filtering, we are all now experts at clicking the *delete* button and sending junk mail into oblivion. Effective, meaningful surveys should never be the result of bribes or shotgun email blasts. A well-cultivated list of willing participants is the only path to surveys that offer the steering you need to keep your business on the road.

Handcrafted outreach and person-to-person engagement are on orders of magnitude *far more meaningful* than a long, multifield survey form.

Some of the methods for capturing survey data include:

- ► Speak with a prospective customer and obtain permission to send them a survey.
- ► Add a survey to your website that includes fields for the name and email address of the person completing the survey.
- ► Set up surveys on your social media profiles (many have native survey/polling tools).

▶ Exhibit at trade shows related to your industry and ask attendees to complete surveys (or capture their email *and permission* to send them the survey later).

Do you like free stuff? For surveys small or large, I use Google Forms. It's free, intuitive, and easy-to-use—the servers are always fast, and I can receive a handful or thousands of responses with no lag or downtime. Google Forms even supports branding. I use Google Forms for surveys and *anything else* that requires a form, e.g., RSVP responses for company events, contact forms, and more. Responses are stored in a Google spreadsheet. If you have a Google account, then there's no separate setup or registration; you can start using Google Forms immediately. For details, visit: https://forms.google.com.

You can also conduct surveys and engage in business scuttlebutt on social media. Social media adoption is extremely rapid and *social selling* is a real "thing" now. Social media platforms make money through commercial advertising, which opens up doors for you. Be warned before spending a mint on digital advertising, however—many mature wholesale distribution businesses know a little secret you'll quickly discover—word-of-mouth remains the most powerful customer acquisition tool you'll ever have. A penchant for insanely fabulous customer service paired with quality products and fair prices is the most powerful marketing tool. That said, wholesale distribution businesses are finding customers on social media platforms. It works in part because public social media profiles offer a peek "behind the curtain" into people's lives and that of their businesses. While not generally considered a social media platform, LinkedIn feels quite a bit like one. LinkedIn is a professional networking service that had 630 million members as of June 2019. While a basic account is free, a premium one isn't cheap (visit their site for the current pricing—job seekers pay the least and sales professionals pay more). LinkedIn Sales Navigator is a sales tool that allows you to find key stakeholders at companies and reach out to them. You can ask to connect with other LinkedIn members and they may or may not accept your invitation. Busy executives may not. Direct connections are considered "1st degree" who can message each other without a premium subscription. For nonconnections, you'll need to use InMail credits, a limited number of which come as part of a premium subscription. If the member responds to your InMail message, you'll receive the credit back. If not, you use it and lose it. LinkedIn is an excellent tool for my business (full disclosure: I am also an author for LinkedIn Learning). I use LinkedIn to communicate with prospects and close deals. Once I'm connected with someone and know them well (e.g., customers), I use InMail to send links to my customer surveys. InMail never reveals a LinkedIn member's email address so they can say "goodbye" at any time to the relationship. This is one of the reasons it is effective—virtually no spam, you control the conversation, and "big time" company executives are within reach. You can also blog and write articles—both of which are excellent ways to raise awareness of what you are up to.

## Other Key Considerations

All industries suffer headwinds and that means challenging times during downturns. Will an industry continue to be viable tomorrow? In addition to providing *high value* to your customers, you must consider the demands of the marketplace. In certain industries, the growth of disintermediation is a formidable threat. In the automobile industry, certain manufacturers such as Tesla have chosen to operate company-owned showrooms and sell vehicles online rather than through a dealer network. To be sure, there are aftermarket accessories retailers that specialize in serving Tesla owners; however, it's a young market. I tend to gravitate toward more understandable and predictable products with longer sales histories. There is no shame in trying, but be warned that the risk grows when wandering about in unknown territory. Tesla's focus is to cut out the middleman (P.S. that's you, the wholesaler!).

Who are your biggest competitors? Some industries continue to consolidate and are dominated by large, national, and global conglomerates. Look for a neglected niche.

Let's look at the case of Sysco Corporation (NYSE ticker "SYY"), which (in 2018) is the largest global distributor of food and related products serving the food service and "food away from home" industry. Sysco Corporation serves 600,000 locations that include restaurants, health care, educational facilities, lodging properties, and other customers that serve food. This organization is a well-lubricated machine. They rock, and its price-to-value ratio for goods, its service, and its selection are all incredible. In 2018, Sysco Corporation traded $58.7 billion in goods, and as an agent for growth, the company continues to acquire other, large wholesale distributors. How could I compete against them? I'd want to scour their catalog and see if they have any white space. Specialty foods and the farm-to-table movement are really hot right now. I could see opportunity with handcrafted boutique cheese, organic kombucha, or exotic locally farmed truffles.

I believe there's a huge opportunity in the unique, differentiated products niches. If becoming a *specialty* food wholesaler strikes your fancy, then there would be a wonderful opportunity to gain market share and establish your business. Think of the many influential farm-to-table and farm-to-school advocates who are promoting locally sourced food. While a direct sales relationship is common (think farmers markets as one possible sales channel), local producers of beer and wine, produce, herbs and spices, seafood, poultry, and other meats are working with wholesalers to connect with the growing number of businesses that cater to locavores. Specialty food and beverage producers can be found by the hundreds exhibiting at the Fancy Food Shows held in San Francisco and New York (https://www.specialtyfood.com/shows-events/).

Look with intensity at the competitors that are currently in the market. Some industries are very fragmented, made up of a multitude of small, privately held companies. Focus on these industries for a point-of-entry and for long-term opportunities. Niche companies go farther in a shorter amount of time than broader-based firms. Business analysis can be mind-numbing, and you would be ill-advised to bury your head into too many books before simply getting your feet wet.

What would you ask a potential *future* customer?

- ▶ "Are you happy with your current wholesalers? If not, why?"
- ▶ "Would you consider auditioning my company as a potential new vendor?"
- ▶ "What products are you buying the most and would you try new lines from different manufacturers (or farmers, etc.)?"
- ▶ "What problems are you facing in your business?"
- ▶ "Who are the decision-makers and what is the approval process?"
- ▶ "How could I help you run your business better?"

There's no singular approach to surveying people, but one thing a busy company never has time to do is *waste time*, so your outreach needs to be focused and meaningful. Of course, there will be different questions depending on the industry and customer type. Making appointments for a meeting is preferable to emails and phone calls. It's not likely you'll be kicked out of someone's business, but it's easy to make excuses in order to get off the phone.

## Identifying Competitor Threats

In order to identify perceived competitors, internet research should be enhanced with walking trade shows and by speaking with companies in person whenever possible.

These traits are likely to make a competitor a real threat within your SWOT analysis:

- ▶ They provide highly trained, exceptionally knowledgeable staff who serve their customers with great alacrity. Consultive workers help customers find solutions and engage with personalized service that makes it nearly impossible to lure their customers away to consider buying from anyone else.
- ▶ Their operations are meticulously efficient.
- ▶ They offer everyday low prices.

▶ It's easy to do business with them; they serve a variety of customer tastes—orders can be placed online, through an application programming interface, by phone, email, fax, text, etc.

▶ They obsess over customer needs and fill them with "one stop" shopping—forecasting trends and polling customers (it's not mandatory that every product make a profit if its mere availability averts a customer's wandering eye).

People adore companies that provide exceptional customer service, and my instincts tell me that in your startup, this is a core part of what it means to find your niche and how to use exceptional service to your advantage. This seems super basic and simple, yet so many established players become so complacent that they (and their staff) lose sight of how they became a top player in their industry. You'll always need to get the pricing correct so that you have a competitive advantage, but being *cut-rate* isn't a smart business decision if exceptional customer service is what will land you accounts.

>
>
> **tip**
>
> Always obsess about customer needs, not short-term profits. When you mark up special order merchandise, do so modestly. Your fairness will not go unnoticed and is a genius customer retention tool. Obsess about customer needs, not short-term profits.

Focus your energy on things that are easy to understand where you can excel. Selling quality construction 2-by-4s is far less complicated than trading in couture fashion. Wholesale lumber and apparel are pretty much neck and neck in terms of annual gross merchandise volume. Fashion retailers must address ever-changing customer tastes and will require return privileges as a hedge against slow-moving and obsolete inventory. While a truckload of surplus construction lumber can be quickly resold, returns of out-of-season and out-of-fashion clothing, shoes, and accessories may end up collecting dust in a warehouse. As designers fall out of fashion, the value of their creations tumbles in lockstep. Once you identify competitor threats, you can then use that information to determine how you will both do it *better* and also *differentiate* your company to win over new business.

As you place your competition under a microscope, be mindful of your industry SWOT analysis as well as company-specific examination. You may find that there are lessons to be learned in wholesale categories that may not at first appear to be related (*psst*—that's how you chart trends). For example, while confectionery and tobacco are worlds apart, they share many of the same opportunities and challenges. Both are nonessential goods, so consumers may stop purchasing these products if they expect their income level to be adversely affected in the future. Both industries suffer from unfavorable public attitudes. Some health professionals and consumers argue that both sugar and nicotine are equally addictive. Confectionery manufacturers are expanding into sugar-free products that use perceptually "better for you" sweeteners (such as all-natural stevia extract), and thus the industry is opening more doors for health-conscious customers. The tobacco industry continues to take hits and is extremely vulnerable. Electronic cigarettes were once viewed as a less-harmful alternative to combustible tobacco, but reports of vaping-related illness cases have been gripping headlines. A wholesaler evaluating the marketplace must be vigilant and add these points to the analysis.

## Checking Out the Competition

A friend in business recently bought me lunch (I offered to pay, but he grabbed the check), and as we ate and conversed, he casually mentioned that a plastic tumbler manufacturer approached him about licensing four animation characters that he developed. "I was turned off by his website; it didn't look very good," he said. I spent the next 30 minutes sharing some relevant stories about *six- and seven-figure* deals I closed with obscure, under-the-radar factories that either had no websites or that had very poorly managed ones. In the world of manufacturing and wholesale, some industry segments place little or no value on their public-facing image. These firms don't seek to attract end users. The companies that end up retailing their goods are those that work on the beautiful marketing needed to entice retail buyers.

Researching the competition is crucial, but I am skeptical of how much you'll learn about your industry adversaries from their web presence. Here are some of the stones that you may wish to overturn in order to gain the desired *threats* examination about each perceived competitor in your SWOT analysis:

- ▶ Sign up for their newsletter to maintain the pulse of what they're up to.
- ▶ Follow them on social media.
- ▶ Make purchases from them.
- ▶ Examine their online reviews.
- ▶ Set Google Alerts so that you'll receive immediate emails about news stories related to them.
- ▶ Follow news coverage in the media with a focus on trade magazines (you can identify which magazines are relevant and useful by speaking with the organizers of large wholesale-oriented trade shows—lists are found through the local convention center(s) in your city).

- ▶ Read annual reports if the firm is a publicly traded company.
- ▶ Ask their customers for intel.
- ▶ Speak with trade associations about them.
- ▶ Search court records (most are online now) to examine any legal activities the company has engaged in, e.g., defending or initiating lawsuits.
- ▶ Search trademark registration records online at the U.S. Patent and Trademark Office to study what new products the company may be launching.
- ▶ Talk and talk (and talk) with people in the industry (i.e., *business scuttlebutt*).

In the SWOT analysis, threats must be examined under a microscope. This can include speaking with suppliers and customers, attending conferences, and if you're taking really bold and dramatic action, hiring employees away from your competition to diminish their foothold on your market. And just ask people, even your competitors. You might be surprised how open and candid people can be.

## Analyzing Industry Data

Since 1939, the U.S. Census Bureau has been conducting the Monthly Wholesale Trade Survey (MWTS) in order to provide regular estimates of sales and inventories within the wholesale trade industry. The MWTS polls industry firms within the U.S. These include merchant wholesalers that take title of the goods they sell, jobbers, industrial distributors, exporters, and importers. Excluded are nonmerchant wholesalers such as manufacturer sales branches and offices; agents, merchandise or commodity brokers, and commission merchants; and other businesses whose primary activity is other than wholesale trade. View current and historical wholesale trade data by visiting: https://www.census.gov/wholesale/index.html. The 2018 MWTS reported more than $6 trillion in total wholesale trade (which represented an almost even 50–50 split between durable and nondurable product sales). If you're new to the jargon, *durable goods* are products that yield utility over time rather than being consumed in one use (e.g., cars, books, tools, furniture, etc.). *Nondurable goods* are used rapidly or in a single use (e.g., fuel, wine, medication, paper products, clothing, etc.).

This is how the federal government breaks them down:

*Durable Goods*:
- ▶ Automotive
- ▶ Furniture
- ▶ Lumber

*Nondurable Goods*:
- ▶ Paper
- ▶ Drugs
- ▶ Apparel

- ▶ Professional equipment
- ▶ Computer equipment
- ▶ Metals
- ▶ Electrical
- ▶ Hardware
- ▶ Machinery

- ▶ Groceries
- ▶ Farm products (but not farming equipment)
- ▶ Chemicals
- ▶ Petroleum
- ▶ Alcohol

These are the major categories of goods, and any products that do not fit into these categories have gross merchandise volume that is small enough that the census groups them into a "miscellaneous" category.

It's prudent to examine the MWTS to spectate sales fluctuations to identify trade headwinds. Certain industries, such as office supplies, face the real threat of contraction as more office work becomes digital and in an effort to be socially responsible, people are endeavoring to print less. Trends like these will bear out in the data, so pay close attention to what this and other government reports tell you.

There is no right way to do what needs to be done when it comes to interacting with prospective and actual customers to perform market research and gather intel. Checking out your competitors, asking prospects what they look for from a wholesaler, and analyzing the competition will eventually become a routine and come naturally to you. This will involve stepping out of your comfort zone and trying things. Once you open your doors and your company becomes more successful, never lose sight of how you got there in the first place. Be ever-vigilant and continue applying the techniques you've learned in this chapter as long as you run your company.

# Raising Money

"Avoid using borrowed money."

I mean it wholeheartedly. That said, this is how I prefer to live life. I also advocate *living with less*. While I never recommend operating a company with obsolete equipment or unreliable delivery vehicles, I persistently question every purchase and expense. "Is this absolutely necessary, and will this be a profitable decision?" I don't carry credit card balances, and I have zero business loans. I have borrowed millions of dollars from banks to acquire real estate and will continue to do so.

If you want to start your own business and don't have any capital to get going, then start small and work your way into bigger deals. An entrepreneur who lacks any banking and borrowing savvy should never borrow money unless they are fully prepared to lose every dime of the loan and still be ready to pay it back in the future. I would be doubly concerned if you are a person who rents an apartment and drives a shiny new luxury car, shops at high-end stores, eats out every night, and has zero savings. One of the reasons I have always managed to stay flush is that for every $10 of profit I earn, I save eight of them and either reinvest those eight dollars in the business or park the money in a low-cost S&P 500 index fund. Keeping profits invested in liquid investments allows me to rapidly deploy those funds when a lucrative deal crosses my path. But that's just me. I'm not a financial advisor, so you should always seek the advice of a pro before you make your own investment choices to benefit your business. You can, of course, start close to home and look to people you know or your local bank for a startup loan. Loans from family and friends tend to be unstructured and open-ended. If the loan gets into arrears, you'll live with the fallout in a very personal way that will never occur when borrowing from established lending sources. Things could get awkward. By all reports, from many wholesalers, your first year in business will probably be a very hard one. You will need working capital to function and accomplish anything at scale because startups and growing businesses are usually operating in the red. Lenders make money by lending money. Their credit decisions have very little to do with how long you've been their customer or how white your smile is; creditors care about your ability to repay the loan and make the payments in a timely manner.

Banks are no longer the only go-to source for business loans. The lending landscape has evolved considerably over the years. There are many options for business financing. In this chapter, we'll explore various ways you can get the cash flow flowing for your wholesale business. You have a wide variety of options ranging from credit cards to angel investing. Let's take a look.

## Credit Cards

Yes, you can use credit cards to help fund your business. That said, know that you should proceed with caution and know exactly what you're getting into when you sign that card agreement. You pay for the goods with a credit card (not a debit card), and you resell them during the period before the bill is due, pay off the card, and keep the profits. The *grace period* is the time during which you are allowed to pay your credit card bill without having to pay interest. The Credit CARD Act of 2009 requires that if issuers have grace periods, they must last at least 21 days. The grace period usually applies only to new purchases. While this sounds like a wonderful strategy for securing some "float" on the money while you hustle a deal that's already in motion, if your buyer falls through and there are no returns privileges, you're stuck paying the credit card bill while you scramble to resell the merchandise to someone else. Credit card interest rates are generally in the crushing double digits. Since the merchant card processing fees are paid for by your supplier, these fees are passed along to you in the form of slightly higher prices. Most credit cards do not give a grace period for cash advances and balance transfers; instead, interest charges start right away. If you pay in full, avoid all interest, and can secure pricing that's the same as cash, then using a credit card as a short-term means of financing a deal makes sense. Note that to get a grace period on purchases, most card agreements require that you pay the new balance by the payment due date every billing cycle. If you do not, you will not get a grace period until you pay the new balance for two billing cycles in a row.

## Raising Capital Working with a Partner

Working with a business partner is a realistic means to raise immediate capital for starting your business. Think hard before partnering with family members. It can work beautifully or become highly divisive. If you share the same values and have complementary skills with someone who has money to invest *and* prior business experience, a partner can propel things along quickly. Two heads may indeed be better than one. It helps to have a track record together before you go into business. Carefully define each partner's roles and responsibilities and engage in a written agreement, ideally one that is prepared by a talented partnership attorney. Transparency and candor are paramount in a business partnership.

Give serious consideration to how much time each person will commit to the business as well as how much money each will inject into the partnership. A "silent" investor who merely invests a portion of the initial startup capital should receive less than someone who *both* funds and works at the company. This is negotiable. Poll other established partnerships for ideas. There is no playbook for handling partnerships per se because each arrangement is different. Partners should be advised that there is no guarantee of any return on their investment and that the venture involves substantial risk. Look for potential partners who are former entrepreneurs or executives, making use of their experience and networks.

Forming a partnership is one scenario where I recommend you seek out the services of an attorney who is a partnership specialist.

## Angel Investors

Wealthy individuals working independently or in angel groups (or angel networks) provide capital for business startups. These angels customarily receive convertible debt or ownership equity in exchange for supporting startups throughout the initial, high-risk stages of launch and initial operation. Angel investment is most commonly associated with the rich region of Silicon Valley; however, there are a growing number of angel investment clubs, networks, and crowdfunding sites. The Angel Capital Association (https://www.angelcapitalassociation.org) has 14,000+ member accredited angel investors. While the world of angel investing seems very fancy and "corporate," an angel investor could very well be your local dentist. Many high-income professionals dabble in the world of angel investing.

In the U.S., angels are generally accredited investors in order to comply with current U.S. Securities and Exchange Commission (SEC) regulations. If you're curious, you can look up the official meaning of an "accredited investor" which is defined in rule 501 of Regulation D of the SEC.

## Venture Capital

Venture capital is often referred to as simply "VC" and is a type of private equity financing for early-stage firms that exhibit (or have already exhibited) high growth potential. While I am skeptical you'd secure venture capital to start a wholesale distribution company selling something *everyday* such as canned food or car parts, there are oodles of cool and innovative products out there that require distribution, and should your situation prove to be uniquely positioned for incredible sales velocity and growth, your company may be a candidate for venture capital. Procuring venture capital is unlike raising debt or taking out a loan. A lender expects to be repaid whether you succeed or fail—with interest. Venture capitalists take an equity stake in the company and their return depends on the profitability of the business. Most venture capitalists formulate an exit plan which means that they profit by selling their shareholdings when the value of the business rises to a certain "trigger" level. There are typical stages in venture capital financing, and if you believe your venture warrants it, then speak with an investment banker or a fundraising consultant to explore this further.

Finding a venture capital firm that chooses to invest in your type of business requires that you talk with these companies, and you'll find articles and the names of venture capital investors at https://www.entrepreneur.com.

## Crowdfunding

Crowdfunding is a growing method of funding a venture by obtaining small amounts of money from many people using online sites. This form of alternative finance is mutually exclusive of traditional sources of funding such as capital markets and banks. Friends and colleagues have used crowdfunding with mixed results (most did not appear to reach their fundraising goals). I do not trivialize or dismiss crowdfunding as a way to raise money; however, the crowdfunding world has become *crowded*. If you have a large number of cheerleaders in your orbit, you could set up a crowdfunding campaign and send invitations to these family, friends, and colleagues—asking for their financial help with your business by purchasing stock in your company. Selling stock in your company is a *regulated* activity if your solicitation takes on certain characteristics. The ability of an entrepreneur to raise money in the U.S. by selling interests (i.e., securities) is contingent on ensuring that it is done in a "private offering" and not in a "public offering." A public offering would require registration of the securities. There are tools available for the entrepreneur that do not require SEC registration and are available for small-scale fundraising efforts. The Jumpstart Our Business Startups Act (the "JOBS Act") allows for startups and small businesses to raise capital through formal securities through crowdfunding. The JOBS Act crowdfunding provisions enable new and petite companies the opportunity to raise capital in a streamlined, inexpensive manner by making low dollar offerings of securities (e.g., stock shares) to a "crowd" of interested investors. Title III added new Section 4(a)(6) to the Securities Act, which provides an exemption from the registration requirements of Securities Act Section 5 for certain crowdfunding transactions. Regulation Crowdfunding, which prescribes the rules governing the offer and sale of securities under Section 4(a)(6), permits an issuer to raise a maximum aggregate amount of $1.07 million in a 12-month period. The SEC put these rules into place to help businesses raise money as an alternative to bank financing. To learn more, reach out directly to the SEC.

## Automated Lending and Cash-Flow Solutions

Automated lending and cash-flow solutions are part of the growing number of ways business owners can obtain credit for operations. With these companies, a computer (not a person) evaluates factors such as gross merchandise volume, time in business, social media activity, and credit scores. As artificial intelligence becomes ever-more sophisticated, these services are going to continue to prosper. Lending is one area of business where a computer can do a pretty darn good job of replacing a human being. Automated lending also means lower-cost loans. These are computer solutions and are developed by technology experts—with loans underwritten by licensed banks (to comply with government regulations).

## Trade Financing

The field of trade financing includes factoring, when a business sells its accounts receivable to a third party for a discount. A trade financing partner is a business specialist that focuses on working with transaction-related businesses such as wholesalers. I always prefer to grow a business from available cash-on-hand and I avoid loans like sour milk and stinky cheese. If there is a near certainty that surveys of retailers in your chosen industry are clamoring for the wacky-widget you just invented and you can only manage the incredible order volume with borrowing, don't ask your rich aunt or trust-fund cousin for money—seek the help of a factor, which is a company that specializes in lending cash against wholesale distributor invoices. Factors are business and loan specialists that know your industry and in most cases know your customers and their payment reliability and habits. The experienced factor will work with your market research and their prior experience with your customer to determine just how much money they are willing to advance on any particular sale, whether $1,000 or $10 million. In the early years, I used factors with exceptionally good results. They are expensive, but making a good profit on a really large sale is better than a huge profit percentage on a tiny sale. Factors will help smooth out the cash flow.

Trade financing is a *trillion-dollar* industry globally. These highly entrepreneurial lenders extend working capital to sustain rapid growth. When I first started my company, I worked with multiple trade financing companies with excellent results. Trade financing companies were easier to work with than banks during my startup years.

For a wholesaler, the trade financing options include:

▶ *Inventory financing*—a revolving line of credit that is secured against inventory. The inventory acts as the collateral for the loan and, once sold, is the means for repaying the debt.

▶ *Purchase order (PO) financing*—funding that pays the supplier to manufacture and deliver goods that have been ordered. The customer generally pays the purchase order financing company directly, who then deducts the principal and interest before sending the rest to the wholesaler.

▶ *Shipment financing*—this is part of what is referred to as supply chain finance (SCF) and includes pre-shipment finance, post-shipment finance, and supply chain finance. These tools are typically used by wholesalers with global supply chains. As deals accumulate, wholesalers can free trapped working capital. Unlocking working capital allows wholesalers to extend terms (credit) to buyers while being paid early.

Global supply chain finance (GSCF) is also known as supplier finance—it is frequently used by import/export wholesalers. Receivables management is an asset-based lending industry and is quite complex—a subject that could fill an entire book in itself. When your business grows to a level that warrants lending of this character, you should be speaking with a consultant or expert within the field to identify the potential supplier financiers that can support you appropriately.

## Bank Financing

I put bank financing in the last position because, in candor, I found banks *mostly* unwilling to lend money to my business when I was starting out. I had no issue securing car loans and obtaining home mortgages, but business capital from conventional banks was nowhere to be found back then. This is no surprise because one in three businesses with employees doesn't survive two years, and about half of companies fold within five years. The U.S. Bureau of Labor Statistics publishes a report known as *Business Employment Dynamics* that provides numbers for business "births" and "deaths" to support these facts.

Banks love collateral and will be far more inclined to engage in asset-based lending. That said, here are some banking solutions for businesses:

- ▶ *Business line of credit.* A revolving line of credit that is ideal for all short-term capital requirements, e.g., inventory purchases or supplier payments; interest accrues on the outstanding balance.
- ▶ *Commercial line of credit.* For large working capital needs and "big" companies.
- ▶ *Term loans.* Used to purchase equipment, capital goods, or consolidate debt; the repayment is generally handled with a fixed payment amount of principal and interest, amortized over an agreed-upon repayment term (collateral is usually required).
- ▶ *Small Business Administration (SBA) guaranteed loans.* While the SBA never loans money, the federal government will guarantee a small business loan, allowing your local bank peace of mind to make the deal with you. If you default, the bank can recover their money from the SBA. Loans can be petite or as large as $5.5 million. The SBA requires that you operate a for-profit, U.S.-based company, that you have invested your own money in the business, and that you were not able to secure financing conventionally.
- ▶ *Trade financing.* Banks also offer trade financing. This includes but is not limited to the following financial products:
  - *Standby/performance letters of credit.* Assures a counterparty within a financial transaction that you will fulfill your end of the bargain in situations such as a lease, security deposit, purchase invoice, or project performance.

- *Commercial import or domestic letters of credit.* Allows trading on superior price and terms because the bank will guarantee payment.
- *Documentary collection.* Where the exporter's bank collects funds from the importer/wholesale distributor; exporters permit their bank to serve the role of collection agent for payment of the goods shipped to the wholesaler.

Most retail bank customers work with national and global banks. These behemoths are well-known because of their persistent advertising campaigns. You will find an ATM for these banks nearly everywhere you go, which makes them attractive for retail customers (i.e., people who do not own businesses). In my experience, big banks are great for their convenience, cutting-edge technology, and if you want to borrow money to buy a home. I have found that local, state-chartered banks are hungrier for an entrepreneur's business. You can obtain a list of state-chartered commercial banks from the agency in your state that governs charter banks. When I wanted to borrow $587,000 to refinance a commercial property I own and was attempting to do so after the fallout of the 2007–2008 financial crisis—no big bank wanted to do the deal. I got creative and printed up postcards on my printer using 5-by-7 standard card stock, addressed them to *every* state-chartered bank in California, then applied stamps and mailed them out. The postcard said very little but provided a few key points about the loan I was seeking. I received 14 responses, and after sharing the financial data for the project, five loan offers were made. The loan was underwritten by a bank 130 miles away. The moral of the story is that charter banks work with borrowers that are often overlooked by the "big guys."

Oodles of retired (or laid off) corporate executives tap the equity in their million-dollar homes to start a business. Banks have made the process quite simple with a thing called a home equity line of credit (HELOC). The banks even give these asset-rich, unemployed folks a charge card and a checkbook to use for tapping into their HELOCs. A HELOC is a loan set up as a line of credit guaranteed by the equity in a primary residence—relatively easy to obtain when the equity in a home is considerable. Near the top on your *getting started* checklist should be the source and amount of funds to begin your enterprise. This critical information will greatly affect your marketing plan. A wholesaler of jet engines will need to carry *hundreds of millions of dollars* in inventory. Before you rush out to meet your bank's branch manager and tie up all the equity in your home to start a wholesale distribution business, I'd recommend you test the waters and gain some experience. You're starting a completely unproven, new business venture. The risk of business failure is always substantial. Borrowing against your primary residence is folly unless you have *substantial business experience* and have an equal amount of experience with financial matters and business loans.

# Pinpointing a Startup Number

Determining startup capital can be daunting. Some key points to consider when determining initial capital requirements include:

- ▶ The type of business—what will be sold
- ▶ The amount of inventory to be held
- ▶ Supplier terms (i.e., how long vendors allow for payment—the "float")
- ▶ If the wholesalers' customers pay cash or if terms are extended to them
- ▶ Rent
- ▶ Equipment and supplies (and this may include a delivery van or truck)
- ▶ Utilities
- ▶ Licenses/permits
- ▶ Insurance
- ▶ Salaries
- ▶ Advertising and marketing
- ▶ Printing
- ▶ Website development
- ▶ Professional services (accounting, legal, consultants, and who else?)
- ▶ Repairs and maintenance

Some line items have crystal-clear costs, such as licenses and permits, monthly rent, and any other line item you can apply a number to easily. There are one-time expenses (e.g., setup costs), and then there are monthly expenses . . . and even quarterly and yearly payments for taxes. Ask yourself what it will cost to build out the space and set up your warehouse. Will you have signage? Are there any expenses that need to be specially labeled on your balance sheet? For example, a security deposit collected by your landlord is not an expense, and you place it on your *balance sheet* as an asset—but it must be included in the total figure required to get up and running.

Entrepreneurs must use the scuttlebutt method of curating information from firsthand sources from discussions with other owners, competitors, and industry experts. Be curious and ask a million questions. You will gather tidbits of information from many sources and

**tip**

Keep a written record of accounts payable. I use QuickBooks to track upcoming bills. A common newbie mistake is forgetting to set aside sufficient funds to cover accounts payable. You must estimate the funds needed to pay for these purchases so that you're not caught short.

form a material conclusion to determine how much money to start out with. The U.S. Small Business Administration provides help in figuring out startup costs. Scan the QR code in Figure 4–1 for an example that they put together that can serve as a guide.

FIGURE 4–1: **The SBA Guide to Startup Costs**

# Correlating Inventory and Financing

There is a clear connection between making wise inventory decisions, increasing revenues, and using lines of credit (and other funding sources) smartly. Over the decades I have peeked inside the warehouses of many wholesale distribution companies. It never ceases to amaze me how many businesses allow their deadstock to occupy high-value shelving space. The higher the wholesaler's rent, the more valuable every inch of shelf space becomes and yet there is a rampant hoarder mentality with businesspeople. Even the most talented, smart, and hardworking business owners have attracted these fleas. Slow-moving and completely dead inventory should be cleared out, usually at any price, to free up space for more lucrative, faster-moving products. Tying up a single dollar in deadstock is a mistake. There is a common mentality among human beings to keep items that we perceive could be of value in the future. I have seen the madness of this as a landlord. I own a real estate development business that operates self-storage units. The one and only time I had to auction off the contents of a storage unit, the rent had been paid for years, but the tenant fell in arrears, was given ample opportunity to vacate the unit, but didn't. After many months of unpaid rent, a public auction was held to liquidate the items. The contents of the storage unit amounted to less than $1,000 worth of personal property, yet the tenant had paid thousands of dollars each and every year to store it. This same illogical, dangerous, and harmful mentality is ubiquitous in the business world. You can work hard, but you must also work smart.

Proven sellers and fast-moving goods should be brought into inventory. These can be financed when absolutely necessary. Only buy what customers want and in quantities that you can move quickly. Just-in-time production is rooted in Japanese manufacturing culture that seeks to reduce the time it takes to get things accomplished within a supply chain. Short-cycle manufacturing, continuous-flow manufacturing, and demand-flow manufacturing are also systematic processes under the umbrella of just-in-time production. Wholesalers should take the lead from these lean manufacturing and management movements in order to reduce on-hand inventories to their absolute lowest possible levels without allowing business opportunities to slip through their hands.

Let's examine some fictional companies in a realistic scenario. I'll explain the value of just-in-time supply chain philosophy and why it will save money and reduce capital needs:

Wholesaler Wakiza Distributing is purchasing nearby, farm-direct canned Jerusalem artichokes that are packaged immediately after harvesting. Wakiza Distributing receives a modest discount on both the product and freight when placing big orders. Wakiza Distributing has a $1 million commercial line of credit that is indexed to London Inter-Bank Offered Rate (LIBOR) and is presently costing 7-percent interest. Wakiza Distributing only pays interest on the outstanding principal.

Wakiza Distributing buys $200,000 in wholesale canned artichoke hearts monthly from Hardy Chokes Farms in Castroville, California—the artichoke capital of the world. Because artichokes are *always* in season, the price and availability rarely fluctuate within a growing year. There are few market pressures that affect price and availability, and the moderate California weather provides virtually no surprises within the supply chain. Wakiza Distributing's sales are always strong because its customers are busy restaurants that use canned artichokes in entrees and at their salad bars. Business is booming with no end in sight.

Wakiza Distributing orders $2.4 million in product from Hardy Chokes each year and receives a 5-percent volume discount on any order over $50,000 with no further discounts beyond that. It's not difficult for Hardy Chokes to sell their product, so discounts are merely offered as a courtesy for their larger customers as a standard within the industry.

Wakiza Distributing was placing $200,000 orders once per month and reordered when their inventory reached the 10-percent level because Hardy Chokes's delivery truck can bring a new shipment to Wakiza Distributing within 24 hours. At various times of the month, Wakiza Distributing's shelves were either full or 75-percent bare. Because Wakiza Distributing does not trade in many products, when they have open shelf space, it stays empty between their monthly shipments.

Hardy Chokes requires payment on their wholesale invoice within net seven days, which means Wakiza Distributing enjoys some float and that keeps borrowing from their line of credit to a minimum. That said, they still carried an average $100,000 balance on their commercial line of credit because Wakiza Distributing has considerable inventory left over by the time the farm's invoices come due. As Wakiza Distributing's customers placed orders, they could pay down the borrowed money used to cover the farmer's invoice until eventually the line was paid down until the monthly cycle repeated.

At the recommendation of a consultant, Wakiza Distributing started placing more frequent, smaller orders of $50,000 each and now reorders just-in-time before their supply of artichokes is sold out. Wakiza Distributing masters the timing in such a way that only a couple of days pass from the time the Hardy Chokes truck off-loads their shipment at Wakiza Distributing's dock until that very same product ends up in the larders of the local restaurants, hospitals, schools, and other customers that Wakiza Distributing serves.

Wakiza Distributing deployed a simple *kanban* board scheduling system to track their entire ordering process because their office is very small and a visual on-the-wall system works best for them. Kanban is a visual work flow process that helps you visualize your work. In Japanese, kanban means billboard or sign board. Recently, it started getting recognized by Wakiza Distributing business units across various areas. As a result, Wakiza Distributing can now carry three to four times as many products, their shelves remain full all year round, and they work with many more local farms—offering other canned, always-in-season vegetables, such as beetroot, cabbage, mushrooms, and carrots, sourced within a same-day or next-day delivery orbit.

By changing order frequency and sticking with locally grown products, Wakiza Distributing is now able to buy and sell substantially more gross merchandise volume of canned goods and has nearly zero balance on their commercial line of credit because they can buy and resell the goods before their farm invoices come due. Wakiza Distributing saves $7,000 in interest payments each year by eliminating the $100,000 balance on their line of credit.

This scenario is quite real and is how a just-in-time process works in a wholesale distribution business. For slower-moving products, wholesale distributors can place rush orders from their suppliers rather than keep items in stock. Fewer companies "go big" and stock up because rent and the cost of funds make doing so less practical than accepting a slightly smaller profit. Carrying costs of inventory must be juxtaposed against the additional profits of having a factory discount. Often the discount disappears after footing the bill for the credit line interest payment.

While it is an absolute impossibility to give individual guidance for determining how much money is required to start and operate through profitability, I hope that the aforementioned knowledge sparks a sufficient amount of curiosity so that you can evaluate your individual situation and come up with a clear plan. Don't do it alone. Engage in plenty of business scuttlebutt before moving forward.

## Getting Profitable

I'll start the discussion of getting profitable around some basic and essential tax topics. Bear in mind that investors and lenders are injecting funds into your company with the hope that what you're doing will turn a pretty penny. Raising capital is always easier after your business is turning a profit—injecting more money to grow (isn't that the rub . . . you need money to get started!). Getting profitable also means keeping as much money as you possibly can. If you use an IRS form 1040 and complete a Schedule C for your sole proprietorship, you'll be facing the tax rates for your individual tax bracket. At any rate, the government will still come calling for a big chunk of your net profits. The goal of every businessperson as it relates to this often-neglected subject of taxes should be to pay the least amount of tax that is legally permissible by properly reporting every dime that will offset taxable income. Even taxes are tax-deductible when attributable to your business.

The expenses that you incur or pay for starting a business or merely investigating the creation or acquisition of an active business are considered business startup costs according to IRS Publication 535. You can handle research costs in multiple ways. You can elect to amortize research costs, deduct them as current business expenses, or write them off over a ten-year period.

You incur bad debt if you cannot collect money owed to you, and debt becomes worthless under IRS rules when there is no longer any hope it will be paid. "Reasonable measures" must be demonstrated that all efforts to collect have been exhausted, like credit sales. Common bad debts for wholesalers are the result of credit sales to customers, i.e., sold goods that have not yet been paid for and are on the books as accounts receivable (or notes receivable). After a wholesaler fails to collect the invoice and a reasonable period of time has passed, it can be written off as a business bad debt for tax purposes.

Debt (when used with caution) is a tool for making money just as a can opener is a tool for opening cans. Debt (both borrowing and lending) is a primary ingredient in the business soup. Many expenses that cause you to incur debt are tax-deductible, may require you to capitalize, or may not qualify for a deduction at all.

The IRS requires a business expense to be both "ordinary" and "necessary." Ordinary expenses are those that are commonly incurred in your industry, and a necessary expense is one that is helpful and appropriate for your business. Expenses do not have to be indispensable to be considered necessary. A very simple example is that of printer paper. A wholesaler in luxury handbags and fine women's accessories prefers to print and mail customer invoices rather than use free email. The paper used is fine, linen paper, and the envelopes are custom-printed by an exclusive print shop that specializes in upscale stationery. Beautiful postage stamps are used. While the presentation is stunning, these expenses are not indispensable to the wholesaler's business, but are considered deductible because they are both helpful and appropriate, plus common to the particular luxury level of wholesale trade.

Expenses can be added to the cost of goods, such as warehouse overhead, freight, storage fees, and direct labor (including employee contributions to pension or annuity plans). Companies that trade more than $25 million annually must capitalize the direct costs and part of the indirect costs for resale activities. Indirect costs are rent, interest, taxes, storage, purchasing, processing, repackaging, handling, and administrative costs. If you are "going big" then you'll need to speak to your accounting professional about these nuances. Expenses that are added to the cost of goods can't be deducted again elsewhere. If the IRS discovers that you're renting a boathouse at Lake Tahoe and deducting it as a business expense, they'll probably start asking some fair and reasonable questions about how a vacation rental fits into a wholesale business. You typically cannot deduct personal, living, or family expenses; however, you are allowed to deduct the expenses for the business use of your home and car.

## Capitalize Costs

You must capitalize some costs rather than treat them as expenses. The IRS considers startup expenses, business assets, and improvements as long-term investments and you must capitalize them on federal income taxes. Items that you expect to last more than a year that are not a minor cost are capital expenses. When you capitalize expenses, you recover your cost by depreciation. Business investments are capital expenses, which are also referred to as CAPEX. Capital expenses are considered assets in your business. Under most circumstances, there are three types of costs you capitalize:

▶ Business startup costs
▶ Business assets
▶ Improvements

If acquired property's useful life is longer than the taxable year, you must capitalize it. CAPEX line items must be amortized or depreciated over the life of the asset. Amortization is the process of gradually writing off the initial cost of an asset over a period of time. Depreciation is the reduction in the value of an asset with the passage of time, due in particular to wear and tear. The IRS defines the amortization or depreciation period based on the rules within the Internal Revenue Code. CAPEX creates or adds *basis* to the asset or property (in the case of a building) which, upon adjustment determines the tax liability in the event you sell that asset. Basis in the context of business and U.S. tax law is the original cost of an asset, adjusted for factors such as depreciation. The basis of an asset can be affected by CAPEX. An asset's basis can increase or decrease if changes occur during its lifetime.

The cost basis of assets is a CAPEX and comes into effect when the money is spent to do things like acquire fixed assets, repair/restore/adapt/upgrade an existing asset to improve its useful life span, convert an asset to a new or different use, prepare an asset to be used in business, and spend capital for starting or acquiring a new business. Here are a few CAPEX examples for a wholesale business:

▶ A used delivery truck is acquired for $5,000 and you repaint and brand it for another $1,800—the *basis* is now $6,800.

▶ 100 secondhand pallet racks are purchased for $12,000 and a contractor is hired for $2,500 to install them—the *basis* is now $14,500.

▶ A new mini-split HVAC system is acquired for $5,000 and the contractor charges $1,500 for installation—the *basis* is now $6,500.

▶ A new sign is installed on the existing warehouse—the *basis* of the cost of the building is raised by the materials and labor cost of $2,700.

Tracking your asset basis matters dramatically to your profits. Virtually everything you own and use in a business is considered a capital asset under IRS regulations. The IRS methodologies for handling depreciation of capital assets is complex and is explained in 110 pages in IRS Publication 946, *How to Depreciate Property*. If you are a petite wholesaler and have no interest in learning the ropes of depreciation, then place the entire matter into the hands of your capable accountant. If you are thirsty for the knowledge, you can explore Publication 946 to expand your knowledge on the subject. Any businessperson setting up a large company must understand depreciation and the IRS rules that apply to handle depreciation.

Expenses appear on the company's profit and loss statement as incurred during the appropriate month. Capitalized costs are amortized or depreciated over multiple years.

Capitalized expenditures are placed on the company's balance sheet. Some costs can go both ways and the business owner decides. Capitalized interest is spread out over the asset's life span, and above certain IRS limits, CAPEX may be treated as part of the basis for the business, which will benefit the owner at the time of sale of the company.

The many nuances of the tax code are found in IRS Publication 535, *Business Expenses* (search engines are your friend!). Even if you hire an accountant or use sophisticated business tax preparation software, you will benefit greatly from understanding these essential accounting and tax topics for businesses. It will be very harsh on your bank balance to wait until you've accumulated a stockpile of cash just to find out that you've missed out on important offsets to your net profits that will reduce your tax bite. Learn early and avoid venting later.

**tip**

Uncle Sam generally doesn't require a physical receipt for deductible business expenses that are less than $75. You never need to keep a pile of de minimis receipts! But you must keep *good* records. A good record of a $2 parking meter expense or a $35 inkjet cartridge could be as simple as maintaining a spreadsheet or journal.

When venturing into the world of financing, you face many considerations. Examine every scenario that comes to mind. As shown with Wakiza Distributing, it is possible to make one very small adjustment (in their case, increasing ordering frequency) to substantially reduce the amount of working capital required. Intensely competitive industries require business owners to constantly evaluate and reevaluate everything. There are two very important lessons in the Wakiza Distributing example: the first was that they did not require as much capital to efficiently operate their business, and the second was that they could use their new ordering strategy to increase the number and gross merchandise volume of what was being sold to increase profits. Dealing factory direct (farm and factory direct in the case of Wakiza Distributing) at competitive prices improves profits. The more mouths to feed in the middle, the fewer bites each person enjoys from the pie.

Getting to a profitable place relates to both how much profit margin you can squeeze from the fruits of your labor, as well as running your business in an incredibly efficient and lean manner—avoiding taxes on the profits however you (legally) can.

## Financing Next Steps

Experienced businesspeople can borrow money at the right time and should do so if there is a high probability it will increase profits predictably. With experience comes skill, and borrowing money is a skill that took me years to learn. For your first startup, consider it a lab, and in this lab you'll be experimenting—a lot. Don't gamble with other people's money during the learning phase of opening a business. Seek proof of concept—place a toe in the water and feel things out.

As you consider how you will secure your financing and what you will do once you get it, you should ponder these questions:

- ▶ Have you spent sufficient time studying the industry?
- ▶ Did you engage in enough business scuttlebutt before proceeding?
- ▶ Is the industry seasonal, and have you considered how that impacts cash flow?
- ▶ Is the industry vulnerable in any way?
- ▶ Do you have a formal business plan?
- ▶ Did you settle on a startup total required to open your business?
- ▶ Do you need to raise money?
- ▶ Should you lease initially to conserve your available cash, just in case you need it?
- ▶ Do you have enough self-control to leave your credit cards in the dresser drawer and just use a debit or charge card?
- ▶ Can you identify a savvy partner with money to invest who syncs up with you perfectly at every level?
- ▶ Do you know a rich dentist or other professional seeking a tax shelter who is willing to go out on a limb (and knows the risks)?
- ▶ Are there angels or venture capitalists in your purview?
- ▶ Do you *really* need to sell stock in your company (e.g., crowdfunding) or can you weather the initial storm while you seek profitability?
- ▶ Will your bank offer trade financing with attractive terms?
- ▶ If banks have turned you down, would an SBA-guaranteed loan program be a viable option? Would you be able to continue to pay off the loan in the event your business folds?
- ▶ How much borrowing can you avoid by working with suppliers that offer terms?
- ▶ Will your suppliers offer additional financing beyond terms?
- ▶ Do you have an essential understanding of accounting and taxes to avoid getting into trouble with cash flow and the government?
- ▶ Is a member of your family both rich enough and "cool" enough to be your angel investor?

In the next chapter, I'll discuss finding your business's home and getting set up. Whether you work from the corner of the bedroom or make decisions in a boardroom, the next chapter will help you spark ideas for how to select the location for your startup and put all the puzzle pieces together.

# Setting
# Up Shop

The question that I'll pose before diving into this chapter is: Do you have enough money—cash dollars—to open a warehouse (or another type of wholesale home)? The question is simple enough, but there's another, closely related question: Just how "big" do you want to get with this new wholesale distribution business? You can start with little more than a small, cheap space and a sign that says you're in business, or you can invest a considerable amount of money to create a high-profile, corporate-looking, professional image. The latter will require a good amount of planning and budgeting on your part before you sign a lease and start curating potential construction contractors. Looking "big" may also be counterintuitive for your chosen industry. A jewelry and gemstone wholesaler can meet clients in a secure, shared office space or showroom and store inventory in a small, high-security office with a safe. Wholesalers in the jewelry trade often share resources to avoid overhead, and most of these sellers have little desire to pay the high rent associated with fancy locations because their customers—the retailers—are handling the sale to the retail customer. I conducted a site visit at a massive apparel wholesaler that deals with low-price goods, and their pallet racks rose sky-high. Every warehouse shelf was completely filled. Wholesalers of small items, on the other hand, commonly call on customers at their own business location and many never have customers visit the site where goods are stored. Bulky items require adequate storage space.

The decision to stay small or go big is something you'll have to grapple with yourself. This has a lot to do with the product and industry you have chosen. It would be fair to say you have an idea already how big you want (or need) to go and this chapter gives you the tools and advice to pave the way forward properly.

Some possible scenarios for you might be:

▶ Work from home (spare room, basement, garage, a shed out back, etc.).
▶ Work from your existing office or store if you have a running business.
▶ Open a warehouse in a cheap part of town.
▶ Create a high-profile business with a warehouse and finished offices where clients can visit.

The possibilities are endless—where you set up shop is totally dependent on what you want to sell, how much space you need, and how much you can spend. In this chapter, I'll walk you through some of the location possibilities and go over some considerations to keep in mind when you are deciding on a place to run your wholesale business.

# Working from Home

The simplest and most inexpensive way to get started is to get going in your own cozy cottage. As long as you can attract clients, working from home can be a great blessing because you will have virtually zero startup costs. You can have a very efficient and streamlined business working from home. But there are some drawbacks. The advantages are wonderful—starting at home is super low-risk for a wholesale newbie. A homebased wholesaler can easily partner with a Third-Party Logistics (3PL) to receive, store, and ship massive quantities of merchandise while staying at home at the nerve center of the company. You forfeit some margin when you outsource; however, any profit you make is found money because you'll avoid all the major costs of getting going. Having credit terms (usually shortened to just "terms") and liberal returns policies with your suppliers will compound the benefits. If you are a supercautious person, working from home will be your best bet when starting out. You'll want to discover if this new career is the right fit for you before pouring lots of money into a larger, rented or purchased space. Clearly this advice would not apply to a seasoned executive opening a well-funded, large-scale wholesale startup operation.

## Working at Work

What about hanging your shingle at work? If your boss is cool like that, then why not offer to pay rent on idle space at your employer's location? Most established companies have spare storage space. It's difficult to serve two masters, but you can assure your boss that you would do much, or all, of the work over lunch and/or before/after your normal work schedule. This isn't retail—incoming and outgoing orders are large, wholesale trades. So customers aren't going to be traipsing through the office, disrupting your employer's business.

Why would any boss allow this? There are scenarios where this works. The arrangement is worthwhile for the company because it generates income on otherwise idle space. If you work at a job with any amount of downtime, you can make a fair argument that this is a logical fit for your job. If you work for a small, entrepreneurial company, you can earn the admiration and respect of your boss and make some extra money at the same time. Pay your employer a percentage of the profits to really spark their interest and engagement.

If you're already your own boss, it's even easier. Do you own your own retail store? If so, then piggyback on the existing shop. Add additional storage such as a shed or shipping container if there's enough room. A standard shipping container can be used out back and away from the public view as a secure way to store inventory. Shipping containers are large enough for shelving units and will hold oodles of products. Items requiring climate control won't work in an outdoor shed or shipping container. Wholesale trade from a retail store is a beautiful idea—you'll enjoy greater buying power because the gross merchandise volume will rise and margins will grow. Synergize efficiency by trading in wholesale products that are available from existing vendors. I've seen owners operate a retail store, a wholesale business, and an ecommerce business all from one location. Reworking an existing location is cheaper than setting up a new one.

# Leasing or Buying a Warehouse

Do you have big bucks or a rich relative, or will you plan to raise lots of money? A slick, professional-looking warehouse with fancy offices requires a lot more planning. Planning includes, but is not limited to, a lease agreement, branding, design/layout, and build-out/ renovation costs. Consulting firms and specialized contractors will reduce friction and make everything seamless.

With thinking big, comes bigger overhead. Your need for ideas to bring in new business will be much more intense and urgent. You will need to sell a lot more to cover your expenses.

## *Location Is King*

Earlier I remarked about the possibility of leasing or buying in a more industrial part of town, and that most certainly makes sense if you require lower cost warehouse space and don't have an image to uphold. Other considerations come to mind such as the local zoning, distance from your home, traffic and accessibility, work force demographics, utilities and other costs, vehicle parking, proximity to eateries for your employees, and the flavor of the community.

Location matters. As a real estate developer, I've acquired attractive, commercially zoned land in the Midwest sitting on a truck-accessible road for $1,900 per acre. The same year, the average cost of land per acre in New York was $5.2 million and in Los Angeles was $2.6 million. If you're in a part of the country with a low cost of living, your monthly overhead will be relatively low, too. The biggest overhead expense in any business is usually labor, with rent typically second—mutually exclusive of the cost of goods. Wholesalers that call on customers prefer to be near them, while those that ship *everything* find homes in cost-effective locations with good access to shipping.

Sam Doria is the founder and president of Premier Shipping and Fulfillment, a contract third-party logistics and end-to-end commerce company. Sam helps entrepreneurs with turnkey solutions. Premier Shipping and Fulfillment eliminates the need to own a warehouse by offering scalable climate-controlled secure storage, cloud-based inventory management, and order fulfillment.

**tip**

It's an easy decision whether you should keep a high-rent retail space for a hybrid retail-wholesale business when the retail sales are so-so. You should divest yourself of a business that has failed to prosper after a long time and a lot of effort. Move the wholesale business to lower-cost digs and dump the retail program.

"Currently, we have one warehouse on the East Coast of the United States. Our future plan is to have four warehouses across the country, located near California, Texas, Illinois, and New Jersey. This creates an effective distribution network that can minimize shipping distance. Minimizing distance is crucial when working with large shipments in wholesale."

Consider that the higher rent you pay for a fabulous location will reduce the amount of money you will have to shell out for advertising your store when you operate both a retail and wholesale business. Conversely, if your retail business has gross merchandise volume that is far greater than your wholesale division, you'll want to look at moving the wholesale operation to a separate, lower-rent area.

Consider the size of your town and the cost of doing business. In Burbank, where I live and work, rent is staggering. How important will your location be to capturing customers? With the higher cost of living, wages and benefits will be incrementally higher. If all your competitors are paying their employees half as much as you do because they enjoy lower cost of living based on geography, you may not stay in business very long. Much hinges on whether or not your sales depend on personally calling on your customers. If customers come to your place of business, you'll have to maintain a neat, organized, and professional appearance. Impressions are important, and perception is reality.

A wholesaler that has large trucks coming and going daily needs shipping docks. Bigger companies require multiple bays so that multiple trucks can be served at the same time. A smaller business won't need docks, however, the freight trucks serving these locations will require hydraulic lift gates, which will increase the cost of pickup and delivery.

I'll be covering a lot of ground here and this buffet of information is designed to get your mental gears moving. Here are some key points to be thinking about:

- ▶ Rent or ownership costs
- ▶ Cost of living
- ▶ Accessibility
    - Distance from suppliers
    - Distance from customers
    - Accessibility for shipping and transportation services
- ▶ Environment
    - Weather and seasonal impact
    - Security considerations
    - Built-in amenities to handle any and all of these issues
- ▶ Scalability and capacity
    - Is there room for growth in the same location? In a location next to it? Or will significant growth require a completely additional or new location?

- Is there room for growth for your team? Will you need a headquarters, office or storefront, or will that be integrated into the initial space?
- How much space do you need to start? How quick will your product turnover be, and how will that affect the storage space you need?

And don't debate these considerations to the point that you become paralyzed and cannot make a decision on any location. There may never be an ideal site—typically no such thing exists, and you'll make do with the best location you can find that fills most of your needs.

## Consider Your Lifestyle

When you sell from home, you can take a break or a vacation at any time as long as your buyers are being serviced. When you open a business location, you no longer have the luxury of selling when and if it suits you—you have to keep up sales to pay for the persistent overhead. You can't simply lock the door and take a vacation without having someone to mind the business. This may seem pedestrian, but most business newbies fail to realize that owning and operating a business is like a marriage, with tremendous responsibility, and you should give this reality careful consideration before making the leap. If you have never operated a successful business before, I must discourage you from making the immediate move to a high-profile business storefront that costs a lot of money and requires you to be front-facing all day, every day. Consider selling part-time from home at first and learning the ropes of being a wholesale distributor. You can gradually evolve your business into something bigger and move to a grander location. For example, Genuine Parts Company has enjoyed steady growth for nine decades, and in their first year, sales topped $75,129. By the second year, sales grew 303 percent to $227,978.

You can grow your wholesale business similarly, if that's what you want to do and your lifestyle and family situation fits with your business goals. Most everyone has a family life of one sort or another. If you live with other people, whether a spouse, significant other, or family members, others will be impacting and influencing your business. Positive or negative energy will have the expected effect on your attitude, on your very plan to become an entrepreneur.

Working from home in an unsupportive environment is a recipe for failure. Without positive emotional support, your business won't be fun. Lack of family support may even promote failure. This could actually be one of the reasons you might want to open a warehouse or store-warehouse hybrid—to separate your business from your personal life.

If you have the house to yourself during the day, then working at home will be much easier. But if others are around, it is only natural for the family magnet to drag you into this or that project and pull you away from your duties.

Jealousy and envy are part of human nature, and if you live with anyone who is not completely in favor of your work at home, you may find subtle or obvious efforts to undermine your success. Try your best to rally early and committed support for your plans to start and grow a business. If you're getting positive vibes, you can give it a try and see how things go. But when you start spending hours defending your use of a portion of the residence as your office and explaining why the garage is always bursting with merchandise, it's time to consider separating your business from your home life.

You will know what is right for you. My philosophy in business has always been to seek the path of least resistance with family, friends, and colleagues. If something is too hard in your dealings with these people, it's probably not the right way to go. Do what comes naturally and easily. I don't mean that this venture of yours will be a cakewalk—I'm simply suggesting that your decision to work from home or should not be based on your natural instincts and feelings.

## Investigating Prime Locations

While it is possible to start a successful wholesale distribution business from just about anywhere (even your basement or spare bedroom), entrepreneurs who want to grow and prosper must be situated in a well-served logistics market, with few exceptions. A small organic farmer's jobber won't need to worry about intermodal shipping or truck brokerages—the product is highly perishable with a local farm-to-table-loving customer base.

Companies that trade exclusively wholesale and sell retail using ecommerce platforms do not require high-traffic or high-visibility locations. Those that aren't homebased are often in the industrial section of town. Distributors should seek out areas that are rich in industry and close to transportation centers.

Locations vary by the type of product being distributed. As the saying goes, birds of a feather flock together. If you're an industrial distributor, you'll want to be set up where the U.S. industrial base is, typically in the midwestern states. Wholesale distribution companies tend to locate where land is not too expensive and where they can buy or rent affordable warehouse space for the storage of inventory. Wholesale distributors are rarely located in downtown shopping areas. Most are found off the beaten path.

Americans are a diverse bunch of people, and there is neither a typical small-business owner nor a usual way of accomplishing the mission. Business owners are active in their communities, and before you spend a single dime, collect intel by interacting with other business owners in the community where you plan to set up. Here are some questions you can ask to determine a prime location for your wholesale business:

▶ Is the local government (and state) business-friendly?

▶ How could future government regulations affect the business—have things been historically stable? How fair and simple is taxation in the area?

▶ Does the area have affordable and available labor?

▶ Do people want to live and work in the area or is it highly transient in nature, or worse—is the community population contracting?

▶ What are the local union organizing efforts and is there risk that laws might change to aid in these efforts?

▶ Does the community support asset-light business strategies such as the availability of assets and storage facilities owned and operated by third parties to help reduce capital requirements?

▶ If you work with a 3PL company, could you locate your office space close to their facility to stay on top of the business relationship (e.g., conduct physical inventory, check the condition of your product, and monitor the 3PL's management of your business)?

Once you get a feel for these topics, you'll be able to pinpoint the type of area that best suits your business mission, values, and goals.

## The Right Site

Not every distributor needs a cavernous warehouse situated in a major industrial park. Location may not be a critical issue for the small wholesale distributorship where customers rarely visit, and conversely, the business that sells over-the-counter and through a showroom must give plenty of thought to location and appearances. Consider the neighborhood carefully. High-crime areas will have higher security costs—will this cancel the cost savings as compared to a better neighborhood? Customers will not feel inclined to visit you if you're in a rough area. Insurance will cost more. Labor will be more challenging in extremely poor, high-crime areas.

A growing number of younger workers are abandoning cars and driving in favor of other, less expensive means of getting to work. Cities are reorienting their focus on people over cars—looking at quality of life rather than developing communities that require cars. Cars remain dominant; however, the age of the automobile has, by some accounts, reached a peak. Less driving requires multimodalism. The degree of mode shift from cars

## ▶ When in Doubt, Ask Around

Ask around when seeking space. Post on social media and community networking sites letting people know you're looking for warehouse storage and logistics services. Ask the chamber for a list of its members that have large, well-run, and well-managed warehouses. Most companies don't make full use of their warehouses and some may be willing to lease you a portion of theirs. In multi-tenant facilities, valuable goods will need to be caged and locked to prevent the firm's employees from unauthorized interaction with your inventory—some shared facilities have secure storage and others simply let the clients' merchandise sit on shelves where anyone can access it.

to transit, biking, scooters, and ride-sharing depends on the region. Powered mobility scooters that can be activated and rented with a smartphone are reaching many densely populated areas. If the jobs you'll be offering attract workers who drive cars, you'll need a location that's pain-free with easy access to the freeway with ample free or company-paid parking. In areas where workers don't want to own cars, then you'll need to be close to transit stops. There is evidence that younger workers gravitate toward urban environments. If your proposed site is not very close to where the action is, then it should allow for employees to hop on a fast, cheap subway or public transportation system. Finding the ideal location takes time, so get an early start. In areas with fierce demand for sites, the longer you will have to wait and harder you'll have to look to find your ideal spot. To help avoid analysis paralysis, pare down the choices.

**tip**

As you attempt to find an impeccable location, make do with what you've got. If you have a garage, move your car out onto the driveway and set up a desk and a laptop and you're off and running with virtually zero overhead.

The U.S. Department of Labor, Bureau of Labor Statistics reported that the national unemployment rate fell to an incredible 3.5 percent in 2019—a number that was last seen in December of 1969 when I was seven months old. Setting up shop in areas with high unemployment seems intuitive; however, I have found both success and wisdom in attracting workers who already have gainful employment. Low unemployment results in wage pressures; however, all the money in the world will not buy employee happiness. While I don't recommend stealing employees from other companies, offering part-time positions to those with jobs allows them to explore their curiosity about your company without the guilt of leaving their position—and you'll find that when you are nicer, more flexible, and more awesome than your competitor, workers will gladly give you more of their time.

## Lease, Rent, or Buy?

Let's make a deal! "It's just business," they say, and indeed it's true. A lease is a business deal, and once you settle on a location, you will need to sign a lease. Some landlords are kind and generous and keep rent increases fair and reasonable; however, more often, buildings are owned and/or managed by management companies, real estate developers, and institutional investors. Independent building owners will be more likely to treat you like family. Expect corporate types to consistently raise rents to match the local market rates. A lease will establish terms and fix the rate that your rent will increase. New leases should be negotiated before the prior one expires. The pressure of the expiration date will affect your ability to make relaxed business decisions including looking at alternative options. The higher your capital investment costs, the longer you should make the term of your lease agreement. Moving and setting up shop elsewhere at the end of a lease is an expensive proposition. If you just need to throw up some pallet racks, hook up the internet, and buy some supplies, a month-to-month lease would be perfect. Many pop-up businesses seek out their proof of concept by deploying a low-cost startup to see how they do before getting serious.

Signing a lease is the biggest long-term commitment you'll have to make when starting your business. It is not uncommon for a smart businessperson to select multiple locations and leverage landlord offers against each other. When vacancy rates are high, you'll win every time. If it's a tight seller's market, this tactic will fail.

Leasehold improvements are the enhancements made to the space by the tenant. These are any changes made to the rental property in order to customize it for your needs. If this is your first time leasing a space that feels like a blank canvas, these costs often add up fast and are sometimes more than expected. Leasehold improvements should be fully recovered well before your lease term ends. You can never assume a landlord will renew your lease agreement in the absence of the option to do so in black and white. Ownership change is a common reason businesses are forced to leave at the end of their lease. Ask for a lease provision that permits you to sublease the building in the event you voluntarily close the business or move because you grow out of the space. You can then sublet to another tenant and profit from the spread between what you pay the landlord and collect from your tenant.

Be sure to check out your county or local zoning laws before entering into a lease or purchasing a building to verify that the location is zoned for your type of business. As you study the market, keep notes and must-haves so that all your criteria are met with each location you consider.

When it's your first time taking a swing at the ball, start by renting or leasing space. Use professionally managed, flexible, multi-tenant warehouse space whenever possible, or rent less attractive space at a discount as you explore your business idea. There are many hidden costs in operating a warehouse. When the capital outlay is small, you can rent short term, e.g., month-to-month. Real estate developers tear down older warehouses to erect condos, homes, office and apartment buildings, etc.—as land becomes more valuable, what was once low-rent industrial-commercial becomes high-rent commercial, mixed-use, or residential. You can work out a killer deal for your pop-up warehouse in a space that is scheduled for future demolition. Planning and building permits take time, and owners don't mind a temporary tenant to help with cash flow while they work out their construction plans. Never rent if you have to pay for significant improvements out of pocket, but many wholesalers just need secure space to store things. The canned food seller can make do with a forklift and a smartphone, and shuttering location A and moving to location B takes one day for a super-simple business. You don't need pretty or painted—you need room for these space-intensive operations. The uncomplicated business can rent and pay pennies on the dollar for what some might consider unattractive space and terms. Make sure the property is secure and has a good roof. Renting allows you to engage in business location "dating" while you sort out any kinks in your business model. Early-stage businesses can't easily predict future expansion.

Renting or leasing vis-à-vis buying adds benefits and risks. Here's a scorecard:

Benefits of renting or leasing:

▶ Broad variety of locations, sizes, and features.
▶ Lease payments are tax-deductible.
▶ Capital is not tied up in a substantial down-payment (usually much higher for commercial vs. residential buildings).
▶ It's substantially faster to pitch a tent somewhere else when the business outgrows the space.
▶ The owner can wander nomadically and play with different ideas more fluidly.

**tip** ⓘ

Homebased entrepreneurs should look at shared offices and executive suites locations for meeting customers. Customers appreciate the professionalism and will perceive a business as more serious if the conversation isn't consistently derailed by the distractions found at home.

- ▶ Taxes are less complex.
- ▶ There's considerably less to worry about (management and maintenance is usually someone else's problem).
- ▶ If the quality of the area drops or a strategic advantage that existed previously disappears, the business owner can leave and won't suffer the anchor of a declining asset.

Drawbacks:

- ▶ Inevitably, the monthly rental/lease payment will escalate and commercial tenants almost universally have to control increases contractually (because no one but the owner sheds a tear when a business has to pay higher rent or is pushed out—it's very different than residential rentals that have more regulations).
- ▶ The building owner gets richer, and the business owner gains no equity or capital benefit for their business.
- ▶ The business loses all leasehold improvements when the building owner decides not to renew the lease.
- ▶ Buildings change hands and a new owner may not be as cool as the prior one.

One of the things that's neat about the wholesale distribution business is the potential for very low rental rates. A flat-floor warehouse is among the simplest buildings.

When operating a hybrid retail-wholesale business that relies on location and foot traffic, buying a building right away is wise. These premium neighborhoods appreciate at a faster clip than industrial areas. I have made millions of dollars on real estate investment and the concept of *location, location, location* remains a truism today. A property owner enjoys tax deductions for interest, depreciation, and non-mortgage related expenses on a commercial property. Owning puts you squarely in the driver's seat. If you decide to discontinue the business, a prime location is easy to lease.

Benefits of buying:

- ▶ Your rent never goes up.
- ▶ You'll pay zero rent once the building is paid off.
- ▶ Interest payments are tax-deductible.
- ▶ The IRS allows you to depreciate the building (take a tax deduction).
- ▶ You can do with the space as you wish—you have no one to answer to.
- ▶ If the neighborhood is a good one, you can score a profit when you sell the building.

Drawbacks:

- ▶ You have to handle all improvements at your own expense.

▶ You are tethered and moving locations is significantly harder when you outgrow the space or the character of the neighborhood becomes undesirable for your business.

▶ In high-demand areas, the prices tend to be inflated, making monthly mortgage payments (in some cases) higher than leasing—but check this against your tax benefits to see if they balance each other out.

Common sense must always trump temptation. Those who enter the business world during an economic downturn are conditioned to do a lot more with far less, while others who start businesses during the good times must condition themselves to defer gratification. As I write these words, the U.S. is experiencing the longest economic expansion in history. Rather than remodeling your house, buying expensive jewelry, and taking high-end vacations at exotic resorts, put the profits into new real estate investments. There's really

## ▶ Types of Leases

Landlords utilize various lease types. Here are the most common:

▶ *Gross Lease/Full-Service Lease.* The lease payment includes all property operating expenses including taxes, utilities, and maintenance. The landlord takes care of everything.

▶ *Net Lease.* The lease payment is lower and the tenant pays fixed operating expenses. There are three types of net leases:

– *Single Net.* The tenant pays a fixed rent amount, their utilities, plus the building's property taxes, and the landlord is responsible for the other operating expenses (e.g., insurance, common area upkeep, and repairs and maintenance).

– *Double Net.* The tenant pays rent, utilities, property taxes, and insurance, and the landlord is responsible for the other operating expenses.

– *Triple Net.* The tenant pays rent, utilities, property taxes, common area maintenance, insurance, and other expenses. The landlord pays few or no expenses.

▶ *Modified Gross Lease/Modified Net Lease.* In this lease category, the terms are open for negotiation. Modified gross leases are more often used in multi-tenant buildings—e.g., if there is one power meter and the building is subdivided among multiple tenants, each might pay a proportional share of the expenses based on the square footage they occupy. Maintenance and upkeep could be paid by the landlord or the tenant(s), depending on negotiated lease terms.

nothing better than making money in your sleep. Adding additional commercial buildings to your company's investment portfolio generates cash flow and provides options. If the tenant moves out, you can use the space for your going concern, start a new business of your own in the vacant space, or lease it to someone else.

As the world becomes smaller thanks to technology, the buyer-seller connection takes on so many textures. Whatever your decision regarding renting vs. leasing vs. buying, each careful step of the way needs to be constantly vetted by the question "Is this a necessity?"

Speaking of necessity, in the next section, we'll cover the basics you need to know to set up shop.

## Setting Up Shop

As soon as you've found the perfect pad, the blank slate of the space will require layout planning and outfitting. All the little details will need attending to—turning on the utilities and internet, installation of shelving or pallet racks, curating office supplies, etc. The magnitude of the space will dictate whether to handle the design and setup of your space yourself or if you should hire an independent supply chain consulting organization to support the design of your warehouse and distribution and fulfillment processes. A small space allows for experimentation and wandering. For small-business owners, mistakes are corrected easily and with little effort. For well-funded startups, it's important to abridge time—loans start incurring interest, bills come due, and there isn't as much room to play.

Regardless of the size of your operation, there are universal setup considerations, which will include:

- ▶ Determining the working space and storage requirements.
- ▶ Creating a warehouse layout and then evaluating the layout for efficient space utilization (consider multiple layouts).
- ▶ Identifying optimal warehouse floor traffic-flow tactics.
- ▶ Testing and re-evaluation.

Warehouse efficiency lessens costs, but no subsequent solution will resolve serious weaknesses in the initial setup. For the petite business, it's easy to identify inefficiencies on-the-fly and mend them instantly. Just as a speedboat is to a massive cruise ship, larger companies are not so agile. The time you spend upfront is money saved later. Ingredients for success include:

- ▶ Planning for future growth.

▶ Allocating generous space for receiving—to allow for adequate space to check incoming shipments, break down larger pallets, stage items to be returned, and marshal products that require management inspection and approval.

▶ Maintaining a separate shipping area (or dock) so that outgoing orders aren't confused with incoming orders, shipping and delivery trucks aren't crossing paths and getting jammed, etc.

▶ Optimizing picking paths—popular items and merchandise often sold together should be grouped closer to the shipping and receiving areas.

▶ Using forward locations for high-volume items—minimizing trips to more remote locations and reducing the picker's travel distances (having a set quantity of stock stored at floor-level forward locations that are replenished from a larger supply of the same product elsewhere in the warehouse, such as on high racks).

▶ Allocating separate areas to store returns and deadstock (and for food products, items nearing their expiration date that need to be liquidated quickly).

▶ Using barcodes to speed data management and improve accuracy.

▶ Visible shelf labels, signage to identify sections of the warehouse, and use of color-coding.

## Working Essentials

The size and nature of your business dictate the essentials required to get started. For example, everyone needs a computer, a smartphone, or both. A printer is essential but not indispensable. Most businesses are going paperless and many companies have already achieved their goal of printing virtually nothing. The homebased entrepreneur working from a garage needs inexpensive shelving or prosumer level pallet racks, storage bins, a work space (e.g., a desk or folding table and stool or chair), a high-quality wheeled hand truck, and office supplies. If the floor is smooth, level concrete, for seating I prefer a rolling stool with a thickly padded seat.

A larger warehouse will require safely-installed, professional-grade pallet racks, a forklift, work tables, rolling warehouse picking carts, and other material handling supplies. The building will need a loading dock with enough bays to handle shipping and receiving efficiently. Businesses with high-value items use lockable security carts so that only trusted keyholders gain access to contents as they move throughout the warehouse. Offices will need to accommodate desks for management, sales, marketing, and support staff (with space to grow).

"Paperwork" no longer has to be on actual printed paper; however, there needs to be a system in place for handling employment records so that the business stays within the letter of the law. Some companies have co-employment systems in place to extinguish the mental anguish of dealing with human resources and are working with professional employer organizations. A professional employer organization (PEO) is an outsourcing firm that provides services to small and midsized businesses (SMB). The PEO acts as the employer of record for tax purposes, allowing the small-business owner substantial relief from record-keeping and compliance concerns. This means fewer in-house documents and therefore fewer paper files floating around the office. It also means you can sidestep the internal human resources manager and install fewer desks and computers. PEOs allow SMBs the opportunity to offer Fortune 500® level benefits, gain expert HR support without the head count, and stay compliant with the eternally changing legal landscape.

You may have heard of the multibillionaire who drove a Honda and worked from a desk fashioned out of a wooden door. Really rich people often maintain a culture of frugality among their ranks, and in the interest of setting the tone for their staff, they celebrate and work in modest conditions. For the longest time, I used standard pencils and a sharpener because I felt mechanical pencils were an extravagance. I didn't buy sticky notes because I felt they were a luxury item. If you dream of a huge corner office with a fabulous city view, then you should work for someone else because the most successful people in business understand the value of operating lean. Pointless spending will result in an under-accumulation of wealth.

This is more than simply a rant or a teacher's lecture, but sage advice from someone who has tried and failed in the business many times. Buying status objects and living a status lifestyle compel you to keep up with your colleagues. Hyper consumers must constantly maintain the high income needed to afford their luxuries and are vulnerable to failure. Spending tomorrow's money today is a leading cause of debt and a lack of net worth. So, when thinking about whether you need that aquarium or pinball machine for your office, ask yourself:

- ▶ "Is this really necessary?"
- ▶ "Is this indispensable?"
- ▶ "How can I accomplish more with less?"

What are the office essentials you require to get the job done? Fewer startups are investing in office equipment. Cloud services delivered over the internet are the norm—accounting, telephony, customer relationship management, tax preparation, and many other aspects of business can be accomplished online with zero investment in software and no fancy servers.

Work has become untethered without the need for the complex office cabling of years past. A comfortable desk and chair in the corner of your warehouse may do just fine.

Laptops and phones now operate for an entire day—some even longer—without being plugged into an outlet. Wifi and cellular data make work mobile. Modern mobile phones can be configured to act as a "hotspot" permitting computers and other devices to connect to them, allowing access to the internet. Low-cost unlimited data plans eliminate end-of-month billing surprises. If a DSL or cable modem is required, the services are blazing fast and today's wireless routers reach farther than ever before and operate at breakneck speeds. Let's take a look at some of the common office expenses.

## Communications

Cloud-based contact center services make telephone equipment completely unneeded these days. Incoming calls can be answered by a virtual auto-attendant and complex customer interactions handled without friction. These call center services can query databases and serve customer needs, e.g., tracking the status of a shipment. Call routing is managed by voice commands and the proper person located with a simple verbal request, reaching them by mobile phone. I spent over $12,000 for my first office phone system in 1988, and today's cloud contact center services are now available for fractions of a penny per minute of actual usage with zero upfront equipment cost. Many businesses still use toll-free numbers, but I'm skeptical you need one. Virtually everyone has free calls on their mobile phones nowadays. More support is handled by email, live chat, and social media.

Starting a wholesale distribution business today involves far fewer upfront decisions and startup costs than in years past thanks to cloud services, outsourcing, and gig providers (e.g., smartphone apps that instantly schedule messengers who handle small to large merchandise deliveries nationwide).

## Interior Office Space

If you'd like a little privacy while doing deals, you can erect a pop-up office within your warehouse. Many vendors offer quick-ship integrated modular office systems that come in a variety of configurations, colors, and sizes. The best of these are constructed of acoustical materials to ensure privacy when closed-door meetings are required. Most prefabricated offices have options for AC/HVAC systems for added comfort. A quality, comfy chair that allows you to sit at just the right height is a must.

## General Computing

When it comes to computers, some people simply swear by their brand-name favorites and I have never been one to gravitate toward expensive computers. I am faithful in my reading of online reviews and I go deeper than simply looking at stars—I read lots of the individual comments before making a purchase decision. My goal is to do everything in the cloud. I store virtually nothing locally and use Salesforce CRM to store mission-critical data—I can grant and restrict user access instantly and the information is secure. I love Google Suite (G Suite) cloud computing, productivity and collaboration tools from Google—email, documents, large file sharing and storage, and robust calendar management and sharing are all part of the G Suite ecosystem. I manage most of my to-dos on the calendar, and when a task isn't completed the day it's due, I can instantly bump it to another day—with text, email, or push notifications. G Suite connects with Salesforce CRM so data flows in perfect sync.

Using all cloud-based solutions allows me to use ordinary laptop and desktop machines. In the context of cloud computing, the internet connection speed and reliability are far more critical than the horsepower of the computer. Laptops have secure logins to prevent unauthorized access in the event I accidentally leave it behind somewhere. I store nothing important locally within my on-the-go computer in case I inadvertently drop it or it is damaged in my luggage while traveling. If you absolutely insist on storing data locally on the hard drives in your office, then you must purchase server-grade hard drives designed to operate 24/7. Consumer-level equipment fails rather quickly—a typical spinning hard drive has a high probability of failure within three years of consistent use after being placed in service. If your warehouse lacks climate control, you should *never* place a computer server in it. Never store important company data on computers in a hot warehouse. The probability of computer failure increases dramatically at higher temperatures and in dusty environments. Computer cases are fan-cooled and virtually no one bothers to regularly vacuum out their company computers to remove the accumulation of dust that gets inside them (yes, even laptops have system cooling fans). A solid-state drive (SSD) is a type of storage drive that has no moving parts and costs more—but without a spinning platter their life span will go well beyond that of their mechanical counterparts. Look at using a server-grade SSD if you ignore my warning and decide to keep mission-critical data in the office instead of in the cloud. Factory warranties for SSDs typically are based on either years of use or terabytes of data written, whichever comes first (e.g., a warranty might be the earlier of ten years or 600TB).

The wonderful thing about running a business entirely in the cloud is that you can simply swap out a dead computer with another one and be back in business in a jiffy. Companies that work in the cloud have substantially reduced their IT expenses by forgoing the need for a high-paid staffer or vendor handling computer upgrades and repairs.

I noticed that my computers suffered sluggishness after upgrading my Windows operating system. After investigating this, I determined that performance improvements were gained by making a few adjustments.

## Operating Systems

If you are a techie, then you can apply some quick hacks to make your Windows operating system faster. If you are a MAC user, then please carry on to the next section (I don't know enough about MACs to be of any use). Most settings can be accessed by pressing the Windows key on the keyboard ⊞ and then typing keywords into the search box. For example, type "background apps" and then turn off all the background apps that are slowing everything way down. In the delivery optimization section of Windows updates, turn off the feature that allows downloads from other PCs. Doing so will prevent your bandwidth from being used to give Windows updates to other PCs on your network or on the internet. Within Windows privacy settings, turn off every setting that allows activity tracking or that permits Windows to suggest content to you. Go through all the Windows permissions and turn off every feature that is not essential to you. I also turn off location and notification services that are in no way important to what I am doing. All this extra stuff causes friction. Every one of these features is an anchor on your computer's performance. Change the power plan under the power options settings to high performance and turn off file indexing. Explore YouTube and online Windows forums for tips on how to dramatically improve your computer's performance without having to purchase third-party optimization software. If you haven't already discovered this trend, please allow me to share—software prices have been dealing with the "race to the bottom," and as a result, the support options offered by many publishers have suffered. I am curating virtually all the answers to my technology questions from public forums where fellow users help each other. If you are an ultra-techie, then look at the Windows 10 debloater PowerShell script authored by Sycnex that you can download and run without cost from GitHub—for advanced computer users only.

## Internet Access

When connecting to the internet, I have experimented with both DSL and cable internet services and find that cable internet is more reliable and far faster than DSL. Be mindful of the fine print because the cable company salesperson automatically added a telephone line to my order that I didn't want or need and wasn't aware of until the first bill arrived. I imagine that infrastructure will evolve to the point that everyone will have access to fiber-optic gigabit internet connections in the very near future. For wireless connectivity within my businesses, I prefer Google Wifi's™ scalable mesh router system in lieu of renting the router offered by my local cable provider. We simply chucked all our Cat 5 cabling and strictly use Wifi™ connectivity everywhere. It's fast and very secure. Google

Wifi is low-cost and far better in every respect than the more expensive options within the marketplace. Google's mesh wifi delivers constantly strong and reliable signals by passing the connection along to individual access points and dynamically optimizing the clearest channel for the highest possible speed available. Equipment from Google is set up using a smartphone and took minutes to get up and running unlike the more complex brands of routers and access points I had purchased in the past. The administrator can even throttle or block usage at certain times of the day or for specific devices to limit usage. Unlike most dual-band 2.4 and 5GHz routers, Google Wifi automatically selects the band that delivers the best Wifi.

## ▶ Finding Bargains

When it comes to outfitting a warehouse, buy as much as you can secondhand. Durable items such as picking carts and metal task tables have incredibly long service lives. Look for deals everywhere. eBay has a distance-based search feature that allows you to identify items for sale near you. Bid on these local bargains and pick them up to save on shipping. There's no need to splurge on a new desk when people are literally giving them away for free on Nextdoor and Craigslist. Invest in a computer scanner that converts paper into PDFs and a cross-cut shredder. Scan all paperwork, then upload the scans into Google Drive or store them somewhere secure, then shred away. If you truly need a filing cabinet for any reason (I cannot imagine why), then you'll also find plenty of free or cheap used ones out there. Retain paper copies of high-value contracts, property documents such as deeds, and anything that seems really important.

There's really no model for outfitting a new business that can be universally applied. Idea adoption and stakeholder buy-in ensure a home run. Tools work only if people use them. Before buying everyone a computer, make sure their role requires it and they are likely to use it. Some all-in-one printers can print, scan, fax, and copy. If you select one of these machines, go for a model that's based on laser-toner technology. Machines that use toner are less expensive to operate than those that print with ink cartridges. If you feel compelled to have a dedicated fax number, then opt for a virtual one. Cloud fax services provide a fax number where received faxes are emailed to you as a PDF—you'll avoid the step of having to scan and store faxes. To send a fax, you simply upload a PDF and provide the fax number you're sending to. On the subject of printing, before you ask your bank to order preprinted checks, I'd like to mention that I never use them. Cloud payroll programs print directly on cheap, blank check stock available everywhere. With the installation of an inexpensive third-party plugin, QuickBooks also prints directly to the same blank check stock. Enjoy the savings!

I'm recommending Google Wifi, however, your local internet service provider will rent you a router and you may find that it does a wonderful job for you. These technologies evolve rapidly and some industry experts predict that the latest mobile kind of network, called 5G, will soon allow both residences and offices to connect to the internet at incredible speeds without the need for bulky modems and separate routers.

## Printing

When it comes to printers, unless you simply must maintain an upscale image with color invoices, a fast, small laser printer will do just fine. I have a printer that's been in service since 2006 and is still used every day. I have many printers now that my business requires them. Check toner prices and calculate the cost per page by dividing the price of the cartridge by the estimated number of pages it will yield. The supercheap ink printers cost less than the manufacturer pays to make them in order to lure you into buying them and you end up paying too much for the ink. Avoid these false bargains. If you need more than one, buy printers that use the exact same toner to keep life simple. If your company cannot operate without a printer, then always have two in case one suffers downtime.

## Operations Software and Systems

Busy companies will require software to handle the management of payroll, receivables, payables, and inventory. In a perfect world, this can come together within a single solution, but in practice, most businesses have to work with the best solutions across multiple vendors. Warehouse and inventory management systems are very specialized and cater to specific industries. Review and evaluate Warehouse Management Systems (WMS) and Transportation Management Systems (TMS) before you open your doors. You may or may not need them. It all depends on the complexity of your business and your transaction volume. A WMS allows teams to wrangle the routine activity within the four walls of the warehouse. The WMS will connect with the most popular accounting programs such as QuickBooks. A TMS handles supply chain management allowing streamlined communication and visibility from point of order to final delivery—handling the booking and management of freight forwarder shipments. Both WMS and TMS solutions are robust, require training, and are ideally suited for companies with multiple employees. While there are WMS and TMS solutions for the little guy, my instincts tell me that small operators would do better handling low-volume work with spreadsheets and documents. A middle step would be to configure a customizable CRM such as Salesforce to handle the data workload. Salesforce is fully customizable and data objects can be rapidly set up and configured to store and manage custom data types such as shipment and purchase order logs. Salesforce also has third-party installable packages to handle most business requirements. Before you pay a dime for any solution, snoop around and talk with industry peers—engaging in more business scuttlebutt. There is absolutely nothing wrong with a manual system to get you started and out of the gate.

## Vehicles and Transportation

Operating and maintaining a company vehicle is complex. Ponder all these costs and considerations:

▶ The cost of the vehicle (lease, cash purchase, or loan payments)
▶ Annual vehicle registration fees
▶ Insurance
▶ Fuel
▶ Preventative and routine maintenance
▶ Repairs
▶ Driver's payroll, taxes, workers' compensation, etc.

When you're small, starting out and making a handful of deliveries each week, you can make local deliveries yourself, but then who will mind the business when you do? Will you pass along the cost of delivery to your customers or offer free delivery? What's the minimum order to earn that free delivery?

If you ship pallets, then develop a list of all the local independent truck drivers in your area with lift-gate vehicles. Ask around, but it's not too hard to find them—their trucks are big. Photocopy a note and put it in the door handle or on the windshield. Independent truck drivers have downtime and carry their own insurance.

If what you are sending isn't that large, then partner with people locally who own vans, pickups, or box trucks. Post notices on Nextdoor and Craigslist. If you know a reliable driver who doesn't own a vehicle, you can rent a moving van or truck as needed, but be sure to purchase the optional insurance in case of a mishap.

Early on, outsource deliveries as much as possible. You need to gain a greater understanding of your company's average order size and delivery volume. You can offer customers free delivery on specific days of the week to help ensure a robust dispatch schedule. As volume increases, you can offer free delivery on more days. Consult with an expert bean counter to determine the right time to buy one or more company vehicles. Even if you own one vehicle, you'll need a Plan B when it's in the shop for repairs and maintenance. When you do purchase company vehicles, be mindful of operating costs. A large truck is expensive to operate—can you fill it or would you be better served with smaller vehicles such as box trucks and cargo vans? If your vehicle is running partially filled, then downsize. If it's usually full, having two smaller vehicles may make more sense or outsource just the overflow.

Need more ideas? There's power in teamwork—partner with other area wholesalers in noncompeting industries to handle your deliveries. If you sell candy, partner with the beer and wine distributor—you may find synergies such as selling to the same customers.

As tempting as it may be to purchase the lowest-price delivery vans and trucks for your business, you must sharpen your pencil and study the overall cost of ownership. Nobody is driving big-block V8 delivery vans anymore. They're cheap because they cost too much to operate and nobody wants them. Examine the vehicle's fuel efficiency and compare it to the estimated mileage your delivery drivers will be racking up on the vehicles. Cars, like all deescalating assets, will eventually age and need replacement. The acquisition cost includes the purchase price, tax, and delivery fees that must be amortized over the vehicle's useful service life. Study your competitors and see what vehicle models they're purchasing. Before making any purchase, speak to multiple independent mechanics about the reliability of your chosen model. The dealer is beholden to the automaker and may not say bad things about the brand. My close friend and business colleague traded his gas-guzzling domestic van for a fuel-sipping import that was twice the price. He experienced less maintenance, and with the money he's saving on fuel, he remains substantially ahead—plus with virtually no downtime, the van is a trusted and reliable asset. A closing thought—check insurance rates across all potential models because they will vary. Safer vehicles have lower rates.

In the next chapter, I'll talk about something that makes the average business owner cringe—finances! Everyone has to face the music on the facts and figures of accounting (and taxes) if they wish to remain aware and financially healthy in their endeavors.

# Managing
# Your
# Finances

I n everyday business management, a wholesaler deals with a plethora of facts and figures. Cheap computers and useful software have substantially reduced the bookwork of companies—a fact many entrepreneurs now take for granted. In 1988, I spent thousands on computers and a DOS-based invoicing and accounting package, and many more thousands on a coaxial cable-based network.

While '80s software worked better than using a typewriter to prepare invoices and reports, it was so much more complex to use than today's intuitive programs. A laser printer was really expensive back then—big bucks! Computers are now untethered and software is really smart. An app can provide instant accounting reports by examining a picture of purchase invoices and receipts captured on a smartphone, assigning general ledger expense codes by examining the user's prior decisions using artificial intelligence and without typing.

Today's accounting software is super cheap as a result of popularity. More people are using the same tools. Although sameness is not saneness in every aspect of business life—when it comes to accounting, following the herd helps retard costs.

If you look at how most older small companies handle their daily routines, you'll usually see a patchwork of different software solutions cobbled together—an invoicing program from one vendor and a warehouse management system from another and so forth. For the established business, even logical change such as consolidating software solutions is challenging because it's like changing a plane's jet engine in midair.

Few people love the financial and accounting facets of their business and some folks downright despise them. Some owners hate paying their accountants and some accountants hate both their clients and the accounting profession. In-house accounting staff at small firms are saddled with work that has nothing to do with accounting because owners feel the need to justify a worker's salary. This phenomenon stems from the fear caused by allowing part-time freelancers access to sensitive books—fearing competitors will learn trade secrets when bookkeepers work for multiple companies. External accountants must cope with the high cost of doing business and also the ongoing software upgrades required to prepare compliant tax documents. The work that owners expect from accountants requires effort and cost, but many want to pay peanuts while expecting caviar. A carefully selected freelance bookkeeper will maintain a tight lip and do a great job while allowing the business owner to pay for only the time and service required. This generates far more satisfaction for both parties because the owner pays less and the bookkeeper isn't burdened with unrelated busywork.

A wholesaler must turn inventory over rapidly which is the byproduct of high-demand products offered at modest markups. Vendors are paid for goods sold to the wholesaler and buyers are invoiced for what they purchase. Sometimes collection efforts are needed to catalyze timely payments. Working with creditworthy customers means on-time payments and fewer hours spent collecting from elusive buyers. You will painlessly extract coins from the pockets of merchants when dealing in fairly priced, honestly traded, and high-demand goods—if it's easy for your customers to sell it, then it's just as easy for them to eagerly pay you. It's just one factor to consider in your overall financial management plan.

In this chapter, I'll walk you through some basics that you'll need to know as you manage finances for your wholesale business.

## Determining Markup

The "buy low, sell high" adage is far easier said than accomplished because price transparency is frictionless and at every buyer's fingertips. I once received 17 pallets of video games and took some time to tinker with different price points until I found the right balance between the minimum order size and the price at which I could offer every buyer without sitting on the goods. My goal was to move everything out within 30 days and I did.

Margins vary dramatically between sectors—with consumer electronics and pharmaceutical wholesalers working on razor-thin margins, and consumable and perishable goods dealers often making double-digit returns. Gypsum Management and Supply, Inc. is a wholesaler of construction materials including drywall, framing, suspended ceiling systems, and related building products. According to its 2018 annual shareholder report, Gypsum Management and Supply, Inc. enjoyed a robust gross profit in excess of 32 percent on more than $3 billion in sales. As a company grows, it's hard to keep earning double-digit margins, but this public company does it.

The spread between the price paid and the price sold can generally grow through buying power because the price that a wholesaler can ask is controlled by market conditions. It is easier to seek discounts from the factory than it is to secure higher prices from a buyer. If distributor A charges $1 for a package of light bulbs, then so must distributor B and which of the two distributors receives the business is a matter of customer tastes—who they like better—what credit terms are offered, how friendly the distributor's staff has been, who may be related to whom, and so forth. I once lost an account for reasons unknown and upon querying the buyer was told he gave the business to a friend—who later lost the same business back to me due to lackluster service and slow handling of orders. The wholesaler whose service is so friendly, accurate, and fast will never lose a customer over the matter of a few dollars here or there—but large price differences will be noticed when a competing company's sales representative starts showing price lists.

A business owner who wishes to keep a customer for life must also lower prices in lockstep with the cycle of business. When a source charges less and a healthy margin is secure, the buyer's cost should drop in lockstep. Having this level of integrity speaks loudly about your character and will not be forgotten when other firms solicit your customer's business. And never be quiet about price reductions—explain their logic and reason.

Every new business struggles with markup because their buying power starts off weak and therefore their margins are much lower than where they can and will be in years to come. A well-funded bank account will be needed in the early years so that a sufficient number of accounts are added to grow sales volume large enough that the wholesaler's supply comes at a lower and lower cost over time. Honestly traded merchandise correctly bought and sold requires no bribes or gimmicks to move it.

With the invention of speedy internet, buyers at every point within the supply chain and at every corner of the planet have become experts at finding the lowest price for everything. Those who did not train for this marathon lost their breath years ago and shuttered—blaming technology for the decline of their businesses. These same individuals held high prices—living in big houses, driving luxury cars, and eating at fine restaurants on the backs of their customers. Behind every heartbreaking retail store closure is almost always a backstory of accumulation of unneeded debt, wasteful spending, and a failure to evolve. The shuttering of underperforming retailers with poor sales and decreasing profitability will pull down everyone upstream in its wake—suppliers, bankers, employees, and even the communities in which they operate. The wholesaler must remain vigilant—persistently reviewing the state of their buyers' businesses. Sudden increases in order size may be a good or bad thing—if the retailer is about to go under, the unpaid invoices could be wiped out at the conclusion of a bankruptcy.

So many people have asked how I became wealthy. I have been asked this question by family, employees, friends, and colleagues—and I give the same answer to all. I made more money last year with my investments than I did with my business. My company has a Vanguard brokerage account and any funds that are not at work are parked in an index fund that tracks the S&P 500. Having financial strength allows me to make rapid company decisions without the fear normally associated with risk-taking. A dollar of profit invested back into more profitable fast-moving and certain inventory makes the most sense. If trade financing is in place and if that financing works as a line of credit, idle cash should be used to pay off credit lines when more stock isn't required on the shelves. While business is the source of my cash flow, investing keeps me strong in every economic climate. A business owner should never carry interest-bearing debt while sitting on a pile of cash.

A wholesale business that has challenges moving merchandise should apply any combination of these tactics:

▶ Cast a wider net.
▶ Lower the price.
▶ Stop carrying the product and replace it with another.

Determining markup involves study. Competing prices should be reviewed. The profit margins of public companies in the same and similar industries should be reviewed to provide a baseline. Figure 6–1 reveals gross profit margin percentages for select companies (in no particular order) as shown on their 2018 SEC 10-K reports. Vehicle products and maintenance, repair, and operations (MRO) industries enjoy some spectacular margins while the pharmaceutical wholesaler is earning single-digit returns.

Business owners must accept lower margins on popular products as compared to the higher margins earned on goods that are slow-moving, hard-to-find, or customized. It is common sense and common knowledge that greater competition places pressure on sellers

| Company | Sector | Gross Margin (percent) |
|---|---|---|
| Graybar Electric Company, Inc. | Electrical, communications, and data networking products | 19.17 percent |
| Henry Schein, Inc. | Health-care products for dental and medical offices | 27.23 percent |
| Reliance Steel & Aluminum Co., Inc. | Metal products | 28.45 percent |
| TESSCO Technologies Inc. | Wi-Fi, Internet of Things, wireless backhaul, and related products | 20.72 percent |
| HD Supply Holdings, Inc. | Maintenance, repair, and operations (MRO) | 39.28 percent |
| Performance Food Group Company | Food and food-related products | 13.01 percent |
| Beacon Roofing Supply, Inc. | Roofing materials | 24.82 percent |
| AmerisourceBergen Corp. | Pharmaceuticals | 2.7 percent |
| LKQ Corp. | Vehicle products (e.g., replacement parts and accessories) | 38.52 percent |

FIGURE 6–1: **Gross Profit Margins for Public Companies Engaged in Wholesale**

to lower their prices. Newly launched and hot items will enjoy a period where customer appetite is strong enough that an entire industry can enjoy strong sales and equally healthy margins for a time. Drivers of wholesale sectors follow a consistent flow pattern. For example, even though consumers may be searching for healthier dietary choices, high-calorie foods continue to fill retailers' shelves—millions of people refuse to give up chocolate, cookies, and ice cream! Certain products will always have generous margins, and since there is an upper limit to consumption, the high-margin business operator should not lower prices hoping for an unqualified increase in sales. There is a price point at which going lower only reduces the bottom line. This is a bit of a conundrum because startups must compete for business but should not bankrupt themselves in the process. As the good times roll, an operator must also sock away capital in order to weather the storm of periods of depressed retail sales—which in turn, results in factory production curtailments that trickle all the way down the supply chain. Owners must be nimble—adjusting operational scale to suit the economic climate. A wholesaler should expand operations during the best of times and protect the business from folding in the worst of times.

## Creating a Financial Map

To steer the ship, a wholesaler requires financial maps. To pay the piper, the owner must precisely tally the work.

My outline for what's required in these areas follows these key points:

- ► Daily/weekly stuff
  - Check cash position
  - Prepare a flash report, if applicable
  - Process payroll
  - Invoice accounts receivable and collections
  - If cash and checks are involved, record and reconcile against receipts
  - Review low inventory levels, place orders, check for stale items (mark down or dispose of deadstock when the shelf space costs more than the nonmoving items)
  - Record received inventory
  - Key in and schedule accounts receivables for timely vendor payments
  - Scan/code/file receipts (could be moved to monthly, if desired)
  - Back up data (daily)
- ► Monthly/quarterly stuff
  - Reconcile bank statements against the accounting software

- – Review and take action on delinquent accounts
- – Pay vendors
- – Forecast inventory requirements
- – Prepare a profit and loss statement
- – Prepare a balance sheet
- – File periodic tax returns (sales and use tax, payroll tax, etc.)
- – Forecast and pay estimated income taxes
- ▶ Annual stuff
  - – Write down (i.e., charge-off) uncollectible receivables
  - – Review inventory and write down unsellable product
  - – File forms (W-2, 1099-MISC, etc.)
  - – Finalize full-year financials
  - – File annual tax returns

The larger the stakes, the more time will be expended on business finance (and more sweat will pour in the process). For global sellers, their advising accountant will gravitate toward International Financial Reporting Standards as a framework. U.S. sellers use Generally Accepted Accounting Principles. Whether or not you formally understand and adopt a financial framework, your accountant is required to do so and by extension, you'll be following standards of accounting in your business.

Whenever possible, use flash reports (which you'll read more about later) to evaluate your company's financial condition—however, this is not an all-or-nothing situation. Accounting programs will generate instant profit and loss statements and balance sheets to help provide financial clarity and understanding. When delegating bookkeeping, look at the line items and apply course corrections as needed—I once had a bookkeeper put an asset on the profit and loss statement instead of on the balance sheet. When I politely mentioned it to her, she was quick to defend her action as being "in progress" and it quickly moved to the right general ledger code.

## Credit and Cash Flow

Each party in the manufacturer-distributor-customer supply chain must manage cash flow. Like a crème-filled cookie sandwich, the wholesaler can become squeezed in the middle—coping with the short payment terms of the factories and other suppliers while retailers take their time to pay them. Interest payments for in-place trade financing adds up quickly, so cash-flow management requires an eagle eye to ensure that money is flowing harmoniously.

Here are some tips:

- ▶ *Make payment very easy.* All banks now offer free inter-bank money transfers (not the same as a wire, which still costs money). Offer a variety of free payment services—the most popular ones change frequently so ask your customers what they prefer to use and sign up for it (these services make their money on the interest they collect while floating money between the parties).
- ▶ *Encourage early payments with a discount.* If your factor charges you 3-percent per month you would be wise to offer a 3 percent discount for fast customer payment (e.g., ten days) because the buyer will likely push a 30-day invoice to 45, 60, and sometimes 90 days.
- ▶ Stop shipping when customers haven't paid in 60 days even if you fear the loss of their business.
- ▶ Use and enforce clear, reasonable payment terms.
- ▶ Maintain delivery records until customer payment is tendered.

In the same way your vendors ask for personal information, credit references, and bank details, you must ask for the same from your buyers—carefully screening customers. Even when payments are made on time, conduct periodic checks to ensure that your buyers are still creditworthy today. Dun & Bradstreet offers business credit files, however, new businesses won't have established credit. Every company is assigned a D-U-N-S Number for tracking purposes. Other credit reporting agencies offer credit risk assessment reports for businesses, but I've found that most companies offer a courtesy credit limit for most buyers and raise the credit limit based on multiple factors—e.g., length of the relationship, order history, promptness of payment, etc.

Asking buyers for permission to run a personal credit report isn't unheard of but may be viewed as intrusive. It is wise to check court database records for any lawsuits against both the company and the owners (e.g., law suits for nonpayment, etc.).

References should be called and asked about their experiences working with the prospective buyer. Liberal terms and returns policies from the factory will allow you to extend credit to your buyers, but this becomes a house of cards if the buyers you elect to do business with are slow-to-pay . . . or worse, go out of business and never pay at all. We have all heard and read news of massive retailers that folded and this happens to businesses of any size. According to the Small Business Administration's Office of Advocacy, approximately half of companies with employees will fail within five years of opening their doors. It is not unheard of that a business about to shutter will continue placing orders until the bitter end even if they never intend to pay for the invoices. While this is certainly an illegal act and a form of theft, proving intent is nearly impossible and virtually no one is ever prosecuted by authorities for failing to pay a wholesale invoice when they walk away from a business.

# Taxes

According to the Internal Revenue Service, every business should apply for a Federal Tax ID number. States have varying requirements, and virtually all of them require the payment of income or gross receipts taxes. A couple of states do not levy corporate tax at all. Your accountant knows what to do and should be consulted prior to making sales and storing products—there are tax implications for just holding an item in inventory as well as on the profit earned in a trade.

According to the Tax Foundation, 45 states plus the District of Columbia impose a sales tax in order to raise revenue. Many local jurisdictions also impose a sales tax. Alaska, Delaware, Montana, New Hampshire, and Oregon don't have a state sales tax. Appropriate attention must be given to all applicable registrations and tax obligations—not just for a compulsory business license, but also for remittance of income tax, employment taxes, excise tax, property tax, sales and use tax, self-employment tax, and estimated tax. While not every one of the preceding will apply to all businesses, the failure to make timely payments will deal a heavy blow when penalties and interest are assessed. Import/export wholesalers deal with fees referred to as duties—depending on the context, this may be called a customs duty, import tax, or import tariff.

While you are not required to collect sales tax (or pay sales tax to your suppliers) when trading for resale, there is a record-keeping element to the process.

The sales tax is avoided by providing adequate documentation in the form of a resale certificate. The certificate indicates that the purchaser will be reselling the merchandise and that they will collect and report tax on the final sale to an end user. A resale certificate form is provided by the collecting governmental agency, however, most states permit the certificate to be in any form (including digital and online), so long as essential information is collected and appropriate signature is captured (wet or digital) certifying that the merchandise is being purchased for resale. In rare situations, a seller's permit is not required but a legal reason must be given. Contrary to popular misbelief, generally, a nonprofit's sales and purchases are taxable. If an audit occurs, the wholesaler will be held to task—having to provide documentary evidence the sale was handled correctly. When appropriate proof that the sale occurred in wholesale trade is absent, the distributor may be required to pay the sales tax—wiping out precious profits . . . a hard-earned lesson. Taking someone's word that they are tax-exempt is not legally defensible in an audit.

Consulting with a certified public accountant on day one is not only smart but will save you headaches down the road. Everyone misses something and no one can think of everything. When meeting with your accountant, come prepared, listen, and make notes—their time is precious and their fees only become expensive when meetings are haphazard and protracted. The accountant's advice will translate into action items and deadlines—which can be managed on a simple calendar. As for internal financial matters, most operations use a freelance (typically remote) bookkeeper to handle the preparation of flash reports, profit and loss statements, and balance sheets. It is very rare for an accountant to do this busywork. The best accountant is a highly skilled strategist whose job includes finding out how to legally help you avoid paying taxes. It is a mistake to ask the accountant to do data entry and bookkeeping tasks.

In the chapter that follows, I'll challenge you with ideas for product sourcing and managing logistics.

# Acquiring and Managing Inventory

Managing inventory will be your biggest challenge as a wholesaler. What will you stock? What will you drop-ship? And how can you run your business more efficiently than your competitors? A wholesaler faces ferocious competition and must, therefore, accomplish much more with far less. A lean operation means using tools that serve customer needs with fewer employees and lower stock levels. For those in a niche, unique goods and high availability will trump economies of scale and efficiency. It's a race to the bottom if you focus on inventory that's readily available everywhere.

The good news is you have options. For example, you can operate as a curator, dropshipping substantially all orders. This model won't work in the fresh produce business because you'll be quickly pushed out of the middle as the grower and retailer finally meet each other at the time of the delivery. You might be able to control the relationships contractually for a time, but eventually, that business model is headed for failure. Dropshipping works well when customers sell at high margins and require concierge-level service. Drop-shipping fails when the retailer is a high-volume, low-margin business and prefers to cut out wholesale distributors and source as directly as possible from the factory.

You can also use your warehouse to keep all your products under one roof. Having "everything" in stock with deep inventory only works if your gross profits are in the triple digits. If you rely on trade financing, the interest payments to carry on-hand inventory will eventually sink you. There are substantial risk factors in not having what a customer needs when they come calling and, conversely, headwinds when you cannot unload merchandise within a reasonable period of time.

Handling inventory properly requires forecasting so that customer expectations are swiftly met and capital isn't trapped in deadstock. The smallest business owners forecast using experience and intuition. At this scale, inventory audits are conducted visually and by the owner. In the field of inventory management, products are tracked using a *stock keeping unit number*—referred to as an SKU for short. With a small handful of SKUs, there's no need to invest in a pricey warehouse management system. Businesses up to 100 employees use QuickBooks, although I am in no way endorsing QuickBooks as the one-size-fits-all solution for inventory management and forecasting.

In this chapter, I'll explain how to manage inventory, how to manage just the right stock levels, how best to handle the logistics (moving) of goods, and some tips on creating a fulfillment plan.

## To Stock or Not to Stock

I never wish to patronize; however, please remain skeptical of any ad or video that makes high claims regarding special opportunities and riches to be made in stocking up on secret products. Snake oil salespeople are alive and well today, even in the wholesale distribution business. You will begin a very perilous journey when you start buying wholesale systems and joining the inner circle subscription programs of the individuals claiming to be gurus in the field. Telltale signs of baloney include the requisite private plane, exotic sports car, or mansion playing co-star as the backdrop in the ad. These alleged influencers monetize at every turn—making money on affiliate links, ad clicks, and subscription fees. Before you stock up on the products mentioned by one of these "experts" or head over to a global sourcing website they've recommended and start importing goods, reflect on just how easy something is. The easier it seems, the more people have jumped into the fray and the harder it is to sell and make a profit. The axiom, "If it sounds too good to be true, it probably is," remains just as valid today as it was in the past, and when heeded, will continue to protect you from boneheaded decisions in the future. The more challenging a business, the less likely a whole bunch of other people have already dived in. That said, dealing with other people is likely to be the biggest challenge you face in business—and the ability to do so is probably one of the most priceless commodities in business. Greater earning power comes from the ability to evoke enthusiasm in customers—and when you solve problems rather than sell to someone, customers feel like they are buying rather than being sold to.

Should you determine that there is a vigorous demand for what you are selling, consider both expanding your sales efforts dramatically and stocking deep inventory. Consider that 1 million units of a product with a mere nickel margin will yield $50,000 in profit. There are very few products that represent disruptive innovation, i.e., something so remarkable that it creates a new market and displaces established products. Consider how the smartphone rapidly replaced the clamshell flip-phone in a handful of years. Even revolutionary products are rarely disruptive. Consider that the five-blade razor didn't replace single-blade, disposable razors because it represents a luxury product that, while truly revolutionary in its design and function, is not affordable to the hundreds of millions of people globally who buy cheap disposable razors. You will always face significant challenges displacing established market-leading distributors because their alliances run deep, they possess hard-earned experience, and they are typically well-funded.

Industries will evolve in time based on gradual changes in customer tastes, and that's something you should pay attention to when deciding what is worth stocking. While vintage vogue might be all the rage with young fashion-conscience customers, most clothing distributors aren't stocking deep inventory of ensembles with huge, padded shoulders—a look that fell out of fashion some decades ago. A new entrant in an industry will struggle with what is referred to as the *zero-sum game*. In a nutshell, the zero-sum game refers to the fact that there is essentially X number of dollars' worth of total business in any particular trading area for a specific product or product category.

The X figure may increase or decrease over time depending on inflation, the rising or falling cost of raw materials, higher or lower fuel and delivery driver labor costs, etc. For example, most kitchens have a food processor and when it breaks down, a customer can expect to pay slightly less for one today than the same product cost ten years ago. Manufacturing efficiencies in the food processor industry have steadily improved. Automotive parts pricing has become more favorable for the same reason. Lower gross merchandise volume doesn't mean fewer units were sold nor does it necessitate lower margin. The $39.95 retail food processor can still net a wholesaler the same per unit gross profit while resulting in lower gross merchandise volume today than ten years ago. In a zero-sum game, it is very unlikely you will generate new demand.

Before deciding how much inventory to buy now and in the future, consider the following:

- ▶ Do you have sufficient statistical data upon which to base forecasts?
- ▶ In the absence of sales statistics upon which to base your forecasting, how can you predict customer demand for any given item? (P.S. don't guess—you may have challenges with initial stocking predictions.)
- ▶ Once inventory turnover has been predictably measured, at what inventory level does having more units in stock actually start increasing the final cost of goods after applying available volume discounts and adding back the pro rata storage and handling costs? The cost of inventory financing must also be added to the cost of goods. Storage and financing expenses are not only real cost of goods line items, but can amount to a significant sum of money that quietly accrues with few neophyte businesspeople taking these costs into consideration.

The clearest way to determine how much inventory to stock at any given time is to ask each customer what they need. The purveyor of janitorial goods such as paper towels, rubber gloves, degreasers, deodorizers, and hand soap bases stock quantities on the average customer usage multiplied by the number of customers served, giving consideration to price breaks and the cost of carrying the inventory before it's delivered.

At the start, a prudent manager will pay a bit more to buy less inventory so that customer usage data can be acquired from actual sales—an analysis of real-world examples rather than making presumptions based on potentially faulty predictions and too-brief sales history. With experience as your wingman, you'll be making just the right volume of purchases for each product your customers require. For the occasional need on an urgent basis, a sharp operator places special orders without regard for profit in order to retain the overall customer relationship that is profitable.

## Use Reporting to Determine Inventory Needs

When products are in stock, customers receive them quickly; this is a fundamental aspect of extraordinary customer service. Full shelves can expose a business to obsolete inventory, higher storage costs because more space is required, and the tying up of precious capital. Wisdom comes from experience. Experience is a warehouse manager's friend. No amount of computer power will replace common sense nor time under your belt.

In addition to wisdom and experience, you can rely on strong reporting to guide your inventory decisions. For example, a *flash report* is an accounting tool that summarizes key company data, such as bottleneck utilization, the status of overdue receivables, the customer order fulfillment rate, and the amount of storage space left in the warehouse. Every company manager should implement flash reports to champion effective leadership. A flash report shines a light on issues that require action. Flash reports can be prepared with a frequency that suits the taste of the owner or general manager of a business, e.g., daily, weekly, or monthly, etc. The report is only circulated internally and usually contains confidential information—for "eyes only" and to be shredded after it's no longer needed. Business experts encourage flash reports to be generated and reviewed weekly, typically every Monday so that the team does not need to wait until the weekend or the end of the month to experience the elevated blood pressure of problem awareness. Flash reports help with critical inventory and stocking decisions, but also identify other metrics regarding the business. What's included in a flash report depends on the manager's needs and may include sections such as the following:

- ► Productivity
- ► Liquidity
- ► Profitability

What precisely fills these sections—the information that a manager wants and needs—depends on personal preferences or established policy. It all depends on how sophisticated the business owners wish to be. Success may be defined as reaching specific goals—and the repeated achievement of these goals. The flash report should inform the team of the key performance indicators (KPIs) which are quantitative facts that aren't colored by bias or personal interpretations. Critical decisions regarding stocking inventory are made from the flash report with the added benefit of intel collected from business scuttlebutt. Like the recipe for a secret sauce, a flash report utilizes ingredients that the master chef selects. The astute bookkeeper or accountant will assemble flash reports using the data generated from existing programs without having to spend endless hours compiling or auditing. Flash reports, as the name implies, are quick and need to be streamlined in such a way that they are not costly to the company and maintain sufficient accuracy to be useful.

The distributor must also factor in the product life span. For the fancy foods wholesaler, a properly stored uncut cheese wheel can last for years—and dried beans will be good for

## ▶ QuickBooks and Their Partners

QuickBooks remains wildly popular for the business owner who only needs to invoice customers and track a small number of product SKUs, cost of goods, and receive notifications when inventory is low. QuickBooks will reveal what's popular, and manage purchase orders and vendors. According to Intuit, the publisher of QuickBooks, 5.6 million businesses use their accounting software to manage their businesses with more than 200,000 QuickBooks ProAdvisor accountants who aid and advise them. QuickBooks Online adoption is accelerating as more users ditch desktop software in favor of the cloud. QuickBooks is popular with SMBs because it also handles payments and payroll—handling end-to-end business management. QuickBooks Enterprise is the advanced offering designed for SMBs with 10 to 100 employees with more complex needs with industry-specific reports and features for wholesale distributors. If what you do isn't super complicated, the QuickBooks ecosystem works or at the minimum will become a starting point for handling inventory matters. QuickBooks financial management solutions track income and expenses, create and send invoices and estimates, manage and pay bills, and generate standard and custom financial reports. QuickBooks is built on an *open platform* allowing third-party developers to create online and mobile applications that connect to and interact with QuickBooks data. Wholesale distributors can work with these third-party tools, either turnkey or off-the-shelf, or hire their own developers to create custom solutions. QuickBooks users enjoy the benefit of seamless integration with TurboTax products enabling rapid, accurate tax preparation. QuickBooks provides both self-service and full-service payroll, the latter handling all tax payments and filings. The QuickBooks App Store is a directory of hundreds of third-party tools that serve the B2B wholesale community. Solutions include self-service online ordering systems that work with real-time inventory levels to avoid sell-out surprises. Apps can be rated for experiential transparency.

Publishers of software face intense competition, and because barriers to entry within the cloud solutions space are very low, the competitive landscape can and will change rapidly. Free or low-priced products offered by emerging companies may look attractive, but time-tested solutions serviced by well-managed providers will deliver the most hassle-free experience.

decades. But even correctly frozen meat kept at exactly 0°F without fluctuation will start to taste bad after too many months in storage and must be liquidated at any price once age sets in.

In a perfect world, inventory will be moved down the road to the retailer before you have to pay for it. When the manufacturer offers 30 days for payment, the ideal inventory level represents 30 days or less of inventory on the shelves. This float cuts capital requirements.

## Filling Your Shelves

The proverb *don't put all your eggs in one basket* rings true today with the same veracity as it did when the phrase was coined in the 17th century. Becoming reliant on a small number of suppliers to fulfill the needs of a wholesale business is perilous at best. Manufacturing is vulnerable to rapidly changing tastes and factory closures are common. While it is excellent for a wholesaler to specialize, having a limited number of major suppliers is unwise. Plan B suppliers are just as critical to disaster recovery when a supplier folds as a data backup for mission-critical company data.

It may be challenging to attract the interest of vendors with robust representation in your trading area. While it could be extremely difficult to wrangle a sales territory away from another wholesale distribution company, your diligence and success—your true grit in making things happen—will stun and delight those within your industry. Success breeds more success and an impeccable reputation for honesty, fair dealing, and diligence will precede you in business circles.

The great thing about successful people in business—they want to be found. High-achievers make themselves available. To find the best companies, look no further than industry trade shows and trade magazines. Exhibiting at a trade show represents a significant investment for a manufacturer and their team will be eager to meet you when you visit their exhibit space at

**tip**

When operating as a sole proprietorship, every purchase is made under your name and this involves an assurance that you will be solely responsible for the payment of all business debts incurred. Vendors frequently ask partners and corporate officers to engage in separate personal guarantees. No one with integrity applies for credit with the intention that they may fail to repay their obligations. As a business grows, it takes on a life of its own—well-established businesses with a long credit history should be able to secure vendor credit without a personal guarantee.

an industry event. A direct email or phone call to a factory will open doors, but there's nothing quite like engaging in a firm handshake. Nothing will ever replace the trust that builds from face-to-face meetings. Lasting relationships that stand the test of time and benefit both parties require hard-earned trust that only occurs with constant rapport.

When you sell products, the factory's reputation becomes your reputation. Before placing an order and filling up eager shelf space, you must carefully evaluate samples. While most people are honest, it is important to not only conduct due diligence and investigate your trading partners carefully, but also to place orders of modest size to test for consistency with every aspect of the experience. Freight partners must be vetted in the same way. Even big-name shipping companies have delivered pallets of merchandise to me with forklift holes poked into the merchandise.

Next, you must establish credit with suppliers so you can buy products as needed and not wait until you have cash on hand. Wholesalers rely on credit from their suppliers and will be expected to extend credit to their buyers. While each vendor has their own credit application, I have found that most will accept the information in any format, so long as the data that's required is present. In Figure 7–1 on page 123, I've provided a sample credit application which contains sections for company information, banking relationship data, and trade references. The conundrum is that credit applications require trade references and startups have none. Therein lies the rub. Solutions to this paradoxical situation are somewhat straightforward. Invoices can be guaranteed by a credit card or a bank letter of credit. Most vendors will extend a nominal amount of credit to most any licensed business—lines are increased over time based on payment and purchase history.

## Managing Inventory Turnover

Remember the adage, "Haste makes waste"—hurriedly buying poorly researched and inadequately studied products causes mistakes that result in lost effort, time, and money. At scale, a company will require software to forecast the correct inventory levels and identify the products that fail to move. Deadstock should be sold off at cost or off-price in order to release the funds originally used to acquire it. A computer provides some reassurance; however, you must also conduct market research. Seasonal businesses and those that are vulnerable to rapid changes in customer tastes require you to remain ever vigilant and engage in ongoing business scuttlebutt in order to amend your forecasting beyond simply running inventory reports.

The *inventory turnover ratio* measures how efficiently a company manages inventory assets. Retarding inventory holdings cuts overhead costs, enhancing profitability. The inventory turnover ratio would ideally be calculated as units sold divided by the units on

# Business Credit Application

## Name/Address

| Last: | First: | Middle Initial: | Title |
|---|---|---|---|
| Name of Business: | | | Tax I.D. Number |
| Address: | | | |
| City: | State: | ZIP: | Phone. |

## Company Information

| Type of Business: | | In Business Since: | |
|---|---|---|---|
| Legal Form Under Which Business Operates: | | | |
| | Corporation ☐ | Partnership ☐ | Proprietorship ☐ |
| If Division/Subsidiary, Name of Parent Company: | | In Business Since: | |
| Name of Company Principal Responsible for Business Transactions: | | Title: | |
| Address. | City: | State: ZIP. | Phone: |
| Name of Company Principal Responsible for Business Transactions: | | Title: | |
| Address: | City: | State: ZIP: | Phone: |

## Bank References

| Institution Name: | Institution Name: | Institution Name: | |
|---|---|---|---|
| Checking Account #: | Savings Account #: | Home Equity Loan: | Loan Balance: |
| Address: | Address: | Address: | |
| Phone: | Phone: | Phone: | |

## Trade References

| Company Name: | Company Name: | Company Name: |
|---|---|---|
| Contact Name: | Contact Name: | Contact Name: |
| Address: | Address: | Address: |
| Phone: | Phone: | Phone: |
| Account Opened Since: | Account Opened Since: | Account Opened Since: |
| Credit Limit: | Credit Limit: | Credit Limit: |
| Current Balance: | Current Balance: | Current Balance: |

I hereby certify that the information contained herein is complete and accurate. This information has been furnished with the understanding that it is to be used to determine the amount and conditions of the credit to be extended. Furthermore, I hereby authorize the financial institutions listed in this credit application to release necessary information to the company for which credit is being applied for in order to verify the information contained herein.

_____      _____
Signature                                    Date

FIGURE 7–1: **Example Business Credit Application**

hand. Software can accomplish this, however in the smaller, less-scrutinized set of books, the financial statements will yield the metrics, and since financial statements only capture monetary values, external valuation of inventory turnover (e.g., auditing a set of books by an accountant or bookkeeper) relies on the values recorded under Generally Accepted Accounting Principles (GAAP). GAAP is the commonly accepted way of recording and reporting accounting data. See Figure 7–2 below for how to calculate inventory turnover.

$$\frac{\text{Cost of Goods Sold}}{\text{Average Inventory}} = \frac{\text{Cost of Goods Sold}}{(\text{Beginning Inventory} + \text{Ending Inventory}) \div 2}$$

FIGURE 7–2: **Inventory Turnover Formula**

The more frequently you can turn over inventory, the more money you can generally make. Lower prices do not always correspond to greater sales velocity. In my experience, dropping the price on easily sourced, everyday items will result in great sales velocity to a point. There is a limit to how much merchandise can be absorbed within a given local or regional trading area. A retail grocer can only sell so many avocados to its shoppers and there is a point at which the wholesaler begins to leave profits on the table as they reduce their price to the retailer. If the wholesaler experiences a surplus of highly perishable inventory such as the rapidly ripening avocado, unsold inventory can be converted into other products such as prepared and frozen guacamole—a product that lasts up to three months in a freezer. A metal fastener has a virtually indefinite shelf life, but olive oil does not. As food products reach the event horizon of their sell-by or best-by date, the value declines with incredible speed. A boutique replacement hardware wholesaler catering to contractors that remodel mid-century modernist homes must carry a vast array of inventory and will experience inventory turnover on orders of magnitude slower than the produce wholesaler. The replacement hardware wholesaler will acquire new inventory for little money from the demolition waste when old homes and buildings are torn down—the cost of goods will be mostly the labor for cleaning and reconditioning (plus the payroll costs and benefits of the employees handling the cleaning and reconditioning), transportation costs, storage costs, and overhead related to the stocking of these items (e.g., the protective packaging materials used for storage and later shipping to the customer). Such a business requires very low rent and a lot of space with extremely high margins. Inventory turnover will be likely molasses-like in such a trade.

# Moving Your Inventory

Before diving into how to move inventory, I will start with a few comments about preparing customer orders for shipping and what you need to be thinking about before product leaves the warehouse—the handling of inventory in-house. One of the most common mistakes made in dealing with shipping is a failure to protect goods before handing them off to the person or company delivering them. Boxes move through conveyors and are jostled and often compressed when piled high with other cartons, forklift drivers run into the side of paletted goods and poke holes in unprotected cartons, products are exposed to dust and moisture as well as substantial changes in temperature and humidity.

In the cold chain, honeybees (indeed insects are wholesaled), medicines, ice cream, cut flowers, and fresh produce must be stored at perfect temperatures without fluctuation as they travel their route from you to the customer inside of a reefer.

Defend goods against moisture and mold. Take preventative measures to protect delicate and sensitive goods so that abuses en route do not cause a loss of precious cargo and capital. Verify the carrier's insurance and ask for a copy. And if your customer doesn't have a dock (or your location lacks one), a lift-gate truck is required for pallet shipments and will involve an additional fee paid to the freight company.

Once you get your inventory in place, it's time to move it. "But I just stocked my warehouse," you say. "Now I need to get the products back out?" Well, yes. That's what wholesaling is all about, after all—moving product. The cost of delivering products of any significant size or weight to customers will be nontrivial. I have been sending out products using a myriad of shipping methods since at least 1988. I have come up with best practices for everyday item shipping that considers both speed and cost. I am presuming that the vast majority of wholesale distributors will get product in the hands of customers in the following ways:

- ▶ Offer local pickup, which is usually referred to as *will call.*
- ▶ Provide local delivery using company employees.
- ▶ Deliver goods using an on-demand service—usually called upon by using a smart-phone app.
- ▶ Ship light items by common carrier.
- ▶ Ship by freight (e.g., truck, rail, ship, or plane).

Bus companies and airlines also offer competing shipping solutions, but I'm limiting the discussion to the most common shipping methods.

Will call is by far the least complicated way of handling order fulfillment. The buyer places an order, a pick list is generated, the order is pulled, and the customer picks the goods up personally—an invoice is generated and paid at the time of pickup, is prepaid, or is sent out and paid at a later time.

The remainder of the items on the aforementioned list involves *logistics*. No matter how you source products, once an order is placed and the wholesale distributor takes on the responsibility to deliver what was ordered, that duty does not end until the customer receives and accepts what they ordered.

A plethora of things can go wrong along the way, such as:

▶ The vehicle has an accident, destroying some or all of the product.

▶ The goods are delivered to the wrong consignee.

▶ Mishandling causes damage (e.g., a forklift pierces the boxes on the pallet, the parcel is crushed, or it's left in the rain and the water ruins what's inside the cartons, etc.).

▶ Some or all of the goods are stolen along the way.

▶ Any number of other possible reasons.

## High-Value and Perishable Goods

Wholesalers of high-value merchandise such as champagne, computers, or fragrances will commit to using an entire truck, and special tamper-evident locks and seals are used for security and insurance purposes. Temperature-controlled shipping is accomplished using reefer containers—for frozen and refrigerated foods and goods that will become damaged by excessive heat such as aquarium fish, wine, or live landscaping plants. In virtually every case, shipments are insured against loss or damage. Reefers have temperature audits and any failure of the system can result in melted and refrozen ice cream or spoiled meat. We have all had a frozen treat that was weirdly crystallized—caused by logistics failure relating to a reefer or poor handling by the retailer.

## Keep Costs in Check

Sending products at the lowest possible price involves shopping around and experience. Sending a package through the United States Postal Service (USPS) across town, even a very heavy one, is quite cheap. When a person can easily pick up the shipment with two hands, a local buyer that's not in a hurry would be ideally served by using a common carrier such as USPS. Additional common carriers include DHL, FedEx, and UPS. I'm using the Roadie smartphone app to request local messengers for affordable same-day deliveries. For crates, pallets, and heavy shipments, a motor freight company, freight forwarder, or logistics provider would be used. While brokers offer a valuable service, I don't recommend using them. Technology sites are rapidly replacing the broker with accurate, instant quotes and immediate scheduling—made possible by connected computer networks that speak with each other using a tool called an *application programming interface* (API). I'm using Freightquote (https://www.freightquote.com) to score amazing rates for less-than-truckload shipments. All my shipping consisting of palleted goods represents less than truckload freight which is referred to as LTL.

Securing discounts with common carriers requires an application and a one-on-one conversation with an account manager. The account manager evaluates your proposed volume and type of goods—taking into consideration average shipment size and other factors and then sets up rates that represent a discount off their retail pricing. Common carriers can come on-demand or will schedule daily pickups.

## Large Shipments

Truck shipments can be moved using regional, national, and international freight companies. Regional shipping can be accomplished by opening up a single account with a well-vetted local firm, but once a shipment ventures further out, things can become a bit more complicated. For example, a third-party logistics provider will work with contracted carriers that include motor carriers, railroads, air, and ocean carriers. Not all ocean freight is headed for other countries—LCL (Less than Container Load) and FCL (Full Container Load) ocean shipments move eastbound and westbound, to and from Hawaii and Guam, and there is ample business trading with retailers off the mainland.

When big shipments need to move to or from another country, it's prudent to speak with a freight forwarder or for full containers, an intermodal freight company—the latter moves an entire container of goods without touching what's inside. Intermodal freight can involve rail, ship, and motor freight—and the container remains sealed as it changes modes. The reduction of cargo handling improves security and minimizes loss or damage.

## When Third Parties Are Involved

Outsourcing is growing in popularity, but even big-name contract warehousing and logistics providers are only as good as their worst employee. Sock wholesalers won't lose any sleep over who is managing their inventory, but a sturgeon roe caviar distributor will require a tightly controlled chain of custody and records to ensure the product is being handled correctly with computerized door-to-door temperature logs.

And what happens when the retailer refuses to pay because of damage during shipping? The wholesaler will be left to negotiate a settlement with the shipping company's claims department and rush replacement goods to the buyer.

## Shipping Options Overview

Circling back to the 360-degree view of handling orders, I have provided a chart in Figure 7–3 that summarizes my use cases for different types of freight needs.

| Delivery Method | Use Case |
| --- | --- |
| Will call (local pickup) | Will call is ideal when the goods are cheap and delivery or shipping would be expensive; it's an excellent option for small orders and customers can be offered a discount for picking up their order since it's less expensive for the wholesaler to rapidly pick goods and hold them for pickup. Labor and supplies for packing/protecting and palletizing are avoided and these savings can be passed along to the buyer. |
| Direct delivery using a company vehicle | Among the most common means of order fulfillment and by far the most dangerous and expensive. A sole proprietor can deliver orders themselves (but this pulls focus away from the business) or can work with a family member or trusted employee. Labor and vehicle costs are considerable as are workers' compensation and liability insurance. Repairs and maintenance add to the headaches and when accidents or breakdowns occur with only one company delivery vehicle, work comes to a halt. Who pays for parking tickets and moving violations? Vetting excellent drivers is costly and time-consuming. This works best with high-margin goods and when order volume justifies multiple vehicles. |
| Direct delivery using a third party | Ideal for the small-business owner with local and regional customers. While I am extremely fond of the Roadie smartphone app, there is a plethora of on-demand messenger and contract delivery companies out there. While most of these companies handle same-day pickup and delivery, some (e.g., Roadie) can service next-day delivery and even cross-country shipments. Orders that won't fit in a van or pickup truck can be handled by an independent box truck or a delivery truck owner. Operators of semis are sometimes willing to handle local LTL shipments in their downtime. Connecting with independent driver-owners is a matter of posting on social media sites like Nextdoor and Craigslist or asking around (e.g., calling the local chamber or regional business development agency). |

FIGURE 7–3: **Use Cases for Different Methods of Fulfillment and Delivery**

| Delivery Method | Use Case |
|---|---|
| Common carrier | A common carrier includes companies like DHL, FedEx, UPS, and USPS. They will deliver packages and goods for different people and companies. They accept responsibility for any loss or damages in the transportation process when insurance is purchased as a separate concession. The maximum weight that common carriers will accept varies and is in the range of 70 to 150 pounds per parcel. The most "common" of the common carriers ship both air and ground. Common carrier shipments are ideally suited for smaller, high-value products and when a customer places a small order. Unless goods are required urgently, surface shipping is utilized. |
| Freight | Freight companies send goods by truck, rail, ship, or plane. While freight companies can have vast networks, their service is far more individualized than that offered by common carriers. Aside from air freight services, shipping through a freight company falls into the zone of handling large shipments. With some exceptions (such as products like jewelry), most wholesalers use freight companies to bring goods in from the factory and some use freight companies to ship to their customers. Less than truckload shipments are the norm—cargo from multiple businesses travel in multi-tenant vehicles. Valuable goods that require the vehicle to travel with locks or tamper-evident indicators will move as partial or full truckloads (or containers when goods travel using intermodal carriers). Locked trucks and containers travel as single-tenant shipments. Merchandise is normally crated or palletized. Forklift damage is quite common so fragile merchandise is crated. Ocean freight is moved in shipping containers. Temperature-sensitive goods travel in reefers. |

FIGURE 7–3: **Use Cases for Different Methods of Fulfillment and Delivery,** continued

## Create a Fulfillment Plan

Having a fulfillment plan is an essential part of talking about inventory. A blend of fulfillment methods is the norm, which compels the business owner to develop the skills needed to make rapid and informed decisions. In my business, I have a simplified set of guidelines which follows these essential rules:

- ▶ Ask local customers to pick up from my facility and incentivize this behavior with a discount that reflects the lower handling and preparation costs I enjoy from not having to ship the goods out.
- ▶ My preferred on-demand same-day messenger service is Roadie for small to medium-size shipments, and for larger orders, I call on one of the local independently owned cartage companies.
- ▶ Ship most lightweight orders by USPS and heavier shipments under 150 pounds by FedEx Ground.
- ▶ Use Priority Mail Express or Priority Mail to ship urgent packages that are required within one to three days.
- ▶ For all domestic crated or palletized freight, bid and schedule the job at https://www.freightquote.com.
- ▶ For global logistics, such as container freight, I shop around and speak with brokers and freight forwarders (who have relationships with intermodal freight companies).

A small-business owner should avoid owning and operating delivery vehicles or asking employees to use their own vehicles to drop off customer orders. When a non-owned vehicle is used, special insurance coverage is needed. On a small scale, it's simpler and less costly to use on-demand delivery services that carry their own liability insurance. While I use Roadie, there are many firms to choose from that offer same-day commercial delivery and messenger services.

In the next chapter, I'll discuss the operational aspects of running a wholesale distribution business and how to streamline what you're doing for top efficiency.

# Optimizing Operations

Now that you have a 360-degree view of the whole-sale distribution industry, consider the economic potential and what product lines interest you— and where the low-hanging fruit exists for profitability. You'll now examine how to operate your business—the day-to-day activities, required tools, and business mandates. You must identify predictable, potentially profitable sources of supply (i.e., your vendors/factories/suppliers) and determine where to find customers. Mastering your business processes will also be an important facet of operations.

Knowing how to work with suppliers will also be a key to your operational success. A *supply chain* involves the transformation of resources, raw materials, and components into finished goods delivered to the end customer. An understanding of the supply chain empowers you to pay the most attractive price and avoid too many middlemen in the journey along the way. Success requires hard work, and the time you commit to vetting suppliers yields returns in the form of quality products, reliable delivery, excellent payment terms, and favorable future offers from vendors.

In this chapter, I'll discuss the importance of ethical sourcing, evaluating and grappling with the various costs associated with operations, the workplace, delivery and vehicles, and technology. I'll also prompt you to start thinking about trimming costs with outsourcing, measuring and tracking what you're doing, and studying what the big players are up to and how to improve what you do by knowing what they do.

# The Start of the Chain: Ethical Sourcing

The number of operational factors to consider may initially confuse or overwhelm you, but with experience, you will become an expert in navigating the roughest waters, many of which tend to churn around the issue of safety and fair labor. For example, consider a report not long ago from the U.S. Food and Drug Administration (FDA) that confirmed significant levels of extractable lead in the glaze and decoration of imported ceramic tableware. The levels reported by local authorities to the FDA exceeded those considered safe because this lead can leach into food and drink that is prepared, stored, or served using these lead-containing products. All major retailers have published responsible sourcing policies to maintain customer safety and the dignity of the people who work within the supply chain, and they'll require you to support all responsible sourcing claims. The wholesaler shares the duty to verify ethical sourcing—making sure that factory workers are safe and treated fairly, and that environmental and social impacts are given sufficient focus. No one should engage in business practices that exploit people, and among the most sensitive concerns is the use of young children for farm and factory labor. Even the most seasoned wholesaler must remain prepared to answer questions from retailers that at any time may seek verification of responsible business practices. The consequences of willful failure to protect end users can be dire. A dramatic example is that of a publicly traded hardwood flooring distributor that paid a $33 million criminal penalty to settle federal charges for knowingly selling import products with illegally high levels of the

▶ **Leaving the Nest**

"Operating very efficiently and turning your inventory over quickly are the keys to making money," says Adam Fein, president of Pembroke Consulting Inc., a Philadelphia strategic consulting firm. "It's a service business that deals with business customers, as opposed to general consumers. The startup entrepreneur must be able to understand customer needs and learn how to serve them well." Fein reports that of the plethora of wholesale distribution startups, statistically, many are founded by salespeople who fled larger companies with their customer list in-hand. "Success in wholesale distribution involves moving from a customer service/sales orientation to the operational process of managing a very complex business," says Fein.

carcinogen formaldehyde. While the company's leaders dodged formal prosecution, the financial impact was painful. Don't allow potential challenges to form a dark cloud over your interest in moving forward with a wholesale distribution business—be informed and act responsibly.

# Weighing Operating Costs

The scrappy entrepreneur bootstrapping a T-shirt business from a basement is clearly financially different from a booming wholesale distributor of power tools with mammoth 18-wheeler trucks backing up to the dock with regularity. Companies that vary in size within the same industry have different needs, and companies within different industries of the same size will also have different financial needs. While you may not imagine your business growing to such a scale as to require the services of an intermodal freight transport company, it's important to understand how they (and other large-scale operational tools) work.

## *Workplace Costs*

Every wholesale distribution business has inescapable operating costs that relate to things like a place to work (e.g., home office, office, or warehouse), an internet connection, a means to talk to customers (e.g., a mobile phone or office phone system), computer(s), supplies, insurance, and payroll costs (if you employ people). Yes, even work-at-home occupations have a home office cost—even if you don't charge yourself rent, the space is costing you something.

## Storage Costs

Storing merchandise comes with a cost. A wholesale distribution business involves warehousing and fulfillment of products. You may not be ready to commit to the investment that's required for a big warehouse. Fulfillment by Amazon (FBA) has become a very popular resource. With FBA, Amazon receives your bulk goods at various distribution centers and you can log into their site to direct shipments to wholesale and retail customers. While FBA is wildly popular for B2C retail ecommerce sales, it works just as well for shipping pallets or even truckloads of merchandise. The contract warehouse model has exploded in popularity as would-be business moguls such as yourself realize the wisdom of outsourcing anything that needs to be done on scale or for a limited time. Third-party logistics companies (3PL or TPL) are available for firms of any size that require storage and fulfillment.

Will you set up your own warehouse or use scalable, on-demand storage? If you score a sweet deal on warehouse space that doesn't have an office, you can hire a local contractor to quickly set one up (and don't forget an air conditioning unit!). Should you enlist the services of a third-party logistics firm in order to bundle storage with outsourced fulfillment?

There are ways to scale and share expenses with other wholesalers. Like fractional warehouse providers, you can fill your vacant warehouse space with the goods of other sellers and charge per-pallet rent like other contract warehouses. As your business grows, you can slowly transition away from being a warehouse landlord. You'll need to survive financially, and this would be one way to elevate revenue. You'll also learn something in the process—which wholesalers move lots of stuff and who is thriving.

## Delivery or Vehicle Costs

Pertinent to the topic of storage is the consideration of time-to-customer when it comes to how much inventory you should store to accommodate immediate deliveries. For local customers, you'll need a means for same-day delivery. These buyers picked you because you are local and they want it now. Do you buy or lease a company vehicle? It is surprisingly expensive to do so. The cost of the vehicle or vehicle lease is layered in with the payroll expense for the driver (which includes the cost of wages, payroll taxes, workers' compensation, and payroll accounting), fuel, liability insurance, training, etc. With advanced artificial intelligence systems and on-demand messaging apps, it is now possible to match willing independent contractors for along-the-way messenger delivery— these are networks that match independent contractors with delivery gigs, and the number

## ► Reducing Costs by Outsourcing Help

Will you liaise with buyers when shipment tracking is needed? Who will be designated to handle a damage claim? There are now millions of people working at home who offer fractions of their day to help with necessary administrative tasks such as hunting down the insurance adjuster to finalize a damaged shipment claim payment. I have hired them affordably on sites such as Fiverr and Upwork with good results. There are multitudes of gig sites filling the role of the expensive employment agency of yesteryear. Wholesale distributors cut staff costs by employing freelancers to handle invoicing, payment processing, order taking, and anything and everything that can be accomplished with a connection to the internet.

of these companies is growing. Given a large enough population of networked drivers, it is a virtual certainty that someone with the correct size vehicle for your shipment is heading to your customer's location the same day. For deliveries that are farther away, a commercial shipping relationship is required—with companies like DHL, UPS, FedEx, and the USPS. A mixture of order sizes and client types will warrant an appropriate variety of package delivery and supply chain options, determined by order size, order value, and how quickly it's required.

## Technology Costs

As I entered the world of business as a teen, I would marvel at the incredible feats of businesspeople—their complex businesses, running smoothly and efficiently with their employees on top of things (I admit also at that age, I was impressed with their fancy cars). How were all these moving parts so well organized and operating smoothly like a fine Swiss timepiece? The answer is: strong operational tools, procedures, and planning. Today, I organize tasks on a computerized online calendar and I track customer interactions with CRM tools. My particular tools are provided by Google and Salesforce and while these are wonderful solutions, their success depends on how well I know how to use them.

You should also deploy simple ordering systems. Make everything easy for employees and buyers. Some people love online ordering and others don't. Be flexible and allow customers to place verbal orders whenever they want. Have order pads around that staff can use to quickly jot down a phone order and always help the customers that call with extreme alacrity. Asking a phone customer to use your online ordering system ignores an important fact—they called you for personalized service!

# The Day-to-Day Routine

Whether you use "sticky notes" or a robust CRM program to avoid chaos and ensure a predicted outcome, you'll need to have routines in place to keep your operational world well-oiled.

As with all sales-driven enterprises, wholesale distributors thrive by selling. In addition, there is a daily ritual of coping with shipping and receiving, handling customer service, keeping up with accounting, and employee management. All these daily concerns require a strong company culture. The high-achieving businesses are those where employees act as company cheerleaders. One reason I quickly fire a bad apple in my company is that they can rapidly rot the entire barrel. To maintain high morale, the employees must accept and be fans of the company culture. Managing that culture is also part of your daily operational landscape.

So, as a wholesale distributor, what do you do in a day? Your daily agenda may include the following:

▶ Checking voicemail, texts, and email messages.

▶ For messages that relate to orders, handling order confirmations and moving the order entry forward—ask customers if they require additional items and share new product information (but don't be pushy or painful about it).

▶ Preparing the delivery schedule.

▶ Organizing shipping picklists and arranging for shipping of common carrier and freight orders.

▶ Reaching out to existing customers to see if anything is needed (customer retention and top-of-mind is key!).

▶ Conducting prospecting for new customers—be consistent, but avoid setting quotas as they can only set you up for failure and disappointment.

▶ Checking incoming shipment status—what's expected, what's late, etc.

▶ Attending to all administrative work and routine chores. Are office and warehouse supplies stocked? Is everything clean and organized? Has the mail been sorted?

▶ Attending to (or mending) any staffing matters, challenges, disputes, etc.

On a less-than-daily frequency, you'll also want to address other mission-critical aspects of your business including:

▶ The management of human capital—management of work force needs, hiring and firing, labor law compliance and employment standards, and payroll tax deposits.

▶ Filing periodic government paperwork, e.g., payroll tax returns, estimated tax returns, sales tax reporting, permit/license renewals, etc.

▶ Bookkeeping (I have used QuickBooks since 2002 and use Patriot Software Company for payroll processing).

▶ Actuarial analysis (risk assessment, force majeure, probability of liability headwinds, etc.).

▶ Strategy and long-term planning.

The recipe for a successful wholesaler cannot be bottled because there is never a one-size-fits-all approach to handling the work. What are the must-dos? I start every day with a good attitude. The rest will flow from there. A tendency to respond positively to something influences your choice of action and how you react to incentives and challenges. Do you get up and handle your business every day hungry to succeed with a do-whatever-it-takes mentality? Be sure to mind your ethics. What things will you need to do on a daily basis

## ▶ Different Systems for Different Needs

I currently do business with Carmelita, a senior in Niangua, Missouri. Carmelita and I have been working together since the 1980s, and she is incredibly organized. Carmelita is a prolific designer and manufacturer of fine jewelry—a product line that I sell with excellent results through ecommerce stores. Although I am a wholesale distributor, I act as the retailer in my relationship with Carmelita. Carmelita owns no computer, has no fax machine, and does business via USPS and through a landline phone. Her records are all written by hand, and she is perfectly organized—running a highly successful manufacturing business. We make money together and enjoy working with each other. She is also legally blind.

A distributor needs tools, and routines are one of the tools for success. Carmelita is proof that success can occur in the total absence of high-tech equipment and dealing with a disability. A company system that is adopted and used is a successful one—even if it isn't high-tech. The cleverest idea will fail if the people working under you do not embrace it. I use software to run my business, but not everyone can use technology, and in some instances, you will have change-resistant staff. An edict for change isn't going to work; you'll have to lead the team and get each person in your organization charged up about using the tools that you've decided are best for your company's future. There is absolutely nothing wrong with paper systems, so long as the team uses them efficiently and everyone accepts them. The same is true of computerized systems. There are firms that work with hybrid systems—some folks use paper while the data entry team inputs them into the computer system. Just like Carmelita, sometimes you have to go with what works for your particular situation.

in order to become your definition of successful? How you act will affect those around you and that means customers, staff, vendors, family, and friends—a positive lifestyle is infectious.

To make your day-to-day run smoothly, make use of outside assistance. The free-flowing nature of today's society has generated tremendous interest in the sharing economy, which is often referred to as the gig economy. Leaders in this space are no longer insurgents. We must embrace change because it is inevitable. Why not ride this roller coaster? Creative entrepreneurs were ordering rideshares, and instead of transporting themselves, they would send orders to customers. This inspired startups in the on-demand delivery services business. Instead of expensive dedicated computer servers, people are using cloud computing services so they can shift the burden of hardware maintenance and software upgrades over to the provider and diminish the need to deal with IT concerns. Shared work spaces are everywhere and millions of businesspeople are using them to conduct meetings and step away from the home office—without the need for complex and expensive contractual lease and rental agreements. I have embraced the change by adopting the sharing economy as a reality of business and as a way to inoculate myself from the complex rules and regulations that businesses fear and cope with every day. I prefer to let someone else worry about distractions such as Transport Layer Security, workers' comp, HVAC systems, licenses, and whatnot. For a smaller business, the secret is in sharing resources to maintain a low-stress business and let the vendors and service providers sweat all the small details.

## Tracking Your Efforts

Operationally, your wholesale business will live or die by tracking data about everything from logistics to customer profiles. Predictable business results require you to be organized and for information to become transparent to every stakeholder within your team in a timely fashion. For example, some customers work on a *request for proposal* (RFP) cycle that can be locked down for a period of years. An RFP is a document that solicits vendors to bid on commodity (or service) needs. In 2008, I was serving as the executive vice president of The Chase Group, a successful event services and logistics contractor that provided experiential marketing services to Silicon Valley businesses. The Chase Group (later acquired by Freeman) was very much a wholesale distribution company because experiential marketing (the trade show and events world) involves lots of corporate premiums and giveaways. The Chase Group would buy millions of dollars' worth of small gift items and have them imprinted with the clients' names. Visa issued an RFP for their event service's needs, and I was voted most likely to prepare a successful proposal—I did and won the multimillion-dollar contract. Freeman inherited the deal, and Visa remains their customer to this day. I was very proud to have landed that deal, and it would not have been possible if it weren't for tracking the process using customer relationship management tools (CRM). CRM systems track calls, generate quotes, send invoices, store documents, and provide detailed auditing of what's going on.

The CRM I have been using for the last two decades is Salesforce. It allows for every member on my team to share visibility of what's relevant to them while allowing confidential data to be protected from view. The sales, commerce, and service activities are organized in a secure, cloud-based *SaaS (software-as-a-service)*. SaaS is a software distribution model where a third-party company hosts applications and makes them available over the internet. This reduces the headache of having to manage equipment, upgrades, and patching. The best CRM systems are fully customizable to simplify or expand based on your needs. When you use a tool to track the little details, customers will be stunned and delighted by what you remember—not just orders and basic needs, but likes and dislikes, birthdays and special occasions, etc.

When there is zero margin for error, the CRM tracks and reminds. Sales calls and meetings are scheduled, and when used correctly, a robust CRM will be your engine for success. A helpful alert from the system cues me when to reach out to a customer at just the right time—whether it's an hour, a day, a week, a year, or a decade from now. Larger customers will have an RFP schedule and you might be waiting for several years for the opportunity to bid on a contract to become a supplier. CRM systems prevent absent-minded business losses and ensure you're staying in the game right where you need to be. If you want to go low-tech, you can accomplish the same thing with a calendar or what we used to refer to as a tickler file to bring important action items to the top-of-mind.

## Study the Other Players

What better way to understand a product category than to see how the big players are doing? I engage in spirited debate with fellow entrepreneurs when I cite publicly traded companies in my case studies. As a new, scrappy entrepreneur, you may struggle to see the relevance of the operation of these big companies juxtaposed with your own small operations. I argue both the clear relevance and that a small business can do it better. If a large company within a particular industry is generating double-digit gross profit margins, then a smaller business can do better through differentiation—offering proprietary products, more nimble service, and through a strong connection with their customers. With some exceptions, big companies suffer diminishing returns as they grow, hire more people, and complicate their operations when compared to a smaller company. What I appreciate about the examination of public corporations is the utter transparency of their numbers—these figures are audited by large accounting firms, and as a result of government regulation and scrutiny, the information we can study is quite accurate. Private corporations have no such transparency. The executives of a nonpublic enterprise can engage in unethical and wild puffery with little or no worry about repercussions. There is an endless number of alleged experts expounding the benefits of their special reports and insider secrets hoping to empty your wallet; however, a wellspring of knowledge lies in the annual reports from America's most beloved public companies.

Annual reports are compulsory, and transparent financial data is accompanied by a well-written, enlightening operational review as well as a forward-looking thesis. Let's take a look at an example. Covington, Louisiana-based Pool Corporation is a public company listed on the NASDAQ and traded under the symbol POOL. Pool Corporation is the world's largest wholesale distributor of swimming pool supplies, equipment, and related products and the third-largest distributor of irrigation and related products in the U.S.—pool and irrigation are kissing-cousin industries with retailers and installers working both of these product categories. As of 2017, the company operates 351 sales centers, and 75 of them are in the golden state of California where I live (no surprise, huh?). Pool Corporation reports that approximately 60 percent of consumer spending in the pool industry relates to maintenance and routine repair of installed swimming pools. What caught my attention about the in-ground pool business was the growth. The installed base of in-ground swimming pools grew at a steady clip for 11 years from 2007 to 2017 with no end in sight. I am certain that Pool Corporation will continue to do a yeoman job of supplying retailers with what they need to help pool owners maintain, upgrade, or replace their pools—but there is always room for another wholesaler in a growing industry. Pool Corporation cannot (and does not) serve everyone. I enjoy diving into the details of annual reports because they provide me with incredible knowledge (and strategic advantages in my own business).

Pool Corporation works with its suppliers (i.e., factories) who offer what are referred to as *early buy purchases*. These purchases allow a wholesaler to place an order in the fall at a discount, well before pool season heats up. The wholesaler can later take delivery of product in the off-season months and then pay for the purchases much later, e.g., in the spring or early summer of the following year. What should be relevant to anyone looking to venture into the swimming pool and irrigation wholesale supply industries is that Pool Corporation's gross profit was at least 28 percent from 2015 to 2017—very healthy margins!

Look at industries where the profits are growing on the low branches of the fruit tree and grab them!

While public companies are required to show their financials to the world, private companies are not. It would be harder to really understand these competitors in your industry because these firms could claim success, but things might not be so rosy behind-the-scenes. How can you really know for sure? There are some ways you can learn from these private firms. Here are a few suggestions:

▶ Study their website for clues on what they are doing.

▶ Check out LinkedIn and see who is working there and for how long—frequent turnover can be a sign that the company isn't doing well.

▶ Check out your competitor's online reputation from support threads and reviews about them.

▶ Check news mentions for information about awards, to read press releases, and to spark ideas for your own public relations campaigns.

▶ Stay on top of social media comments relating to your competitors.

How frequently you conduct this research is up to you, but it's wise to carve out time and do this work consistently. It could be monthly, quarterly, or yearly depending on how busy you are.

In the next chapter, I'll discuss one of the largest and most important topic areas for all businesses—human capital. I'll provide tips on attracting and keeping the best employees now and far into the future.

# Finding the Rest of Your Team

A business owner is a true superhero. You're jug-
gling daily life, family duties, chores at home,
social obligations, and, of course, your company
(possibly even a day job). Day one of operating a sole proprietorship means you'll be wearing every hat. You're the
CEO, salesperson, marketing manager, purchasing agent,

inventory manager, forklift driver, data entry clerk, customer service specialist, shipping clerk, returns manager, bookkeeper, PR guru, and morale officer (head cheerleader).

As your wholesale business grows, being the jack of all trades lowers the glass ceiling. Like Superman, you'll need to venture out of the Fortress of Solitude and become an employer to grow your business. Your need for additional help may become crystal clear to you immediately. It's also natural to be uncertain about the proper timing to hire employees. I have been on both ends of the spectrum. Experience allows me to make business decisions with crisp execution.

If it were humanly possible, most entrepreneurs would stick to running one-person operations. Unfortunately, this would severely inhibit company growth and at the same time burn out the average business owner. A growing business must hire employees in order to benefit from the opportunity that growth affords.

Among the most complex and challenging areas of business subsists in the acquisition and management of human capital. An A-player is worth three B-players any day of the week. In their haste, successful business owners often throw untrained, unqualified people into jobs hoping to see from these workers the same grit and vigor that they themselves commit to running their companies. In this chapter, we'll look into what you need to consider when building your team.

## Great Employees Don't Need to Be Perfect Employees

The application of quantitative standards won't yield the best workers, either. Human resource scientists have toiled endlessly in an effort to unlock the secrets of developing hiring techniques based on observable phenomena. Academic testing and a battery of exams fail to identify the best workers. The top students entering the work force won't always deliver top-quality work for the company. Seats of great learning where individuals go to become deep thinkers generate many well-educated individuals who cannot land or keep a relatively basic job. Even the poorly educated employee can rise above their lack of book smarts to become an accomplished manager and leader. Supported by the latest advances in software and AI, a worker who struggles to spell correctly can deliver grammatically-correct, perfectly spelled documents and emails. Spreadsheet formulas ensure that every financial calculation at a company is accurate to the penny. Workers do not have to be perfect to be wonderful. Conversely, a company owner or a manager working under that owner cannot demand that dedicated employees perform their job as well as the owner or manager. Underappreciated workers are certainly headed for the door as readily and rapidly as those who are underpaid.

And the ambitious business owner must hire to expand. America's first billionaire was oil industry magnate John D. Rockefeller and he said, "I would rather earn 1 percent off 100 people's efforts than 100 percent of my own efforts." Rockefeller understood the role of human capital in the economic growth of a company. When a firm is very small, the employees who are hired must be able to switch tasks and cover multiple bases. As the business grows larger, roles become clearly defined, and cross-training is deployed primarily to ensure things don't fall down when someone becomes ill or takes time off.

And a good enough job is no longer good enough for most workers. Financial fulfillment must be uplifted by flexibility. The old 9-to-5 format has become stifling for many people. Workers expect flexible workplaces and enlightened managers. Certain jobs don't require rigid schedules. A billing clerk can work at any hour and usually from anywhere. Digital records permit sales staff to be untethered and on-the-move.

## Should You Hire?

For a business neophyte, hiring people is a big step. The mere mention of payroll taxes and all that legal stuff is enough to frighten even the most courageous person. First of all, don't stress because it isn't that hard to hire. If your business is failing (we all must fail in order to learn and then later succeed), stop contemplating adding a payroll expense and figure out what is required to bring things back on track. You should not increase overhead unless you are already profitable, or you can make a compelling case that you will be profitable in the near future and adding more people will bring greater velocity to your profitability.

Before you post a single help wanted ad, evaluate if you truly need to hire. Take a close look at your workday. Are you spending too much time distracted by personal calls and texts? Do you engage in tasks that provide zero value to your business? Before you hire anyone, take a week, a month . . . or even longer, and carefully scrutinize your actions. Unnecessary activities must be eliminated immediately. Trim off the fatty tasks that serve no purpose other than to fill time. Are you printing extra copies of your orders and keeping them in a file you never look at again? Do you have your phone set up to alert you when messages arrive in your personal social media inboxes? Are you answering personal calls during work hours? Are you surfing the web endlessly—attracted to interesting headlines and seductive ads? Are you piling papers instead of shredding them? Are you stymied by indecision (yes, that's a task!)? Blogger Brandy Jensen has formed this hypothesis on productivity, "Twenty minutes is, objectively, the ideal amount of time—the Goldilocks number when it comes to doing things." I agree with her because I find that I am ferociously productive when I work on tasks in 20-minute stretches.

Here are the signs you need to hire:

▶ Customer emails and voicemails receive replies in days, not minutes.

▶ Unresolved order complaints pile up.

▶ Orders ship late.

▶ Unsold product sits too long and efforts to market items take a back seat to non-sales daily operations.

▶ Your family and friends complain you're spending too much time working.

▶ You've misplaced the joy and inspiration that brought you to self-employment in the first place.

▶ You're seriously contemplating quitting your business even though sales are great.

If you work entirely by yourself, having another person around who is an asset to your business will brighten up your day, relieve many of the pressures of running a business, and grow profits. But a poorly screened, hastily selected helper will resist your culture and goals. A demanding, drama-filled, unreliable employee is worse than having no employee at all. If you employ more than one person, a bad employee drags down the entire team. Lazy people inspire laziness and spark resentment in others. High standards are highly contagious, just as low standards spread faster than a wildfire after a season of drought. It's up to you to decide if you are ready to take on the responsibility of managing people and the personalities that come with them.

## Are You Boss Material?

Your business must persistently focus on outstanding customer service and a sense of urgency. Employees must align with your goals, be vigilant, and maintain a steady sense of urgency in their actions. No human being can be their best every single day, but a dream team achieves stellar results, which is only possible when your team really clicks. If you expect everyone to be a clone of you, forget it. That's never going to happen. Compelling team purpose requires a vision, clear responsibilities, and a positive team culture.

People love to complain about their bosses when they feel alienated or unheard.

Magic happens when employees enjoy the work, expectations are realistic, and they feel heard and supported. Here are some things all successful bosses do:

▶ Keep the communication flowing.

▶ Avoid the big boss attitude.

▶ Develop a sense of teamwork and camaraderie.

▶ Praise good work incessantly.

▶ Provide honest feedback that never attacks the person.

▶ Allow independent thought.

▶ Give more responsibility.

▶ Avoid being too rigid.

▶ Allow for regular two-way feedback.

▶ Promptly address employee complaints.

▶ Pay people fairly and on time.

▶ Never threaten someone with firing or use money to bend people to your will.

If you feel that you can bring these qualities to the table, and if you're comfortable giving up control of the day-to-day minutiae, then perhaps it's time to think about moving into the corner office.

## ▶ It's Important to Keep Communication Open

Employees look for different qualities in different situations. While a temporary worker may remain distant and focused on the job (knowing they will eventually leave the team), someone looking for a new employment home will hope to find many important qualities in the management and within the workplace. A closed office door shuts out valuable feedback from workers within an organization. My door is both physically and metaphorically always open. A manager of people must regularly talk over matters, see what others are doing, and keep in close touch with the activities within the company. Trust and open communication are priceless and cost nothing to the participants—the most successful managers are superior at listening. Employees should be held accountable for their actions, but the boss must always start each day looking in the mirror to ask "How am I performing in my role as a manager?" before they exercise authority over others. A work environment that fosters creative thinking and challenges the team will grow at an incredible pace. Genuine praise and heartfelt recognition are the least expensive employee benefits and yield the greatest results.

# Mastering the Hiring Process

Mastering the hiring process takes practice. Hiring and managing employees is a subject that covers an endless number of books. It's critical that you keep an eye out for talented people everywhere you go. A wholesale business does not involve rocket science and a sharp learner will pick up the knowledge needed to support your company in a short amount of time. Spread the word to family and friends. Consider new job seekers like recent graduates and applicants without job experience. Avoid the job hoppers; people whose resumes show they can't sit still for very long.

You can post ads on job sites, promote your jobs on social media, and post notices on community bulletin boards. Mention your job openings at every opportunity. Everyone knows someone who is looking for a job. When you're small, seek out candidates who are more likely to be interested in part-time positions, which is great for a small growing company that's not quite ready for full-time employees. A job becomes more attractive than most when it's completely flexible. As long as the work gets done, you can do it at any time of the day. Students appreciate evening jobs and you'll be more than happy to accommodate flexibility in working hours and days. Seniors have a desire to work and stay active and they bring loads of experience and wisdom to the job. Many tasks do not require an eight-hour workday.

Here are some questions you might want to ask during an interview:

▶ Why are you unemployed or leaving your current employer?

▶ If you had a time machine, what would you have done differently?

▶ What's your dream job and why?

▶ What do you look for in a supervisor?

▶ What do you expect in terms of pay and benefits?

▶ Do you have any questions for me?

These are just some possible questions and your list will evolve over time. You should let the applicant do most of the talking and listen carefully. I always admire the warehouse job applicant who dresses in a suit and tie or took the time to put on their best attire, groomed really well, and wrote neatly on the application. A forklift driver or stock clerk who dressed to impress always catches my attention.

I always love curious people and I'm prepared to train just about anyone if they appear eager and curious. While experience is valuable, I'm enamored with people who are willing to dive in and try new things. At some point you have to bite the bullet and give someone an offer. This can be hard to do. Why not offer them a trial day rather than an official offer of employment? Or give someone a part-time position with the intention to hire them full-time if you like their work style and ethic.

Order entry, data management, sales and marketing, accounting, stocking, deliveries and many aspects of a wholesale business can be expertly handled by part-time and flexible shift hiring. You'll also discover that shorter, more intense work shifts are far more attractive than long, boring ones.

# Legal, Tax, and Payroll Considerations

While there is no standard method of paying people and every situation is unique, you'll need to decide how you will pay helpers for the work they perform. If a worker is being paid on payroll (with taxes taken out), then use a payroll service. I use Patriot Software to prepare payroll checks and pay workers' compensation insurance. It takes seconds to print checks on blank check stock or schedule a direct deposit. Taxes are handled seamlessly—on time. No headaches. I used to struggle with all the forms and file them myself. What a mess!

But, do you need to add the high cost of payroll to your budget? Some workers are not considered employees. What if your family extends their helping hands to help get your wholesale business up and running? It is interesting to know that the IRS has an annual gift tax inclusion ($15,000 annually as of 2019). Payments of less than $600 during the year made to someone who is not your employee don't need to be reported. Per the IRS whether an individual is an employee or an independent contractor depends on the "behavioral control, financial control, and relationship of the parties." You don't want to misclassify an employee as an independent contractor, so be sure you ask a tax professional or an IRS employee for help with worker classification.

There are a ton of gig sites where you can hire freelancers, and I'm of the opinion that you'd be safe classifying remote helpers as independent contractors (you'll read about outsourcing later in this chapter). Payroll can take a significant bite into your budget and very small entrepreneurs would be wise to legally avoid hiring employees if the same work can be delegated to a freelancer. If you pay independent contractors, you may still have to file tax forms (1099-MISC for the IRS), but you won't have to tack on the substantial additional cost of payroll taxes, workers' compensation insurance, and payroll processing fees. While I have never done so (I asked a professional), you can file an IRS Form SS-8 requesting a worker status determination to have the government establish if the services someone is providing to you are considered those of a contractor or an employee.

If you become an employer, the IRS requires you to apply for an Employer Identification Number, also referred to as an EIN. You can apply for this online at the IRS website (if you are located in the U.S. or a U.S. territory). The state will have a similar registration requirement if you conduct business in a state that imposes a personal income tax. Most states do; however, the following states do not:

- ► Alaska
- ► Florida
- ► Nevada
- ► New Hampshire

- ▶ South Dakota
- ▶ Tennessee
- ▶ Texas
- ▶ Washington
- ▶ Wyoming

Small-business owners must focus on benefits that are important to their employees. Large corporations will generally upstage smaller businesses when it comes to employee benefit programs. According to the IRS, the provisions of the Affordable Care Act require large employers to offer minimum essential health-care coverage that is affordable and that provides minimum value to full-time employees and their dependents. Most employers are considered small businesses and are not subject to these rules. A large employer is defined as a business with at least 50 full-time employees. A startup may not have the means to offer medical, dental, and vision benefits to their workers. As any business grows, employee retention will hinge in part on the benefits offered. Free snacks, espresso, and soft drinks can only go so far to engage workers. A foosball table is a sweet distraction, but meaningful perks will help to retain employees who support families and want to stay loyal to your growing business. Humans aren't particularly good at planning for an event that's years in the future, such as retirement.

>
>
> **tip**
>
> Hiring someone through an agency will cost a little more but will lift the pressure of dealing with payroll entirely off your shoulders. Experienced wholesalers know the value of early preparation and start adding additional help in advance of the holiday shopping season. Virtually every consumer product category enjoys the boost that comes in November and December.

The IRS offers the small business health-care tax credit for companies that have fewer than 25 employees that offer a qualified health plan to their employees through the Small Business Health Options Program (SHOP) marketplace and pay at least 50 percent of the cost of employee-only—not family or dependent—health-care coverage for each employee. A tax professional can advise on this substantial tax incentive for smaller companies. While speaking with the same tax expert, a small business that doesn't offer group help coverage to their employees can help them pay for medical expenses through a Qualified Small Employer Health Reimbursement Arrangement (QSEHRA). Offer a 401(k) plan at the earliest opportunity.

Can't find money in the budget for employee benefits? Are you 100 percent sure? Then try praise instead of condemnation. Every worker in the world is seeking happiness, and a "thank you" and a smile is the lowest cost and most desirable employee benefit you can offer.

And workers' compensation insurance is not a benefit—it's the law. A caring and dutiful owner will visit with a tax professional no less frequently than once a year to make sure employee benefits are in line with what other employers of the same size are offering. Always focus on being competitive and continue to update your benefits to match what the industry demands.

I contend that incompetence and lack of capital are the chief causes of failure in business. Overpaying for work is just as deadly as underpaying (and underappreciating) employees. For example, a new business with no track record of sales has no business borrowing money (or more money) to fund the addition of employees in the absence of evidence that this action will result in even greater sales sufficient to generate the profits required to at least pay for the cost of the employees and the payroll costs associated with their employment. A person who owes nothing cannot become bankrupt. When you pay cash for everything, you are never going to end up in bankruptcy. One way you can make sure the work gets done without getting in your head is to budget for outsourcing and use it as needed.

## Considering Outsourcing as an Option

A far better solution than hiring additional people is outsourcing. Scope out companies that offer specific services. There are inventory firms that will hand count and report on product in stock. There are retired individuals who will gladly divide bulk goods, weigh them, and seal them in retail packaging. There are endless ways to deliver product to customers without processing a single W-4 form or printing a single paycheck. While there are a plethora of hacks claiming to know the secrets to marketing, there are also a few really superb individuals who work with multiple clients and are able to spread the good word about a wholesale business to appropriate new customers.

For example, you can consider delegating some tasks to a virtual assistant. Virtual assistants are self-employed experts who work from a remote location. Outsourcing appropriate roles to virtual assistants will dramatically reduce cost and headaches for a business owner. Payroll is expensive and involves tax, insurance, and liability considerations. Whenever legally permissible, contractors should be used. I recommend using virtual assistants for market research, data entry, email management, customer service, content writing, and any job that can be done well without having to be in your place of business. To ensure you get what you pay for when hiring unsupervised workers, pay for results, e.g., a data entry clerk working at home can be compensated a set amount for each order, invoice, or document entered. For hourly remote workers, I use Hubstaff monitoring software—a tool that tracks activity and time, and captures screenshots of the worker's computer activities when they're on duty.

There is an endless debate within the wholesale community surrounding the subject of how to pay for outsourced labor. Owners of many SMBs are filling roles with contract and outsourced temporary workers. A simple request for proposal (RFP) including the job requirements will allow interested parties to bid on the work. It is quite common for contract workers to expect and demand large retainers and guaranteed payments. Due to the fluid nature of business, contracts and retainers should be sidestepped in favor of payments based on progress with a right to parachute out of the relationship if the work isn't satisfactory.

I prefer paying flat rates or compensate for piecework. The wholesaler of shelled nuts would be wiser to pay a flat rate per finished bag to the outside vendor who divides bulk products into retail packages. This clear and predictable cost is then added to the cost of goods. Offhand I know of a very large company that buys over-the-counter medications, sundries, and personal hygiene products in large quantities and then seals them into individual blister packs for sale to liquor and convenience stores, hotel gift shops, and gas stations—with staggeringly high markups. We have all seen these products hanging on retail racks in these business establishments.

The multimillion-dollar boutique replacement hardware wholesaler would easily suffer runaway employee labor costs by hiring and training workers to perform triage on demolition waste. Painted antique hinges need stripping and polishing and brass drawer pulls need cleaning and grading. Restoring old hardware requires oodles of skill and tons of experience. The task of painstakingly removing old paint and polishing is ideally suited for the patience of a retired individual working at home paid for their services by the piece.

Anyone who is legally an employee must receive no less than minimum wage, but if you offer the piecework option with a guarantee of no less than the minimum wage, your worker will have a strong incentive to increase output which generates greater profits for you.

## Deciding What to Delegate

Once you have some staff in place, do not delegate anything that is boring, an emergency, vaguely defined, highly confidential, or requires boatloads of planning. That said, delegating mindless tasks is a surefire way to have your best and brightest employees heading out the door for good. Once you have eliminated all unnecessary busywork, then think about what you'd like to delegate to your employees. Allow a member of your staff to try their hand at new tasks—things they've never done before. Let the forklift driver cross-train to learn how to do product research and purchasing. See if the receptionist is interested in learning how to pick-pack-and-ship orders. Keep it interesting and be open-minded to new roles for existing people. Products that involve specialized knowledge or care in handling will involve longer and more costly training.

While it makes total sense to delegate routine tasks, employees will crave interesting projects. An employee who is consistently challenged is more likely to remain engaged and less likely to leave. Many (if not most) company owners are the sales engine in their companies. Delegate time-sucking tasks so that you can focus on wooing new business and schmoozing existing customers (to score even more business!).

## Thinking About How Much You'll Have to Pay

A fair rate of pay shows that you value your employees. The starting point for determining how much to pay someone begins with an accurate job description. Someone certified in the latest CRM software will expect a higher rate of pay than an individual who provides warehouse labor—yet a warehouse employee handles valuable inventory that should not be left in the hands of the lowest-paid worker. Scope out market rates for different positions by engaging in business scuttlebutt and reviewing online job postings. Virtually every job applicant will tell you how much they were paid at their last job, so use the interview process to gain a sense of their expectations regarding pay and benefits.

Every worker must start their employment journey in an entry-level position. Even the Ivy League university student who has completed a well-respected MBA program but who has no prior work experience within a chosen profession is starting entry level, even if their job title sounds high and important. The *knowledge, skills, and abilities* that are required of workers are referred to as KSAs. KSAs for a forklift driver will include the knowledge of the forklift and warehouse principles, skill in driving the forklift without causing damage to inventory or equipment, and the ability to maintain warehouse records. When posting job ads, KSAs that are required should be included in the job description—serving as the compass for applicants, employees, and you to assess the probability for success in the job. If an applicant meets the KSAs that you need, you can expect to pay market rates. Someone who is totally green can be paid a training wage but will either expect market wages upon completing training or will leave to go work for your competitor. That said, I would not recommend on-the-job training for someone wanting to learn how to operate a 9,000-pound forklift. One wrong move and property and lives are placed in jeopardy. Forklift operators should receive formal training to protect employers from liability and safeguard people and property. Specialized training of this type can be administered by a school or acquired directly from the manufacturer themselves—and trained skilled workers expect higher pay. Higher pay is warranted because poorly trained employees make costly mistakes and underpaid people will perform lazily and steal time or worse, steal company property.

When examining rates of pay and employee value, an employer must also consider intangibles through qualitative study—looking at employee worth in the absence of counts or measures. A credit or office manager who consistently and accurately judges the integrity of customers—extending credit privileges to the most reliable, prompt-paying buyers and avoiding the laggards—is an exceptional asset.

Timely payment from a reliable customer is tied directly to how well the team performs. The person taking the order must do so accurately, the person pulling and palletizing the goods must do so meticulously, the driver has to provide damage-free delivery and be prepared to prove that delivery actually occurred. Any misstep by a person working on the team will result in the withholding of payment and a real possibility that company expenses, including payroll, will not be met. For these reasons, paying employees well is essential so that they will act like owners. Determining pay involves business scuttlebutt as well as collecting salary expectations from applicants.

## Tips for Finding Employees

A genuine smile and an expression of sincere interest is the two-way street that helps retain employees. An employer who makes a game out of paying the least amount possible for workers while sleeping at the top of a hill in the most expensive neighborhood in town will experience high turnover. Tightwad bosses become rapidly unpopular and highly resented. At the same time, a highly skilled worker with years of experience will flock to a startup whose owner has a reputation for honesty and fair dealing. Smart workers know that a new company on the rise must conserve capital and cannot pay as much as larger, more established firms. The family feel of a smaller company is very attractive to many people. Flexible hours and a comfortable working environment are equally seductive. A kind manager who is genuinely interested in their workers will earn the highest level of loyalty. A manager who is glad to see their employees will have employees who are equally happy to see them.

Hard-learned lessons should be infrequent. A major investment in employee training will be instantly lost when that employee leaves to check out greener pastures. Just as any landlord would be a fool to charge a tenant below-market rent, an employer is just as much a fool to pay below-market wages. Genuine praise goes a long way however no amount of gratitude will pay your employees' monthly household bills—and quite predictably essential expenses increase over time and so must employee wages.

Look at the most commonly used job sites. Always cultivate people you know. Ask those who are currently employed. Speak with competitors as well as owners in unrelated industries. Guessing is one of the poorest tactics used in business and yet so many business leaders heading up enterprises large and small use this useless tool every single day in sourcing candidates.

Whenever possible, promote from within the company. Current employees should be allowed to apply for a position if they meet the qualifications. Hiring outsiders without asking current workers can cause long-term bitter resentment. If a current member of the team isn't looking for a change, it is very likely that they know someone who is job hunting.

With the exception of dangerous work such as the operation of a forklift, most positions within a wholesaler's business are easily filled with eager, hard-working, and curious individuals of all ages and from all

**tip**

The written tests I have used since 1988 in my own business are yours for the asking. My email is borntodeal@gmail.com.

walks of life. While it is certainly not an absolute requirement, I recommend administering formal testing for typing ability, math, filing, and spelling. Much is revealed to a hiring manager when reviewing answers to essential high school level academic questions. These tests must be proctored and copies should not leave the office because answers could end up online or shared among applicants.

Websites for testing typing accuracy and measuring typing speed are easily found by searching the phrase "typing test" online.

Even a high school dropout can possess a genius mind. When I query applicants about why they dropped out of school, the answers vary but can be generalized into a few categories—they had to care for a child or sick relative, finances required that they work full-time, a de-motivating school environment or issues with other students such as bullying. These dropouts and individuals with problems in their past (e.g., criminal convictions) should not be overlooked. I have hired poorly educated individuals who scored 100 percent on a filing test—as filing clerks. I have employed former gang members and felons. Everyone has a right to escape their pasts, and no applicant should be judged entirely on their academic achievements or disqualified for a criminal conviction in the distant past. Many states now allow adults to clear convictions from their records after satisfying the terms of their probation. Those who are aware of these loopholes are not required to disclose their past transgressions—so don't penalize someone who isn't as knowledgeable. While I do not recklessly lump together dropouts and those with criminal records, the two subjects are not always mutually exclusive as it pertains to hiring.

Impatient and single-minded managers will often overlook the wealth of talent that exists in the young and old. I see many spoiled and indifferent teenagers. Take the case of the janitor who, in the absence of affordable childcare, brings her teenage son to the job. He sits and plays games on his $699 phone bought and paid for by his mother's earnings— never lifting a finger to assist her in the job. Another janitor is accompanied by his son and together they work to complete the cleaning in less than half the time it takes for each to do it alone. The son is also a teen who buys everything he owns with the money he earns. These are both real-world examples from my own business. Children need to experience the value of hard work. While society has made many wonderful advances to guarantee the well-being of children, very few academic situations prepare young people for the world that lies beyond school. Every state permits minors to work with the proper work permit and for a limited number of hours.

Young minds develop habits and a household that encourages children to earn their keep will build the character needed to win as adults. Parents who teach their children the wonder of work will raise adults who lose all respect for anyone who refuses to work. To find highly motivated people for your team, speak with the hardest working individuals in your community. While being a high achiever is no guarantee that a person will have equally ambitious spawn, it raises the probability into more certain territory.

Seniors excel in so many areas. While any worker can live an unhappy life and seniors are no exception, someone who has retired with a pension and social security benefits can still work without fear of losing benefits as long as income limits aren't exceeded. Older employees who possess a positive attitude and hunger to learn new skills should be at the top of your applicant lists. Mature workers have a strong commitment to quality, are punctual, and exhibit a strong work ethic. While it is impossible to generalize, older workers typically have strong people and customer service skills, lower absenteeism, broad work experience, and high job loyalty. Older employees also tend to have a "whatever it takes" attitude and will usually stick around past quitting time until essential tasks are done and dusted.

**tip**

College students can gain valuable experience working in an industry that mirrors their major and in some cases can intern at no cost to the company in exchange for college credit. Many cities fund work experience programs and subsidize the salaries of high school and college students in order to help them gain hands-on experience.

Casting a wider net can also identify excellent workers. Even a modest relocation allowance to move an out-of-towner could be sufficient to entice a job seeker. Look to communities with high unemployment within your state or to faraway places that feel similar to your community. Out-of-state employee prospects who have never lived in your state may struggle with acculturation—many become homesick and return to what's familiar. How different a new place feels is a strong determinant in missing home, not distance. Burbank feels a lot like the town I grew up in—Falls Church, which explains why I have felt comfortable living and working here (I started out my California odyssey in the heart of Los Angeles which feels nothing like Burbank). Environmental differences, urban density, as well as differences in dress, customs, humor, and food will all affect how well someone blends into your working space.

And interviews should not feel like an interrogation. Any unemployed person who comes to an interview with hat-in-hand looking for a job may have had difficulty finding work and will naturally feel nervous. A manager who wants the best employees to join the team must first welcome all the best candidates. An excellent worker may simply have poor interviewing skills. There are also wonderful workers who can be found hidden within an emotional chrysalis. Children with difficult childhoods grow up to become socially challenged adults. A person who has lost faith in themselves will feel hopeless about their ability in a job. With each unsuccessful interview, this individual will sink further down the rabbit hole and their interviews will become less and less motivated. On the other side of this coin are high-demand applicants with several offers from other larger and better-known companies. A cold, business-like interview is a sure way to scare off even the most desperate job seeker. An interview must leave every interviewee feeling like you want them to be a part of your organization and not simply another business transaction. People must feel warmly welcomed at every touchpoint. If it's hard for you to smile, you'll force yourself to do so at every moment in your waking day—to do so will almost certainly immediately and dramatically improve your chances of hiring the best workers and keeping them.

Managers must apply common sense and weave in a bit of vision when screening for a job. Every seasoned employer has been misled by an elegant, beautifully written resume or held high hopes for the applicant who is expertly adept at interviewing but a lazy worker. When interviewing job seekers, have an open mind, an open heart, and engage in careful listening

## Retaining Valuable Team Members

As I write these words, American unemployment is at a record low of 3.6 percent as reported by the Bureau of Labor Statistics. I have engaged in many spirited discussions with colleagues and friends related to hiring—these fine individuals scratch their heads in wonder, curious how I have employees who have worked for me for as many as a dozen years who remain very happy in their jobs. There is no mystery to the cause of this phenomenon—I work hard to understand the individual needs of each employee within my company. I am a daily student of what moves and motivates these dedicated workers. One weekend, I assisted one of my employees with moving an RV she purchased. I ordered a 2-inch tow ball and attached it to a rental pickup truck and easily put her new purchase right where she wanted it. I found the project very easy and fun—something she had been struggling with that was causing her substantial stress. Another employee in my business was deeply troubled by an issue that had been haunting her husband for weeks. He is an independent motor freight truck driver, and one of his customers filed for bankruptcy. The money this financially troubled firm owed him was substantial, and he feared he would never be paid. Tears of despair became tears of joy when I identified an attorney willing to file all the required court paperwork on a contingent fee basis—with his legal fees to be paid only if he recovered the money, and he did.

In the next chapter, I'll share marketing tips to help you broadcast your message to the world.

# Getting the
# Word Out

Two of the most common errors that newbies in business make in the area of business promotion are making the incorrect assumption that customers will magically find them and also failing to commit sufficient time and/or money to the promotion of the new business. A third and often fatal error for going concerns is the paltry or nonexistent budget that is carved out for promotion. Well-established wholesalers know all too well that customer attrition and changing customer tastes mandates the hunt for and acquisition of new business opportunities. Take the example of public company W.W. Grainger, Inc., a broad line, business-to-business distributor of maintenance, repair, and operating (MRO) products. W.W. Grainger, Inc. has been around since 1928, and according to the SEC, the firm traded more than $11 billion in goods in the calendar year 2018. W.W. Grainger, Inc. spent $241 million on advertising in the same period. Their advertising budget is a hair over 2 percent of their sales, net of returns. I would imagine that a startup could easily spend many times that figure on initial promotion without being foolish or reckless. In time, sales will grow, driving down the advertising expense as a percentage of total business. Even the greatest promotion in the world will generate zero results when directed to the incorrect audience.

In this chapter, I'll share my proven tips for developing the marketing skills that will help you earn more customers, we'll look at different ideas for conventional advertising, and I'll explain how to get into social selling. You'll even learn how to score free, unlimited marketing opportunities with public relations and promotions.

## Advertising

While it is always possible to be clever and creative, low prices and a sterling reputation will sell far more pallets of goods than clever and out-of-the-box ads. Direct-selling and word-of-mouth remain powerful allies to the wholesaler. I contend that specializing in awesome customer service and offering great value will always rapidly expand a business to the fullest potential. Take an entirely unrelated industry—restaurants. For nearly 30 years, a local diner in my neighborhood languished. It looked run-down and sad, but I tried the place out anyway. I asked if cards were accepted, and they were not. "What restaurant doesn't accept cards?" I asked myself. The diner eventually closed down, and a new restaurant opened under a new name offering virtually the same menu. Within one year, there were lines out the door virtually every day. I sampled the food, and it's wonderful—served by eager people with great alacrity. The new owner recognized that the only competitive advantage they required wasn't fancy ads—they don't advertise at all. The new owner focused on being amazing at what he does. One of the advantages of word-of-mouth is that it works very fast and costs nothing.

Experienced wholesalers don't engage in broad-audience advertising. The shotgun approach to promotion is guaranteed to gobble up money and offer little or nothing in return. The cleverest ad copy and stunning visuals will fail to engage an audience unless it's the correct audience. Time-tested methods for connecting with retailers include running ads with trade magazines and working with industry-specific trade development organizations, networking and exhibiting at industry trade shows, and through direct sales (e.g., calling, emailing, and mailing to prospects).

According to the Bureau of Labor Statistics, the 2018 median pay for advertising, promotions, and marketing managers was $132,620 per year. Not every startup can afford such a healthy salary, and outsourcing is only as good as the provider. In a small work environment, advertising, promotions, and marketing manager roles are handled by the same person—and as a company grows larger, the needs for each area become sufficiently demanding that separate workers are needed. Sensitive products such as alcohol, tobacco, and firearms may be legal to sell for qualified vendors but are not always legal to advertise, and the person managing the promotion of sensitive goods must also possess the requisite knowledge for their legal sale. Ignorance in this area is never bliss—rather it becomes an expensive legal lesson. While informed adults are the best judges of their own interests, courts have gradually increased free-speech protections for commercial speech in their decisions, but it is always best to solicit a written opinion on advertising controversial products such as alcohol. The temperance movement has varying influence depending on where you live.

Many wholesalers choose not to advertise at all and propel their companies forward with word-of-mouth referrals and through prospecting. Technology's invasion into advertising has increased the noise of advertising by orders of magnitude from what it was just a decade ago. The innovation and rapid change of the internet have spawned disruptive technologies that reach audiences with less friction and at a lower cost. Free video platforms are being leveraged by firms to demonstrate products, engaging and delighting customers.

While there is no customary ad budget nor a one-size-fits-all approach to business promotion, a wholesaler should set aside a percentage of their bottom line each month and earmark this slice of the profit pie for various forms of promotion. The Coca-Cola Company is the world's largest nonalcoholic beverage wholesaler and according to their 2018 annual report they incurred more than $4 billion in advertising expenses against nearly $32 billion in sales—13 percent of their revenue is spent on getting the word out. Similar behaviors are observed with wildly successful companies.

Most of the small wholesalers I've talked with find keeping a robust website updated challenging and therefore turn to content management systems such as WordPress or third-party ecommerce solutions such as shopping carts that allow customers to place wholesale orders in a self-service environment using established payment gateway systems. Due to the fiercely competitive nature of these categories of solutions, providers of digital advertising cross-promote with the vendors of content management and ecommerce solutions.

Door knocking, direct mail, and traditional advertising methods remain staples in the sales toolkit, however, there are thousands of discouraged and hungry salespeople pounding the pavement on a daily basis—many who will give up the profession entirely in due time. When someone can clearly and convincingly demonstrate how their product can solve a retailer's problems, they will make a sale. Customers prefer the feeling of making a purchase rather than the uncomfortable reaction to being sold. A businessperson who merely hopes to help himself but has little interest in how he can help his customers will always struggle in retaining buyers.

While the variety of social platforms is endlessly evolving, I have found very little by way of success in promoting a wholesale business in this way. Retailers are a different breed than the retail customers they serve—there is the right time to connect with them and most are busy tending to their business and won't stop to pay attention to most forms of digital advertising. A retail buyer who commits substantial time and money to attend a trade show is far more engaged in the ritual of meeting potential new wholesalers than he or she would otherwise be in the thick of daily business life.

Salespeople are quick to give costly product samples without a clear strategy for vetting the prospect or a plan for landing a sale. Another challenge in the promotion of businesses is the lack of diligent follow-up. Unfulfilled promises account for more damage to a business than almost any other challenge a company faces—and it is an ailment with a free and simple cure. Top salespeople in an organization are rarely the best-educated or most tech-savvy but they know how to stay on top of their prospecting and their promises are fulfilled. The most successful tradespeople are humble and make many friends in the pursuit of their business. Highly effective people treat the work of selling as a marathon, not a sprint. When lesser committed individuals have moved on to try other things, the master of promotion is consistent and a competent shepherd of their company. I have found a simple online calendar serves as one of the best ways to stay on top of reminders—and in this technique, I have managed to follow through on important callbacks with unparalleled precision. Case in point is the interviews in this very book. I was successful in scoring Q&A sessions with leaders of billion-dollar companies by contacting the appropriate people to schedule the interviews and articulating the clear mutual benefit to these iconic firms—they would receive excellent exposure for their company and the readers would benefit from their sage advice.

Free online business directories and review sites are frequently overlooked. How many times have you checked the online reputation of a business before buying their product or using their service? Claim your business page on every online directory and keep these profiles up-to-date—accurate and well-presented details about your business will set you apart. Busy business owners tend to allow these profiles to decay with time and their business starts to look irrelevant and cobbled together.

If you've never been in business before, you may very well become alarmed or discouraged by the onslaught of solicitors knocking on your door, calling your phone, and filling up your inbox. Most business communication today is solicitation from others. It amuses me how angry managers and workers become in the act of being solicited—yet they become equally angry when others act similarly. Despising the conduct of other people who are seeking business opportunities will put a frown on your face that will be seen by the prospects you yourself elect to pursue. Enthusiasm engages everyone around us. A smart wholesaler is always open to being sold and in this openness will find many future business opportunities—sometimes in unlikely places. Why not ask these very same salespeople what's been working for them and the sales techniques that are landing the most business opportunities? An animated greeting to every salesperson who approaches you not only perpetuates your good name, but also places you squarely in the minds of these individuals who will contact you in the event their company closes its doors and they are looking for employment. And if these friends in business should remain employed long into the future, you can still pick up both customer and employee referrals from those who appreciate how you've treated them. Your example of genuine kindness will spread through your entire organization—your employees will have no choice but to want to be helpful and courteous to each other and to your customers.

Ad salespeople will reach out to you year-round and will sell you something exciting and intangible—hope. The hope that advertising with them will yield a mountain of leads for your business. They'll show you colorful charts in their company's media kit that will all but assure you wonderful results when placing ads with their establishment. Most of these ads will reduce your bank balance and return very little. Occasionally you'll strike gold but just as panning for real gold rarely returns a nugget of gold—or even a fleck, experimenting with advertising is a costly and unreliable customer acquisition tool. Foolish is a long-term contract for multiple ads with no proof of concept in-hand demonstrating the effectiveness of the advertising channel. Moonshots are not smart for little companies—money is far too precious at the start.

Programmatic advertising can also land an advertiser in undesired places—alongside offensive or controversial content. Experienced marketers are moving away from the use of agencies and putting their own hands on their digital marketing initiatives to better control spend and placement—monitoring results in real-time. Performance and brand advertising are quite different in their goals. Performance ads lead to direct engagement in the form of clicks and actions—they cost money when the action is taken. Brand advertising involves videos, text, images, and interactive ads that elevate a company's brand awareness. Customers are increasingly relying on social networks for product recommendations and making purchases. While there are a lot of goofball products and ideas prevalent on these platforms, trusted brands are being promoted in the space. Digital advertising platforms face intense competition and the "in" players change rapidly. With this warning in mind, a business owner must be prepared to change advertising methodologies rapidly to stay in lockstep with market forces and advertising trends within their industry.

The ability to generate cash flows from business activity is a core financial strength in business and startups will need ample time to ramp up sales (i.e., plenty of working capital) so that buying power is increased. A low price on quality merchandise is its best own salesperson and the strongest advertisement an operator can deploy, and this can only be achieved in economies of scale.

Potential ways of spreading the word and scoring more business are listed below, ranked in descending order from what I feel are strongest to those that are weakest for a wholesaler:

- ▶ Word-of-mouth
- ▶ Low prices (turning stock more frequently)
- ▶ Social selling
- ▶ Video product reviews on sites such as YouTube, Instagram, Snapchat, etc.
- ▶ A high reputation for honesty and fair dealing
- ▶ Prospecting (by phone, email, and direct mail)
- ▶ Hiring employees from your competition—they know who the customers are!
- ▶ Press releases
- ▶ Signage
- ▶ Trade shows
- ▶ Public speaking at industry-specific events
- ▶ Selling goods using online marketplaces such as Amazon and eBay
- ▶ Affiliating with trade associations
- ▶ Getting on friendly terms with competitors and welcoming them to your place of business so they will do the same—study, adapt, and improve based on the intel you acquire
- ▶ Sponsoring product demonstrations inside the very stores being supplied
- ▶ A website
- ▶ Blogging
- ▶ Trade magazines

▶ Digital advertising

▶ Traditional advertising (e.g., radio, television, newspapers, billboards, etc.)

"Wholesale to the public" operations can benefit from the deployment of methods at the bottom of my list as digital and traditional advertising is best suited for retail customers, not the business-to-business buyer. A closed mouth is rarely fed, so a loud cry about town to spread the good word of your business will go far—merchants who make more noise will receive more business.

And never knock your competition—every bad word stated about those selling against you will be a boost to their business. Gripe and gossip exude the stench of bitter resentment and desperation. Merchants that work together can find the means for collaboration and co-op their efforts for greater purchasing power and promotion of unity of action among regional wholesalers. Unified wholesalers' voices are a powerful antidote against unfair regulations and rising taxes. A keiretsu can leverage efforts for advertising and promotion and collectively seek better terms on business resources such as trade financing. The size and influence of a group of merchants can grow to the level that allows significant control over an industry.

## Public Relations and Promotions

Those who enter into a new business venture have significant enthusiasm and apply it to every aspect of their new baby. The owner of a startup will be watching dollars with hawk eyes and almost without exception, the expense new owners perceive to be nonessential is advertising. This is so contrary to the reality of nearly every business situation—a fact proven by the substantial ad budgets carved out by well-funded startups where venture capitalists know the drill. Corporations doing tens of billions of dollars in sales also spend billions in business promotion. Two of the least used methods of free advertising are public relations and promotions. While there is a tangible cost to staff time and an owner should always consider their time as quite valuable—these two areas of business advertising are generally without a hard cost when the owner handles them personally.

While placing ads comes with a fee, preparing and sending press releases can announce your new company, share milestones, and disseminate newsy events—without cost. News releases are accepted by regional and national television and radio networks, newspapers, magazines, blogs, and nontraditional news sources—the latter being groups within social networks and hosted by websites. Organizations accepting press releases that are focused on an industry will have the highest impact. Trade magazines are gradually migrating to digital-only distribution which allows publishers to sell advertising within the alerts that

are emailed to willing subscribers. Another mistake that startups make—and I'll surely take heat from publicists for this comment—is the hiring of outside publicity firms. Only the most generously financed businesses should hire third-party companies to represent them to the media. Striking gold in the search for exceptional professionals is rare and challenging—I'm sure to take heat here, too. Far better results come from petite companies when they reach out directly—too many times information becomes lost in translation when engaging in occasional public relations activities with a vendor who is merely an interloper with your business. And, I see no reason to outline how to write a press release within this book because I endeavor to inspire and mentor entrepreneurs—not to formalize something that is likely to change over time. You can readily examine corporate websites and read their self-published news stories to curate ideas for how to present your own announcements to journalists and their editors. Operators of busy companies become too comfortable in their work routines and in coping with daily busywork suffer amnesia—forgetting how they became so busy in the first place. For as long as economics have been studied and taught, experts have proven that business prosperity will forever ebb and flow, which demands that even the most hectic manager with both hands completely full must ensure that they stay on top of building the good name of their company within their industry and trading community. There is no panacea for this—it requires hands-on hard work.

How do you secure free publicity? What you're announcing must be newsworthy. While the local chamber will gladly perform a ribbon-cutting and post beautiful photos of the moment in their newsletter, this isn't truly free—you'll have to pay for a membership—and a chamber membership has its privileges. A story idea must be developed and be truly unique for a journalist to take notice. As with every business skill, writing press releases takes practice. What is unique about the business? How does the company help the community? Is the news relevant and timely? Is the story connected to a holiday or event?

Self-prepared email lists are a good way to promote but should only ever be sent to organizations that welcome them. It is a serious faux pas to spam anyone—and most relevant, legitimate media outlets will provide an email address that is set aside for receiving press releases. Building an internal database is time-consuming and expensive—but very effective at building close ties with the press. Advances in newswire services have opened up the opportunity to use low-cost press release distribution services—beneficial for a shotgun distribution approach but not so useful for handcrafted campaigns.

Promotions are tremendously popular and allow for solidifying customer relationships. Manufacturers and wholesalers alike fund in-store product demonstrations and staff in-store sample stations to introduce new products and elevate existing lines—something that

(surprisingly) very few retailers have the gumption or vision to do themselves. Distributors of regional wines, cheeses, locally roasted coffee, baked goods, and foods and beverages all seek to habituate shoppers to their products—and if what they're sampling is very, very good, consumers will come back again and again to buy their favorites. A wholesale business is most effective when the lion share of the profits are earned from consumable goods.

Buyers also appreciate hosted customer appreciation events—making them feel uniquely special. It's no surprise that some even come to expect these perks. I assert that the cocktail party is alive and well—and one of the least expensive ways to impress customers is to book a reservation for a large group at a swanky local restaurant. Banquet halls and hotel ballrooms are far too expensive and require strangely complex contracts. For some reason the local high-end restaurant that serves both food and alcohol has at least one day of the week they are desperate to fill with eager customers. An open bar with house wine, draft beer, soft drinks plus some popular hors d'oeuvres is far more affordable than catering at a business location or making a reservation for a private room. There's generally no need to make it a private party—the regulars will rarely interfere with the festivities and if the group is large enough, the waitstaff will be exceptionally attentive and make certain everyone has a great time. I am perpetually confused by miserly business owners who have no issue buying ads in useless publications but who scoff at hosting fancy affairs and paying for a little food and beverage for their most important customers. When I opened my doors in 1988, food processors and AM/FM clock radios were all the rage. Twenty-inch television sets with square picture tubes were equally in vogue. Most laugh when I tell this story because every television set today is perfectly square, but in 1988, that was not a truism. I can honestly say that not only did every good customer receive all three of these gifts, not one of them was attracted to another supplier. For the crème de la crème customers, every birthday would be celebrated with a bottle of Dom Pérignon—accompanied by a birthday balloon and handwritten birthday card. Today, everyone is either on a keto diet, exercising temperance, or is adhering to a healthy regimen. Promotions are more complicated today than they were in the past. I track individual passions and hobbies using Salesforce CRM—a program that allows me to easily note the interests of my customers seamlessly and without a piece of paper.

It would be the notion of a fool to imagine they could sell wholesale goods to the largest big-box retailers in America when operating a very small business. The ideal customer profile should be articulated to every member of your team in writing so that each person within the company can keep their eye on the prospects that are likely to convert to customers. Any prospect that does not fit the company's ideal customer profile must be ruthlessly removed from the mailing list to prevent time and resources being applied against these useless leads.

For direct-mail promotions, the compiling of prospect lists must not occur in a vacuum—if you've always had success with local, independent gift shops then your promotions should be directed to more independent gift shops. A common error with businesspeople is imagining that they must hire professionals to develop their promotional materials. If the money is available, sure, why not? But more often than not, the best marketing efforts are those that actually occur with frequency which forces economy-minded owners to use pre-existing templates to hold costs down. Have you ever wondered why the most popular word processing programs have vast libraries of free marketing templates? No one is going to know that your postcard mailing was generated from a template that many other companies also used. The content is far more important than fancy high-end graphics. Mailings do not have to be large to be effective. A postcard is magical for all companies that use it—the recipient can't help but read it—unlike envelopes which are often simply tossed unopened. Between the big mailing campaigns, keep a small stack of marketing postcards within everyone's reach to give to someone or quickly hand-address and mail out to potential future customers. And pay close attention to the employees who distribute the most cards so that praise can be given.

And speaking of cards, the cost of printing business cards has plummeted to an all-time low. A thousand full-color business cards can be had for less than the cost of six lattes. Another big mistake small businesses make is not giving employees business cards. If you do not trust the janitor to represent your company outside the office, why did you hire them in the first place? A business card tells an employee that you trust them implicitly. It is a symbol of agency. This person is entitled to represent your company—and they will do so with integrity and honor knowing you cared enough about their role at the company to have cards with their name printed on them. Everyone within a company has the potential to bring in new business or represent the company in a good way. If the action of printing business cards for everyone, even part-timers, does nothing more for the individual worker than to elevate positive feelings between them and you, it is money easily spent. Consider this very simple example of how cheap a business card really is—a firm with 100 employees spends $2,000 to print 1,000 business cards for each employee ($20 x 100). It will take someone a very long time to hand out 1,000 business cards, so the supply of cards for each worker will last for a very long time in most circumstances. Mind you, some will never carry or hand out a single card—allowing the box of these cards to collect dust in a closet or cabinet at home. And the remainder of the workers, feeling proudly trusted and empowered, will hand out their business cards at every opportunity. Could you buy

100,000 impressions anywhere for as cheaply as $2,000? You will be sick to your stomach when you see how much each click costs for the top keywords searched on pay-per-pick advertising programs—and no digital ad will provide a human being to answer questions and share good stories about your brand in the way a loyal employee would. Chances are that this minor investment will siren in many new customers—but only one is required to return the cost many times over.

I'll address another highly controversial subject—coupons. I'll never say never but I am generally opposed to them. I am not addressing manufacturers' coupons that have nothing to do with the transactions that take place between a wholesaler and their customers. I am speaking of the reckless practice of distributing discount coupons and offering retailers aggressive discounts for using purchase codes on the wholesaler's website. A coupon is very different than a premium—the latter being a token of appreciation for good business. A coupon erodes so many aspects of a business and is in reality not a discount, but a means to shift the cost of goods from one transaction to another, or from one customer to another. The profit that is lost from the use of a discount must always be made up somewhere else and only the novice retailer lacks a clear understanding of this fact. Too often businesses look to discounts as their whole promotions plan, but by the time you consider the effort in producing and managing the campaign plus the discount itself, the entire affair becomes quite expensive. And you are reminding buyers that your prices weren't good to begin with—with the most dangerous byproduct of all being the bitter resentment caused when a loyal customer discovers that someone else received a better deal than they did. Everyday low prices—the lowest possible prices—is an extremely compelling case for a customer to buy now and long into the future.

I try not to brag too much to my competitors or explain my secrets for fear that they will rapidly duplicate my successes and seduce my customers—customer loyalty is hard to come by and it is very challenging to attract consistent buyers in a sea of options.

## Hanging Out Your Shingle

Another endless marketing debate in wholesale circles is the topic of signage. For warehouses in industrial parks and remote facilities, it's hard to say if expensive signs really matter. I once spent $50,000 on a really big sign. That is an alarmingly big number but it was a really massive sign—and I regret the decision. A fancy sign can be counterproductive—sending a message that your prices are high. Today, so much business is conducted without ever meeting the other person that it is really hard to justify a sign that costs five figures. When customers visit a business location, it must be well-organized and clean—including the sign! Can you imagine how expensive it is to clean a high-up sign on a big, huge pole? No sign salesperson will break the bad news to a prospective sign buyer—maintenance for a tall or complex sign will be frequent and expensive. Ever see a sign covered in long, white streaks? That's from birds perching and doing their business—and the tops of clean signs are covered in rows of short but nearly invisible metal or plastic bird-deterrent spikes. I contend that every business needs to be well-organized and clean regardless, but a simple sign is just as good as a fancy one. Businesses that have a healthy amount of traffic should have a road sign as well as good-sized signage at the building. Sign salespeople will push hard for fancy signage, but maintenance is always a concern—and once the sales commission has been earned, you very well may never see that salesperson again. A well-lit and simple sign that's cheap to maintain is the best option. If an expensive service call and a bucket truck are needed to replace a light bulb then the sign is a luxury you had best avoid. I am perpetually confused at the number of businesses that do not invest in just a simple numbered address sign. Have you ever struggled to find a business because the address wasn't on a street sign or printed on the building? Twice a year I pay a woman to paint the street address on the curb by first applying a white background and then using a stencil to paint the numbers in black. This costs me $40 (2x$20) annually. Her price has never risen—in fact, she charges the same today as she has for ten years. The work she does is wonderful. Delivery drivers are always in such a hurry and speed along making their rounds. I have received nothing but compliments on how easy my business address is to find. While many freight companies and customers look for the company name on a sign and verify the name of the business, the first thing that virtually everyone does is check the street address and having the number painted vividly on the curb provides instant guidance for visitors.

And while many business owners wait until they can afford their dream sign, the signage they hope for never materializes—either falling down in priority or becoming a more distant reality as the fact of the high cost of internally lit signs hits the owner squarely between the eyes. Don't have enough money to buy your dream sign? It's important to note that expensive signs will continue to cost money every year with repairs and maintenance. And if the sign company isn't competent, your sign will be made with materials that fade rapidly in the sun. Just drive along and look at the south-facing businesses—are their signs faded and old-looking? I'll bet that many are. What starts out as beautiful, eventually fades and looks weathered—peeling and buckling from the ravages of the sun. Advances in digital printing allow sign companies to print directly onto the surface of all commonly used outdoor-rated sign materials such as non-ferrous smooth metal, magnetic sheet, rigid vinyl, expanded PVC, corrugated plastic, and other substrates. An absolutely beautiful sign can be printed in a shop and installed with very little fuss. The printer's ink formulation must be designed for outdoor use to protect your printed sign from damage caused by the sun's UV light and elemental exposure. Clear matte-finish UV coatings are available to further protect outdoor signs and it is prudent to ask the vendor for a written warranty against fading.

Avoid custom shapes and stick to common square and rectangular sizes. Standard sign sizes work best for a couple of reasons—it makes it simple to print, as well as reprint when the sign exhibits age, and there are stock sign holders that can be self-installed for significant savings over hiring a sign installer. Stock metal u-channel is easily cut to the correct size and attached to the outside of a building. U-channels come with one side longer than the other so that it can be easily drilled and screwed into a wall and a sign slid into parallel left and right channels—plus one on the bottom to prevent the sign from falling down. All outdoor installations must be completed with rustproof materials. Corroded screws will bleed onto a sign as time marches on. Today's modern building materials are clearly marked on their package to indicate if they are rated for outdoor use and the additional cost of stainless steel or non-rusting metals should be spent without a moment of hesitation.

As tempting as it is to get fancy, the most effective signs are simple and easy-to-read from a distance. The font used for a company logo should be selected with readability in mind—a bold sans serif font is the most impactful option. A company sign should never use script or skinny fonts. The person reading your sign will be driving along at a high rate of speed.

A good-sized sign supports recognition for your brand—and will-call areas are another opportunity for signage and promotion. Clever wholesalers doll up their will-call waiting areas with merchandise displays—creating a product showcase. And be sure to clearly mark the warehouse office entrance so that visitors can easily and quickly find you when they come calling.

## Getting Social with Customers Online

According to eMarketer, adults averaged 1 hour and 14 minutes of daily social media consumption in 2018. The figure has reached a plateau and there is a lot of content out there—which means a ton of clutter for users to wade through. I'm skeptical just how meaningful social media can be to the average petite wholesaler who struggles just to get home before bedtime. Social media marketing requires vision, consistency, and a substantial commitment of time in order for it to be meaningful. Many businesses are leaning on social media profiles as an alternative to paying for expensive websites. That's smart when you're getting started.

Simply registering a business on a social media platform will offer little by way of publicity. Posting content—even great content—won't guarantee an audience either. Some platforms, such as LinkedIn, offer online meeting places for professionals in the same industry and with similar interests to build meaningful connections. LinkedIn and most sites refer to these meeting places as *groups*. Spamming on social media is a sure way to turn people off, while the most benefit from social media platforms will come from interactions with the correct audiences at the correct times. People will look at you funny if you start indiscriminately handing out business cards at the movie theater or at a restaurant. No one will think you're odd if you start shaking hands and passing out cards at a business mixer hosted by the local chamber. Social media works the same way—there is a correct time and place to promote your business. Study what other brands are doing to gain greater understanding.

When someone becomes a friend or follower of your company's social media profile, they'll be directly connected with you and see your posting activity.

Social media is about building real relationships. Far too many famous people have been called out in the news for buying fake social media followers and by all accounts, paying for bogus social media fandom is considered fraud. Using social media as a means to notify existing customers about business opportunities is very smart. Social selling is the "in" way to do business and loyal customers who follow a brand online enjoy interesting content and product information. Post photos and videos of new arrivals, share employee stories, talk about nonprofit giving and causes, and allow customers who engage with you on social media an opportunity to humanize what you're doing. Any social media service that allows free direct messaging on a user-to-user basis may pose challenges for door-knocking—most people are online to have a good time, not to be solicited privately. LinkedIn permits member-to-member contact but charges for it—making it harder to do but also more effective. Because so many businesspeople use LinkedIn, the opportunity to make important and meaningful connections is a strong one—and LinkedIn is perceived as a tool for business. Social media enables people to discover, connect, share, and communicate with each other on both computers and mobile devices. Because substantially all the revenue generated by social media sites comes from ads, it's a cluttered space with lots of noise—and the world of social media changes in an instant. No offense is meant to the makers of these innovative solutions, but in my humble opinion, it's harder every day to make sense of how a wholesale company can use social media as a sales tool—seems like a lot of snake oil being hocked on most platforms. I'm partial to LinkedIn but as with every technology, the players shuffle about in their importance over time and an astute

## ▶ Staying in the Good Graces of the Government

Some industries, such as alcohol and tobacco, are subject to marketing and advertising rules and regulations. These restrictions can include laws, statutes, and ordinances designed to protect consumers. Anti-bribery and anti-competition regulations can also bubble up—and privacy/cybersecurity laws may affect the cost of doing business. Nuances for digital marketing include compliance with commercial email rules under the federal CAN-SPAM Act, etc. Failure to comply with laws, known or unknown, could result in civil or criminal action as well as subject the company and its owners to monetary or nonmonetary penalties and/or the loss of permission to participate in government contracting (as well as harm the good reputation of the business). Laws change periodically and managers must be vigilant in the review of changes when they occur. Not only must employees comply, but a business owner needs to ensure the cooperation of contractors and other third-parties in the observation of laws, standards, and regulations.

business owner will engage in business scuttlebutt before sinking the better part of their marketing efforts into any particular site.

When registering on social media sites, it's best to use the same ID on all of them. For instance, I am @borntodeal on the sites I use. Protecting this ID means quickly grabbing these registrations even if you're not active on a particular platform. That said, it is best to focus on building a strong following on a platform before expanding to others—spreading yourself too thin means ineffective and inconsistent results.

# It All Comes Down to Customer Service

A company must be heads down consistently working on the customer experience. The secret to success is no secret at all—every business will live or die based on the customer service offered, and your overall marketing success rides on your reputation when it comes to customers.

It is interesting to note that a simple principle in business that sells more products than virtually any other technique—is to allow the customer to do the majority of the talking and to allow the buyer to feel that the idea of a sale was theirs all along. No amount of customer service will cure an ailing back-office. Customers demand great prices and superior availability. The customer relationship will decay if orders are not filled with extreme and accurate efficiency. There has been an alarming trend toward offshore outsourcing of customer service talent. A call center on the other side of the world cannot walk over to a shelf and explain the texture of a fabric on a bolt. A foreign worker is not culturally in tune with your local buyer. More and more companies that shipped customer support offshore are now bringing precious customer interactions back home—as close to their operations as possible. According to Amazon's year 2000 shareholder letter, the retail behemoth spent an average of $134 per customer acquisition. Would it surprise you to know that Amazon is now a major wholesaler? Bringing new business in the door is expensive and keeping that same customer from heading out the door requires service delivered with extreme alacrity.

In the next and last chapter, we'll glean some extraordinary wisdom from the experts to help bring you to the level of MVP.

# Interviews with the Experts

N ow that we have explored the world of wholesale, it's time to meet some thought leaders in the industry. In this chapter, you'll meet some wholesale-adjacent professionals who have plenty of advice to share about everything from raising capital and choosing the right computer system to running the day-to-day wholesale business.

# Interview with Marco Terry
## *Managing Director of Commercial Capital LLC*

I had the good fortune to connect with a titan within the small and medium-sized business (SMB) trade finance industry, Marco Terry. I had a prior awareness of what he does because I utilized a factoring company with beautiful results when I started my business. His perspective and insights are priceless to anyone starting a wholesale distribution company and are timeless mentorship for entrepreneurs opening their first business in any industry. Here's what he shared:

Q: *What type of business is Commercial Capital LLC?*

A: We are a factoring and purchase order financing company.

Q: *What year did you start Commercial Capital LLC?*

A: The company had a soft start in 2002. I launched a skeleton version of the company as a proof of concept. The idea was to see if this concept would work for me before investing a large amount of capital. I quit my job and worked in the company full-time in mid-2004.

Q: *What did you do before you started Commercial Capital LLC?*

A: Before launching Commercial Capital LLC, I worked in technology. I started my career as an applications engineer for a company that sold relational database systems to government contractors. After four years, I transitioned to a product management role for a telecommunications vendor. In total, I worked for eight years in technology before launching the company.

Q: *Why did you start Commercial Capital LLC?*

A: I have always wanted to be an entrepreneur. This has been clear to me since I was a kid. However, before going into business, I went to college. I was fortunate enough to have the option. I believe having a college degree is a nice safety net. If a business venture fails, you can always get a job.

After college, I worked in the technology field for eight years. I liked the field, and it was compatible with my interests. Actually, I always thought that I would start a technology business. I moved to another field only because I wasn't able to come up with an idea that I thought was worthwhile pursuing.

One day, I bought a copy of *Entrepreneur Magazine's Franchise 500®* rankings at a local grocery store. I went through the magazine systematically. First, I looked for business categories that interested me and crossed out those that didn't.

Then, within each category of interest, I reviewed each business individually. If a business interested me, I would learn more about it. I would schedule a call or, in some cases, schedule a visit. I had a very methodical and disciplined approach.

During my search, I saw that a company sold factoring franchises. I was vaguely familiar with factoring from a college accounting class, so I decided to investigate it. The more I learned about factoring, the more it interested me. Eventually, I was sold on the concept.

Ultimately, I did not buy that franchise. Instead, I learned the factoring business myself by calling competitors (they are all friendly), reading books, and talking to folks in the industry.

By the way, this methodical approach can help you as well. For example, you can use the same process to figure out what type of distribution company you want to start. It can help you zero in on the types of products you want to work with, the markets, and so on.

*Q: What is the coolest thing Commercial Capital LLC has accomplished?*

A: We have provided funding to over 700 businesses throughout our history. We have been a part of helping these entrepreneurs pay suppliers and employees, and grow their businesses. That is the absolute coolest thing we have done. This is also what gives us the most pride.

*Q: Why or why not should the founder of a startup borrow money from family and friends?*

A: I am often asked this question. Getting funding from friends and family is not a binary "always or never" situation. I think it is an appropriate source of funding in some instances. Therefore, I prefer the question, "When is it appropriate to borrow from friends and family?"

I think it may be appropriate to borrow from friends and family if six conditions are met. You will find, however, that meeting all these conditions is very difficult. Your investor friends and family must:

1. Have knowledge of your industry or business. I am a firm believer that one should invest only in businesses and concepts they understand and trust. That is the only way one can determine if the investment is a good fit for them. If your potential friend or family investor does not understand your business, it's best to try to get funding elsewhere.

2. Understand what they are getting into. Most people who start or invest in a business do not understand what they are getting into. They often overestimate their chances of winning and underestimate their chances of losing. This is a dangerous

combination that I have seen firsthand with close family members who lost substantial amounts of money.

3. Be comfortable losing the money without risking their relationship with you. First and foremost, your relationship with them should be more important than any money that they can contribute. Therefore, you have to protect the relationship at all costs. Unfortunately, this is one of the hardest conditions to evaluate. You can ask your friend/relative if they are comfortable losing money. However, you will have to take whatever they say with a grain of salt. People can't always anticipate how they will react to losing money (hint: most react badly). This means that you will always risk your relationship souring if the business fails.

4. Be willing to be as involved (or not involved) as you need them to be. Make it clear to them if you expect them to be involved (or not involved) in the business. This can always be a source of tension, especially if expectations are not met. Just keep in mind that so-called "silent" investors can become very "vocal" if the investment does not work out as expected.

5. Have funds to contribute. Ask for funds only from individuals who have extra money to contribute. If the individual cannot invest in your company and keep their current lifestyle and retirement expectations, don't ask.

6. Be excited about the investment opportunity. Lastly, it is important that your friend (or family member) is excited about the opportunity to invest in your business. If they are not excited about it, then I suggest you don't take the money. Why? Because if they are not excited about the potential gains, they are not making an investment. They are doing you a favor. This can create complications if the investment does not work out.

As a matter of choice, I never took money from friends and family. Instead, I got money the old-fashioned way—by saving and living frugally for over a decade. During the first eight years of my professional life, I saved as much as I could. I did not drive a fancy car, nor did I live in a fancy place. I also didn't travel a lot, except to visit family overseas. This allowed me to boost my savings substantially.

Then, luck favored me. I was able to cash out some stock options at the top of the market, right before the dot-com crash in the early 2000s. The savings I had plus the proceeds of my options were just enough to get me started.

*Q: Explain factoring, purchase order financing, and inventory financing.*

A: From a consumer's perspective, a retail transaction is simple. You pay for the goods and you get them immediately. The retailer gets the money right away and you get the goods immediately. It's very simple. On the other hand, business-to-business transactions are more complicated.

As a distributor, you will be selling to commercial clients who will demand that you give them 30- to 60-day net payment terms. This means that your company must deliver the goods immediately. But your clients will pay your invoices in 30 to 60 days.

Now, let's look at what happens when you buy products from the manufacturer/wholesaler. Your suppliers will often insist that you pay them before they ship the goods to you. This is common with startups because they have a limited track record. Only established businesses get 30- to 60-day payment terms.

This creates a cash-flow problem for you. You have to pay your manufacturers/suppliers immediately but then have to wait a month or two to get paid by clients. In the meantime, you must pay bills and salaries and fulfill new orders. You can see how cash flow becomes a problem soon, especially if you are growing quickly.

One solution is to use factoring. Factoring allows you to finance your net-30 to net-60 invoices from creditworthy commercial clients. Instead of waiting 30 to 60 days to get paid, the factoring company advances about 80 percent of the invoice. Usually 20 percent remains in reserve to cover any potential short payments. The 20-percent reserve, less a small fee, is advanced to you as soon as your client pays their invoice.

You can use the funds from the factoring advance to operate your business. In the case of a distributor, it will usually involve paying suppliers, employees, warehouse space, and other expenses.

Factoring is much easier to get than other forms of financing. Factoring companies base their decision mostly on the commercial credit of your client. Your personal credit does not play a substantial role in the decision, but your background does. Most factors run a background check on all clients.

As you can see, factoring helps you with cash-flow problems related to slow-paying clients. Now, let's say that you get a very large order. In most cases, that would be great news. But what happens if the order is so large that you don't have enough funds to cover your supplier's payment? Do you pass on the order?

If your transaction qualifies, you may be able to finance the transaction using purchase order financing. Transactions must meet the following criteria:

1. Be a large sale to an individual commercial or government customer (e.g., $50,000 or more).
2. Have a single supplier for the order.
3. Consist of nonperishable items.
4. Have minimum gross margins of 20 percent (30 percent is preferred).

5.  Have no services associated with the order.

6.  Have a supplier willing to accept a letter of credit.

7.  Not be the first sale of the business.

Purchase order financing allows you to cover the cost of your supplier. The finance company pays your supplier directly. Once the supplier receives the payment, they ship the product, which allows you to deliver the goods. Once you deliver the goods, you can generate an invoice and send it to your customer for payment in 30 to 60 days.

PO finance companies often request that you work with a factoring company as well. That enables you to factor the newly created invoice and use the proceeds of factoring to pay off the purchase order financing company. That payment closes the PO financing line, and the transaction continues as a normal factoring transaction. The transaction concludes when the end-customer pays the invoice in full.

One advantage of purchase order financing is that you can use it to grow your company exponentially. Most PO finance companies don't set a maximum limit for your line. Instead, the limit is based on the creditworthiness of your client, the reliability of your supplier, and your ability to execute the transaction.

Both factoring and purchase order financing are great options for new and growing distributors. They are easier to get than bank loans or lines of credit. However, this flexibility comes at a cost. The products are more expensive than conventional bank financing.

Once your company becomes more mature and generates a decent track record (three to five years) you should consider other options, such as asset-based lending and supplier financing. These two solutions provide benefits similar to purchase order financing and factoring, but often at a lower cost.

All these financing solutions are stepping stones to conventional bank financing, which is much cheaper (but harder to get) than all these options. Once your company matures past the initial growth phase, you will have a track record of financing that will help you qualify for bank solutions.

Lastly, one additional solution you should know about is inventory financing. This solution is more expensive and complex than the previously mentioned options. It should be used only once the previous alternatives have been exhausted.

Inventory financing allows you to capitalize on unsold inventory that is sitting in your warehouse. Usually you can get an advance of 75 percent of your inventory's Net Orderly Liquidation Appraised (NOLA) value or 50 percent of its value, whichever is lower. The finance company works with appraisers that can determine your inventory's NOLA. The inventory financing company gets paid back as you sell the products that have been financed.

Generally, to qualify for inventory financing your company needs to:

1. Require at least $500,000 of financing.
2. Have an inventory tracking system.
3. Keep good accounting records.
4. Have unencumbered inventory.
5. Be profitable.

Q: *Approximately how much does Commercial Capital LLC charge for each service?*

A: For factoring, we charge 1.15 percent to 3.5 percent per month, based on volume. Note that we have some plans with higher rates, though they are directed to very small businesses (under $10,000 in funding needs) that have higher risk/account management costs. For purchase order financing, we charge 3 percent to 4 percent per month. For supplier financing, we charge 1 percent to 2 percent per month. For inventory financing, we charge 1 percent to 1.5 percent per month. However, setup requires an appraisal and field visit. These can cost from $10,000 to $20,000, which is payable upfront. Some inventory finance companies require a yearly audit/field visit.

Q: *How do you help wholesalers with cross-border transactions? Are there any special considerations?*

A: We work with distributors that buy goods from foreign suppliers and resell them in the U.S. and Canada. These prospects often look for PO financing. There are some special considerations when working with foreign suppliers, which include:

1. We only prepay foreign suppliers with a letter of credit. It ensures the supplier gets paid only if they deliver the product to the client. This reduces the risk that a supplier will not deliver the goods but keep the payment. It also reduces the risk of nonpayment to the supplier since letters of credit are very safe.
2. One of the contingencies we put in the letter of credit is that the goods must be inspected for quality/quantity by a well-known inspection company (such as SGS). This reduces the risk of getting goods that don't meet the specifications.
3. Our distributor clients often tell us that their foreign suppliers only take a "cash" (wire transfer) prepayment. Furthermore, they insist that the supplier does not take letters of credit. These clients always try to make a case for paying in cash and ask us to make an exception. Invariably, we advise clients that we don't participate in those transactions for the following reasons:
   a. Reputable suppliers happily accept letters of credit. It's a well-known and widely accepted payment instrument.

b. Suppliers that insist on a cash payment (rather than a letter of credit) often do so because they have their own financial problems. They may need cash to deliver your order, or worse, a previous order. Ultimately, cash payments increase the risk of suppliers' nonperformance or fraud. We often have to remind these clients that "We are in the business of financing our clients, not their suppliers."

*Q: Are you optimistic about the future of American businesses?*

A: In the long term, I am very optimistic about American businesses. The economy may hit bumps in the road, or even go into serious recessions (such as The Great Recession), but we always recover.

I think there are many reasons for the resiliency of U.S. businesses. One important reason is that the country has excellent business infrastructure coupled with an entrepreneurial mindset. America recognizes the value of entrepreneurship and it's in our ethos.

Unlike many countries, in the U.S.:

1. Anyone can easily set up a company and get a bank account. In most states, you can do it in a day or two.
2. It's relatively easy to access financing. There are several finance companies competing to provide you with financing.
3. We have a wide base of companies that support businesses (e.g., manufacturers, distributors, staffing agencies, lawyers, accountants, etc.).
4. Our laws support business (within reason). This helps us grow when the times are good and recover when the times are hard.

*Q: Can you share any helpful tips you feel readers might benefit from learning?*

A: Here are some things I have learned, in no particular order:

1. Business projections, especially for new businesses, are just that—projections. They are often wrong. Don't get attached to them.
2. Building a sustainable business will take three times as long and be three times as hard as you originally thought.
3. Many of your projects (or products) in business may fail. That is OK. You only need a few runaway successes to make it.
4. If you can, start a business in your free time while you are still employed. It is difficult, but worth it. It allows you to keep your salary and benefits while you get your

business launched. However, stay with your employer only if you are still delivering full value. If you are not, it's time to work at your business full-time. Note: Don't work on your business while you are on the clock with your employer. It may be tempting, but it is neither ethical nor worth it.

5. Save as much money as you can before you start the business. You will need every penny.

6. Don't bet your house or your retirement on a business. If the business goes down, be sure that you can live to fight another day.

7. People (especially your family members) may think that owning your own company allows you the freedom to control your work hours. When this subject comes up, I always remind folks that during the first decade in the company, I was "free" to work whichever 12 hours of the day I chose to work.

*Marco can be reached on LinkedIn: https://www.linkedin.com/in/marcoterry/*

# Interview with Rob Frohwein
## *CEO and Cofounder of Kabbage, Inc.*

Since 2011, Kabbage has been providing small businesses and consumers access to loans through their automated lending platform. I had the privilege of catching up with Rob Frohwein who shared some insights into how Kabbage helps small businesses, including wholesalers, with financing.

*Q: What did you do before you started Kabbage?*

A: I've always been driven by curiosity and have a passion for new ideas, so I did a lot of things! I held several jobs with companies like Andersen Consulting (now Accenture), The Franklin Mint (the largest direct marketer of collectibles at the time), went to law school and practiced for a while, started a radio show, wrote three books on intellectual property, and I started lots of businesses. Nearly all of them failed or at least didn't succeed in the way I first imagined. I learned what running a small business was like—it is the hardest job I've ever both loved and hated.

*Q: What year did you start Kabbage?*

A: 2009-ish. The reason there's not a clear date is that, when you start a business, one day it goes from hobby to job and it's hard to say precisely when the flip occurs. We launched our lending platform in 2011 to help small businesses get access to working capital in minutes.

*Q: Why did you start Kabbage?*

A: I know this sounds like an odd answer, but I had to. For crazy people like me, you're motivated by ideas and you're compelled to start the great ones. Kabbage felt like a great idea and I had a lot of independent validation of that belief from others.

*Q: How do American wholesale distributors use Kabbage?*

A: Many of them are small businesses and need access to capital! When you're in the distribution world, there's often a gap between when you get paid and when you are paid by your customers. You shouldn't have to suffer during that time.

*Q: What was the coolest thing Kabbage has accomplished?*

A: To date, we've helped over 200,000 small businesses access more than $8 billion of working capital. Studies show that 22,000 jobs are created for every $1 billion accessed by small businesses, and every $1 drives $3.79 of economic output. We're proud to make that kind of impact for small businesses and the U.S. economy.

*Q: Why is it or is it not difficult for startup wholesale distribution companies to obtain capital?*

A: Any business that doesn't have a history of getting paying customers, generating revenue, or managing a business has some difficulty. It's important to establish the business quickly so you can access credit for your business.

*Q: Why should or should not the founder of a startup borrow money from family and friends?*

A: The shoulds: It can be easier—your family and friends know you well. And you can get access to capital quickly. The should nots: Asking family and friends for money is great if everything works out according to plan. If it doesn't, holiday dinners can become less enjoyable!

*Q: Do you love to work with small-to-medium-size wholesalers? If so, why and what opportunities are on the horizon for them working with Kabbage?*

A: Wholesalers, restaurants, construction companies, hair salons—you name it—I strongly believe in any small business and the people who run them. For those seeking capital to manage their cash flow or make investments, they can apply for free on https://www.kabbage.com and get a funding decision in minutes. For wholesalers that may rely on invoices for payments, Kabbage recently launched Kabbage Payments, helping small businesses get paid and access the money they earn faster. Any wholesaler interested in learning more can request early access.

*Q: Feel free to share any "wow" facts or figures about Kabbage that would "blow" our minds.*

A: Nearly 1,900 small businesses access as much as $13 million every day with Kabbage.

*Q: Are you optimistic about the future of American businesses? If your answer is "yes," please share why.*

A: Yes, because I deeply believe in small businesses, but also because the data says so. We recently launched the Kabbage Small Business Revenue Index, which analyzes revenue growth by drawing from the 2 million live data connections we maintain with small businesses. Since December 2016, small businesses' revenue has increased by more than 63 percent.

*Q: Why is this a good time to start a wholesale distribution company?*

A: Yes, it's a good time! I say that because I don't believe in timing. You can't time life; you have to go for it. There's always a need for another great business if you're executing well and putting your heart into it.

*Q: What gets you leaping out of bed in the morning?*

A: A whole lot of interesting and different challenges to address and things to do. My job has lots of twists and turns so that keeps every day a bit different than the day before. And the people—I love the team we've built and their absolute commitment to our mission.

*Q: What is your intention in business and in life?*

A: Firstly, to take care of my family. Their happiness is my happiness. Outside of that, I want to make a dramatic, positive impact for a large number of people—employees of Kabbage, small businesses, the communities in which we all live, and the world in general.

*Q: How is your family involved in your company?*

A: They've seen it all. I started the company when my son was 12 and daughter was 9. They've lived the ups and downs with me and they've each contributed at some point. My wife has contributed by being incredibly supportive of my entrepreneurial needs and desires. It's not an easy life. She's spent a lot of time in our offices, helping and engaging with various employees—even leading classes in yoga and meditation. My kids have each interned at the company once, though they have no desire to work there again. I think they don't like being the boss's kid and I don't blame them. They're independent thinkers and doers and will dent the world in their own, unique ways. I'm so proud of them and my wife.

# Interview with Chris Titus
## *Creator and Founder of the Chris Titus Tech YouTube Channel*

I curated many of my Windows 10 optimization ideas from the Chris Titus Tech YouTube channel. Chris Titus took time out of his busy day to engage in a Q&A with me regarding technology choices for startups. Chris Titus Tech has been in the information technology sector since 2003 and has helped set up over 50 companies. Chris shares tips on hardware, software, and his love for Linux and cloud computing solutions. Here's my Q&A with Chris.

*Q: Considering that people will be reading this book for many years to come, what time-tested and long-lasting recommendations can you give about selecting computer hardware for a business?*

A: There are two methods for selecting hardware for a business, and they are leasing vs. buying. While both have advantages, it can vary from business to business.

If you don't have good support or a trusted IT professional helping your business, I would lean toward leasing the hardware. This would cycle your hardware out, ensure you have the latest technology and a predictable cost per month.

However, if you do have someone to assist in a hardware purchase and can support it for years to come, then you can easily save money and purchase a great computer. While I'd love to say one brand is better than another, it is a moving target. Having said that, I'd recommend sticking to a brand name and purchasing a computer that will suit your needs. There is nothing more frustrating than buying a cheap computer and waiting for it to complete tasks because you bought a cheap computer.

*Q: Windows, macOS, or Linux, and why?*

A: This entirely depends on what you know and your needs. Each one of these operating systems has its advantages, and there isn't a clear winner. However, I always look to future-proof myself and businesses I support.

In recent years, Linux has seen a lot of advancements and will start breaking into the desktop realm. While most readers may not know what Linux is, it is important to note that most major businesses rely on Linux servers to run their daily operations. The reason for this is it is secure, reliable, and free of costly licenses. While I don't think everyone should jump ship to Linux desktop just yet, it will soon be a major choice in the desktop space for businesses. I myself have transitioned this past year to Linux desktop and enjoy having greater control over my computer that Windows no longer affords me. A prime example of this is Windows 10's update cycle that is just far too aggressive.

Windows, on the other hand, is still the most used operating system out of the three and has the greatest compatibility. I would not recommend Windows for a startup. More and more programs are hosted in the cloud and are accessed via a web browser. More established businesses that can't get away from some of their legacy applications will continue to use the Windows operating system.

One other factor to consider is how adaptable your workforce is. If your staff are set in their ways and have only used Windows over their career, then you will have issues if they are unable to learn another operating system.

macOS is my last option. While Macs are great for creative types and it has a very consistent experience, it is very expensive and has a more limited selection of software. It should be noted that while I don't recommend it, for those accustomed to the Apple ecosystem, it is an option. Even with a limited software selection, most applications these days are run via web browser and if a business is built with this in mind, they can easily use Macs.

Q: *Can you explain some common tech terms that might come up in daily operations and how to overcome issues with them?*

A: Sure. Let's talk them out:

- ▶ Software bloat/bloatware. This is a major issue with Windows as most Windows machines slow down over time and these days come with far more bloatware that is baked into the OS. If you have a good support team, they can assist with keeping those Windows machines clear of this software and putting restrictions on your computers preventing users from installing programs that don't belong on a business machine. If not properly maintained, Windows can become a bloated mess with each feature update installing unwanted applications such as games and other applications that are incompatible for a business. I find both macOS and Linux have very minimal, if any, bloatware on a fresh installation.
- ▶ Feature creep. Windows is the biggest aggressor of feature creep as the installation keeps becoming more and more bloated. A good example of this is Windows installations now bloating between 15 and 40GB in size when completely patched. macOS on the otherhand has reduced some of its features in the latest iterations and no longer supports 32 bit applications—and overall is rather clean when upgrading the OS. Likewise, Linux also has very good housekeeping.
- ▶ Methods for improving computer performance without applying third-party fixes or using additional tools:
  - – Windows:

- Clean up many of the default Windows store apps. I'd recommend removing games and other bloated MS Store apps. I use PowerShell to accomplish this task and then disable the MS Store afterward.
- Change default settings to minimize the telemetry built into Windows. Chang this to Basic and lessen the burden of aggressive reporting.
- Do not use Windows Home editions. I'd recommend the pro version so you can set GPOs (Group Policy Objects) that disable a lot of the performance killers of Windows, such as Cortana, Suggested Sites & Apps, Error Reporting, Customer Experience Program, etc.
- Disable unneeded startup programs.
- macOS
  - I'd recommend switching off Safari and moving to Google Chrome or Firefox as an alternative. I find Safari is just not as polished as either of these browsers.
  - Go through System Preferences -> Users and Groups and remove startup programs that you don't need.
- Linux
  - Most Linux installations don't require any performance tweaks. It also doesn't slow down over time and is why so many servers run Linux.
- All systems
  - Once your environment is set up, make sure you take proper backups and images of your system. This makes expansion easier and it keeps everything uniform, while also preventing data loss.
  - Managing computers via a domain is recommended.

*Q: Please explain how hardware requirements vary when operating a computer with local software vs. using cloud-based solutions.*

A: The more local software you have will require more resources to run it, where the cloud-based solutions all run from a browser and don't require much if any resources to run. We have seen so many businesses transition to cloud-based solutions because they don't have to buy the large workstations and they don't have to support servers locally to host the applications.

One more benefit to cloud-based solutions is you aren't bound by a certain operating system. This means you can use any of the three desktop OSs or even include tablets and other devices that can save you money by not needing a desktop computer.

*Q: QuickBooks has a large share of the market for accounting solutions for SMBs; do you recommend any competing products, and if so, which platforms do they work on?*

A: QuickBooks is the biggest name in the SMB market and has fantastic compatibility with a variety of line of business applications as a result. However, if you don't need compatibility and you just need an accounting system you should look into FreshBooks, Wave, or Xero. These solutions are SaaS (cloud-based) and don't require any local software. This is where most SMBs are pivoting to and what most startups will use. QuickBooks even recognizes this and has its own cloud-based offering, QuickBooks Online.

Q: *Can you share any helpful tips you feel might benefit our readers?*

A: Evaluate your needs and what you want to accomplish. Don't get stuck doing the same old things from years ago just because you don't know anything else. I encourage many of my viewers to try Linux desktop because it has made me more effective. Learn and try new things; otherwise, you might be left behind.

*Chris Titus Tech authors technology articles and videos that can be found at https:// www.christitus.com.*

# Interview with Brad Anderson
## Corporate Vice President of Commercial Management Experiences at Microsoft

Until I took on the challenge of writing this book, I didn't realize just how Microsoft helped startups. They have many solutions for companies and they work hard to ensure that their products are functional and secure. I had the rare opportunity to interview a top executive at Microsoft, Brad Anderson, who heads up the commercial management experiences division. Here's my Q&A with Brad.

Q: *What enterprise tools does Microsoft offer to help startup companies, such as wholesalers?*

A: Microsoft 365 is a subscription service that ensures you always have the most up-to-date security and productivity tools from Microsoft. This includes familiar Office desktop apps like Word, PowerPoint, and Excel, but it also includes business-class email, business chat/ meetings, online storage, and cloud-connected features that let you collaborate on files in real time. One of the most valuable things it includes is a myriad of security features. The same security tools used by banks, governments, and health-care providers are available in Microsoft 365. This will protect a startup against phishing attacks, ransomware, and other cyberattacks. The subscription model makes it easy for startups to get the latest features, fixes, and security updates (along with ongoing tech support at no extra cost) at a consistent, predictable price point. Microsoft 365 really represents the essential toolkit for startups that need the best tools to communicate, collaborate, and stay secure—all in one simple package.

*Q: Which tools does Microsoft offer that are in the "cloud"?*

A: Every single part of Microsoft 365, and everything we build for small/medium businesses is based in the cloud. This setup gives startups the type of agility, resiliency, and bottomless scale they need to grow at their own pace, and, at the same time, it frees them from ever needing to worry about maintaining servers or on-site infrastructure products.

*Q: Why is security so important for small businesses?*

A: It's a numbers game, and the numbers are stacked against small businesses. Right now, there are 79 million businesses worldwide who meet the "small or medium business" definition of having 300 or fewer employees, and I take this community really seriously because those businesses represent 95 percent of all the companies on earth or, said another way, small/medium businesses account for 63 percent of the work force on our planet. That is a lot of surface area for criminals to attack, and they are getting attacked constantly: Last year, 55 percent of small businesses were attacked, and, in a quarter of those cases, sensitive customer data was breached. This is a disaster scenario for a small business. The average cyberattack will cost a small business $190,000 USD and, after a ransomware attack, only one-third of these small businesses will remain profitable. Perhaps worst of all, these numbers will only increase this year because 90 percent of small businesses do not currently have enough data protection. These huge problems are something we directly address with Microsoft 365 in a way that any small business can use right away.

*Q: Is "cloud" best for a small business and if so, why?*

A: Absolutely, no question about it. Just a few years ago, a small business would have to spend an extraordinary amount of time and money to use all these tools, but now that all this technology can be securely and rapidly orchestrated in the cloud, any business can use them immediately and at a tiny fraction of the cost. Considering how many thousands of small/medium businesses suffer at the hands of cyberattacks, the power of Microsoft 365's security tools makes this a critical part of any organization's long-term health.

*Q: How can a wholesaler leverage Microsoft's AI and machine learning tools?*

A: AI and machine learning are baked into everything we've built in Microsoft 365. AI and ML tools suggest ways to better write and design documents, they help make searches more effective, and AI is at the heart of the vast security tools that respond and defend against threats thousands of times faster than humans can. All of these AI/ML tools continue to get more useful and sophisticated as these global cloud services continue to be used.

*Q: Can you share any helpful tips you feel might benefit our readers?*

A: It's easier than many startups think to set up a professional presence—whether that's setting up a business email with your domain name or using tools for collaboration and meetings. The cloud-based nature of Microsoft 365 makes it possible to start doing this in minutes.

For any startup, the scarcest resource is time; this is where an integrated suite like Microsoft 365 comes in handy. Having a single solution means there are fewer vendors to manage, less support issues, and less administration requirements eating up your time—all the typical things that have distracted a small business from focusing on their real mission. Furthermore, when you are using all the best productivity tools, you have everything you'll need to do your best work and focus entirely on your business. This is a solution that will grow with your business.

## Interview with Rodney Fingleson
### *CPA, Senior Shareholder at Gumbiner Savett, Inc.*

I met a junior accountant named Rodney Fingleson in 1988 who went on to become a senior shareholder of Gumbiner Savett, Inc., a full-service accounting firm. Gumbiner Savett, Inc. provides audit and assurance, tax, business services, litigation support, and business advisory services. Their clients range from individuals and their families to both private and public middle-market companies. Based in Santa Monica, the firm is one of the largest CPA firms in California. I consider Rodney a great friend and a stellar accountant. I was incredibly fortunate to be able to glean some of his MVP tips for wholesale startups and considering how busy Rodney is, I was even more fortunate to be able to interview a man with such a fine reputation in the accounting business. Gumbiner Savett, Inc. also has done much to elevate women in business—one of its shareholders and two practitioners have been named among the "Most Influential Women in Accounting" by the *Los Angeles Business Journal*. Rodney took time out of his busy day to answer a few questions to help guide you in your startup funding journey.

*Q: What year did Gumbiner Savett, Inc. open its doors?*

A: 1950.

*Q: How many employees does Gumbiner Savett, Inc. have today?*

A: We are one of the largest employers of CPAs in our industry and have 110 employees.

*Q: Do you have clients that are wholesale distributors of goods and if so, without sharing names, what industries are doing well today?*

A: Yes, we do, and the clients doing the most wholesale trade within our client roster are selling chicken, meat, diamonds, luggage, and furniture.

*Q: How does Gumbiner Savett, Inc. help a startup determine initial capital requirements?*

A: Our team takes a look at the business plan to develop our strategy for our clients, and then we arrange for them to meet with banks and institutions to lend them money to get started and continue to grow. We have helped clients raise as much as $10 million. We can help clients with investment banking and private equity funds, or if they wish it, to make a public offering. Clients should show a bit of cash flow and practical experience before seeking financing.

*Q: For a business newbie, when does it make sense to operate as a sole proprietor?*

A: The sole proprietor is the most looked-at business by the IRS. Businesses filing an IRS Schedule C are the most audited. It is a known reality in accounting circles that sole proprietors are audited more often than business operators that use other legal structures.

*Q: Is there a "magic" income figure you use as the trigger for when you recommend a more formal business structure?*

A: There is no magical number. It is based on forecasting sales six months to a year into the future—I do not like to forecast beyond one year.

*Q: In what situations do you recommend a C-corp, S-corp, partnership, and LLC?*

A: I always advise my clients to use an S-corp business structure because the income flows through to the individual business owner and they avoid the double taxation that a C-corp suffers. Wholesalers should stick to an S-corp.

*Q: What are the specific SEC-regulated tools available for small to medium-size enterprises that can help them raise capital?*

A: They can use private memorandum to raise capital. It's a presentation but not a public offering. The most we've raised by private memorandum was $10 million. We've also helped people make a public offering and go public.

*Q: Why is it or is it not difficult for startup wholesale distribution companies to obtain capital?*

A: A startup lacks operating history. We recommend that a business establish at least one year of operating history before seeking capital.

*Q: How else does Gumbiner Savett, Inc. help startups raise capital?*

A: We help customers with Small Business Administration loans.

*Q: What role does Gumbiner Savett, Inc. play in the process of an initial public offering?*

A: We act as the outside independent CPA for audit reports.

*Q: Can you share any good news stories about clients that are wholesale distribution companies?*

A: We have helped wholesalers grow and assisted them with private sales. Their exit strategy is critical in the analysis—timing for the sale and future plans after the sale.

*Q: How often do you like to talk to your clients?*

A: We should speak with clients, at minimum, once per quarter to find out what's going on with their company, address any needs, and find out what we can do to help.

*Q: How big does a company need to be in order to use Gumbiner Savett, Inc.'s services?*

A: You have to be a good person; I don't care about the size of your business.

*Q: What was the coolest thing Gumbiner Savett, Inc. has accomplished?*

A: Aside from hiring me in 1979? (Laughs). We have a 98-percent success rate justifying our accounting during Internal Revenue Service audits—that's cool!

*Q: Are you optimistic about the future of American businesses?*

A: Yes, there is a lot of money available for expansion. We see small businesses growing and growing and growing—we are very optimistic about the future.

*Q: Can you share any helpful tips you feel might benefit our readers?*

A: Be honest—always—whether it hurts or doesn't hurt. Planning is critical and it is one of the most important things in business.

# Interview with Marc J. Gorlin
## CEO and Founder of Roadie, Inc.

I had the rare privilege of catching up with Roadie founder and CEO Marc Gorlin who agreed to talk about his brainchild. Roadie operates as a convenient smartphone app, which is a boon to wholesalers who require low-cost fully insured same-day deliveries. I share Marc's vision for reaching into existing resources and surplus vehicle space to move inventory. I anticipate that on-demand delivery services like Roadie will dramatically improve the reach for wholesalers while cutting costs—I love that merchandise doesn't have to be protected so well that it will survive a nuclear blast. My Roadie experiences have been flawless. In this interview, he shares his vision for the "on-the-way" delivery service industry, a few tips, and his pearls of wisdom for would-be entrepreneurs. Here's my Q&A with Marc.

*Q: Who uses Roadie and why?*

A: Roadie works with consumers, small businesses, and big global brands (like Delta Air Lines and The Home Depot) across virtually every industry to provide a faster, cheaper, more scalable solution for scheduled, same-day, and urgent delivery. And we're doing it just about everywhere in the U.S.; we have the largest local same-day delivery footprint in the nation.

*Q: What incredible things can Roadie accomplish for both startups and established companies?*

A: There are five key advantages Roadie offers businesses when it comes to logistics:

▶ *Reach your customers where they are—fast.* Not all your customers live in big NFL cities, and Roadie's crowdsourced model allows you to reach all of them. Roadie also enables you to extend delivery radius outside of a 10-mile city center—often supporting same-day delivery up to 70 miles guaranteed.

▶ *Nationwide delivery footprint.* With over 150,000 drivers nationwide, Roadie has made deliveries in 11,000+ cities and towns and covers 89 percent of U.S. households. Whether your customers are across town or across the country, Roadie delivers.

▶ *Flexibility at scale.* A community-sourced driver fleet allows businesses to flex dynamically to meet unexpected spikes and lulls in demand—in any market, at any time.

▶ *Supports items of any size.* Our driver fleet ranges from sedans to SUVs to cargo vans that can support bulky, heavy, and oversized deliveries.

▶ *Community-focused customer service.* This has been a huge differentiator of ours because our drivers aren't faceless delivery people. They're regular folks—your employees, the woman buying coffee down the street, or the guy at the local service station. They're a community, and we've found that (especially in logistics) community matters. At the end of the day, that level of service and convenience builds brand loyalty and deeper brand engagement with customers, the community, and employees who make deliveries.

*Q: Why is Roadie simply the best?*

A: Our model offers a faster, more efficient delivery model that fundamentally improves the economics of distribution. At Roadie, we're not building a transportation infrastructure, we're revealing one that already exists.

Today, 250 million passenger vehicles will hit the road with 4 billion cubic feet of unused space. Roadie taps into that, creating corridors of deliverability that can solve today's modern distribution challenges. The result is an "on-the-way" logistics utility that's faster and more scalable than anything in the last century. We see a future beyond rigid, asset-heavy logistics models, where untapped resources address delivery demand in a scalable way.

*Q: Why is Roadie awesome for the "little guy" in business?*

A: Customers' expectations for varied delivery options have changed drastically in the last few years. Customers want what they want, when they want it, and if you can't get it to them on their schedule, they'll go somewhere else.

That surge in consumer expectations for convenient same-day and next-day delivery at a low cost has forced small and medium-sized businesses to seek out new ways to compete. Roadie gives them a leg up; we offer independent businesses a viable way to gain that competitive edge without the exorbitant cost incumbent on a bulky, fixed-asset delivery fleet.

*Q: What happens if what I'm sending is damaged or lost in transit?*

A: Roadie offers protection up to $500 at no additional cost on every delivery. We also partner with UPS Capital to offer additional protection, up to $10,000, meaning that our deliveries are backed by the very same protection as parcels delivered by UPS.

But honestly, most of our customers find our single-vehicle system a relief. The painting you spent six months working on doesn't need to be wrapped carefully in bubble wrap, styrofoam, cardboard, and more if it's not going to be jostled by a revolving door of handlers, trucks, planes, and machinery. It doesn't need to be bounced between four trucks and an airplane. It's just going in your Roadie driver's back seat or trunk, where it will stay until it arrives at its final destination. Fewer encounters with the item means fewer opportunities for damage, plain and simple.

*Q: What are the top partnerships Roadie has scored and why did Roadie engage in them?*

A: The best partners for us are those that care about the same problems we're trying to solve. Take The Home Depot, a customer for more than a year and now an investor. They understand that building the Roadie community helps them create a community of their own—shoppers, employees, and local drivers going to, from, and around stores—to bring value to their ecosystem in a new way. The value of the partnership goes beyond funding. Our relationship is symbiotic.

Take another great partner of ours: Delta Air Lines. If your luggage is delayed, it's a Roadie driver who will bring it home to you, and we're able to do that quickly and efficiently. Meanwhile, Delta's long reach and extensive routes have enabled us to easily enter new markets.

It's the same situation with Walmart, whom we work with to deliver groceries. Through that partnership, Walmart is able to offer customers in smaller markets a service that's very scarce outside of big cities. That's great for them, of course, but it also adds volume to our platform in cities where deliveries might otherwise have been thinner on the ground for our drivers.

*Q: What is the coolest thing Roadie has accomplished?*

A: Watching our vision of on-the-way delivery become a reality. Back in 2014, our company was founded on a key question: what would happen if we put four billion cubic feet of wasted space in passenger vehicles to good use? Today, Roadie is the first on-the-way delivery service that puts unused capacity in passenger vehicles to work by connecting people with items to send with drivers already going that way.

And that network is transforming the businesses of our customers. Companies large and small can be more agile and responsive to market demands. We saw this in action recently with one of our Fortune 100 customers: one day this summer, they saw an unexpected spike in deliveries to six times their normal volume. We were able to flex instantly to respond to that demand with an increase in delivery times of only a few minutes. In a fixed-asset model, fleet capacity would have eventually been reached and many of those items would have gone undelivered.

*Q: What gets you leaping out of bed in the morning?*

A: The people, hands down. Roadie is an assemblage of the most talented, smartest, and oftentimes funniest people I've ever had the pleasure to work with; they are simply awesome. And they care deeply about Roadie's mission, our senders, our drivers, and most importantly: each other. Startups are a team sport. They can be incredibly stressful and at times terrifying. Having a committed group of partners in the foxhole with you, knowing they have your back, makes charging out into the world a little bit easier each day.

*Q: Can you share any helpful tips you feel might benefit our readers?*

A: When you're starting anything, get something done every day. Sounds simple, I know. But it's not. It can be easy to get stuck in the mud when you're starting something and hard to feel like you're making progress—so do something every day. It might be as simple as setting up your new email, ordering business cards, or calling five potential new customers in a day to get critical product feedback. If you hold all your days to this standard, you'll have a lot more done as the weeks and months pass by. Eventually, you'll see real progress.

Also, know that the haters gonna hate. Not everybody is going to think your baby is pretty. Many will declare it ugly before even getting a good look. Take in critical feedback and objections as things that need to be answered (especially if they are constantly repeated), but don't let them get you down. It's sometimes strangely difficult for even people who care about you to see the potential of a new idea. Give them time and they'll likely come around. As for those who are just dismissive out of hand with no explanation (and were sometimes rude to boot) . . . they'll never understand, anyway.

## Interview with Melinda Damico
### *Executive Vice President of Vandegrift, a Maersk Company*

For wholesalers who would like to trade across borders, no firm is more experienced than Maersk. The company has been the largest container ship and supply vessel operator in the world since 1996. Vandegrift is a customs brokerage and subsidiary of Maersk that provides importers and exporters with expert advice and services to help them navigate complex government regulations—alleviating the stresses of dealing with customs officials and laws at every point in the supply chain. I had the pleasure of interviewing Melinda Damico, the executive vice president of Vandegrift, and here is the Q&A from our interview.

Q: *If you're a new business starting up an international sourcing program—what's your advice and best practices for international shipping?*

A: It's essential to partner with suppliers and supply-chain professionals with proven and established history in handling international business.

Q: *What are your three top tips for new importers venturing into international business?*

A: Establish clear terms of sale with vendors. Audition vendors with a couple of small shipments to test their supply chain. Actively and regularly monitor inventory.

Q: *What are your recommended top three focus areas for importers as they grow?*

A: Gaining a greater understanding of the level of responsibility of an importer. Understanding the various costs within the supply chain. Preparing to scale their supply chain.

*Q: How can an importer best monitor constant tariff and regulatory changes?*

A: A customs broker licensed by the U.S. Customs and Border Protection agency is the best way to stay on top of changing tariffs and laws. This landscape changes rapidly and a customs professional stays up-to-date on the rules and regulations.

*Q: What is the use case for an air shipment vis-à-vis an ocean shipment?*

A: In general, ocean shipments are less expensive than air shipments. However, depending on the size of the shipment, the cost for air may be less than compared with ocean. A skilled supply chain partner will recommend air shipping at the correct time.

*Q: How does Vandegrift assist with selecting container freight companies?*

A: Vandegrift is a trusted advisor providing individualized customs brokerage and compliance solutions that identify and resolve risk. We are owned by Maersk which has been the largest container ship and vessel operator in the world since 1996. By shipping with Maersk, we keep things all in the family. Bigger is better because Maersk and Vandegrift work on greater economies of scale and our special relationships ensure that our customer's mission is accomplished on-budget and on-time. It's important to find the right company that can meet the specific needs for your business.

*Q: Please provide an example of how an expert customs broker can save money for the importer.*

A: Vandegrift has identified several cost savings opportunities and continues to evaluate ways to save customers money. One way is through the duty drawback program which allows importers to reclaim duty paid on products originally imported and later exported. A common example occurs with ecommerce, where items are sold from U.S.-imported inventory to customers located outside of the U.S.

*Q: How does Vandegrift assist importers with the U.S. Customs process?*

A: Vandegrift helps our importers see a 360-degree view of the import journey. We provide education on how product construction and intended use will affect the requirements associated with importing those items. We handle the required paperwork and processes such as Importer Security Filings and Additional Carrier Requirements to dodge monetary penalties and avoid delays of cargo.

# Interview with Chuck Kradjian
## *Proprietor of V&K Distributing Company*

This last interview was so very special to me and you'll soon discover why. I've lived in Burbank since 1991, and just around the corner from the end of my street where it intersects with Magnolia Boulevard is a discreet storefront with an unpretentious sign that reads:

**V&K**
**Distributing Co.**
MIDDLE EASTERN
FOOD PRODUCTS
(818) 848-1926
VAHE KRADJIAN & SON

For more than two decades, I walked by this store perhaps thousands of times without ever having stepped inside. As I have aged, my sense of adventure has changed, and things that were once of no interest to me have now become curiosities. I'm now exploring the quaint shops that line the popular Magnolia Park retail shopping district. Something beckoned me to go inside V&K Distributing Company—it was the aroma of spices that caught my olfactory senses as I happened to pass by when a customer opened the door. I was curious. While I imagined the business to be strictly wholesale (based on the firm name), to my surprise the aisles of shelving held a plethora of goodies with retail price tags. Large bags of dried fruit for a few dollars, cans of beans for 50 cents, wonderfully aromatic whole bean coffees, dressings, fresh butter for half the price offered at the supermarket, and bottles of exotic Greek extra-virgin olive oil at one-third the price found at local fancy food shops. In addition to a vast array of canned legumes were raw and roasted nuts and seeds—including a massive bag of sunflower seeds for an incredible $1 per pound (my backyard squirrels would soon be over the moon). As I continued to peruse the store, I found rare sweet treats such as homespun pistachio, raisin, and coconut nougat. An entire wall was dedicated to huge bags of herbs and spices—garam masala, smoked paprika, cumin, cayenne, oregano, fennel, and a dozen other imported seasonings—for a few dollars a bag. And oddities such as rose jelly—something I had never seen or savored before.

Locally produced tahini and 50-cent cans of garbanzo beans have become staples on my V&K Distributing Company shopping list. I regularly fry up the halloumi—a very firm, unripe, brined cheese made from goat's and sheep's milk. I'm boycotting the $5-a-tub commercially produced supermarket hummus and making my own—four tubs for less than $2 total! I buy kilos of coffee so my staff can serve it to the guests of my vacation rental business (another of my ventures). I have now learned what the local Armenian residents have known for years— V&K Distributing Company is the go-to store for Middle Eastern foods.

I invited the proprietor, Chuck Kradjian, 56, to lunch so that I could ask him a few questions, and he obliged. We shared a meal and spoke for more than three hours on a Sunday afternoon. Chuck is a husband and a father, and the third generation Kradjian to operate the business. Chuck's grandfather launched eponymously named Khatcher

Kradjian and Fils in Beirut, Lebanon, in the 1930s and by the 1940s, Chuck's father, Vahe, took over management of the company. In his youth, Chuck would sit at his father's desk at the store and help out with the needs of the shop. When the family moved to America, they re-opened the business in 1988 at their Burbank location with the current name. The first year was very difficult and sales were sparse. In time, the good word spread and the quality, service, and value offered by V&K Distributing Company became known statewide. Chuck cherishes education and earned three bachelor's degrees before his father handed him the keys to the business. In his 90s, Vahe Kradjian still works part-time, checking the books and making sure that Chuck has plenty of support.

I had the pleasure of conducting the following interview with Chuck, in which he shares his wisdom regarding the ethnic and specialty food wholesale business.

Q: *At what point did you take over the business, and how did the transition occur?*

A: When we opened in America, I helped out at the shop and handled deliveries. Over the years, as I took on more responsibilities, my father slowly turned over the reins to me. The process was very gradual.

Q: *Under what legal structure do you operate V&K Distributing Company and why?*

A: We operate as a sole proprietorship. I find that it's less complicated for a business of our size.

Q: *What percentage of your sales are from wholesale and retail respectively?*

A: When we opened in 1988, 30 percent of our sales were from wholesale buyers and 70 percent came from walk-in customers. Today, our wholesale business is 70 percent and our retail shop does 30 percent.

Q: *How do you deliver to your wholesale customers?*

A: We bought two cargo vans and paid cash for them. If one is in the shop, we have another one and we're still covered. We use our own employees to make deliveries.

Q: *What do you consider your trading area?*

A: We are mostly a local and regional business; however, we deliver as far as Sacramento which is 375 miles away. The orders are large enough that I can cover the cost of my driver's time and vehicle expenses and still make a good profit. We deliver everything ourselves and find that it's more cost-effective to do so.

Q: *How do you source and what percentage comes from each source?*

A: We love to source locally whenever possible—for example, our tahini is milled and bottled by a local factory. Importers and distributors provide 50 percent of our goods, which are sourced both domestically and are imported. We source 20 percent of our items factory direct. We obtain 20 percent directly from farmers such as our garbanzo beans, which we bring in from Idaho. Restaurants use a lot of garbanzo beans for salad bars and to make falafel and hummus. The jobbers supply the remaining 10 percent.

Q: *What are some "wow" figures you'd like to share?*

A: In one month, we sell 18,000 pounds of garbanzo beans, 10,000 pounds of tahini, 1,600 pounds of coffee, 4,200 pounds of cheese, 430 cases of filo dough, and 850 gallons of olive oil from our 2,000-square-foot store.

Q: *Who are your main wholesale customers?*

A: Restaurants represent 90 percent and grocers make up the other 10 percent.

Q: *Do you advertise? How do customers find you?*

A: We have no sales reps and do zero advertising. Customers discover us entirely by word-of-mouth. Our delivery drivers are the intelligence officers of our company—they see products at the customers' locations that we did not sell them and we then source these items at a better price to offer to our buyers. When someone places an order, I review past purchases and check their stock on everything they usually buy. I find that 90 percent of the time, they add more items to the order. We accept orders by phone, text, email, and fax, but most are placed over the phone.

Q: *How many people work for you, and what do they do?*

A: Aside from my father and me, there are two employees. You must pay well if you want people to work hard. We pay at least $18 per hour. One person handles deliveries full-time, and the other employee stocks and also helps with deliveries.

Q: *Considering how many deliveries you make, have you had any issues with liability, and if so, how did you deal with them?*

A: In all our years in business, we have had very few issues. Our drivers were involved in only two delivery accidents, and both of them were the fault of the other driver. Our insurance didn't pay for anything. We have Berkshire Hathaway GUARD Insurance covering up to $2 million in liability.

Q: *How do you handle your accounting?*

A: We use a simple cash register and send everything to the accountant monthly. The accountant charges us $400 per month for bookkeeping, and all their work at the end of the year costs approximately $3,000. A good accountant is worth their weight in gold.

Q: *If you had a time machine, what would you do differently?*

A: I would have started out better capitalized because we sold very little in the first year in Burbank, and it was a real struggle—covering all our expenses that year was tough.

Q: *Can you share any helpful tips you feel readers might benefit from learning?*

A: Be mindful of licenses and regulations, which can be complicated. Hire a consultant who really knows the business to get you started. Be friendly to salespeople who want to sell you merchandise, and be always listening—you never know who might become a terrific new supplier. For a business of our size, you should start out with at least $250,000.

## Finding Your Success in Wholesale

So many books that aspire to inspire entrepreneurs focus on huge success stories, but even the largest companies start out small. The largest software wholesaler in the world started in the garage of a college dropout. This young man went on to become the richest person in the world, and his brainchild supplies millions of wholesale software distributors and value-added resellers to this day. Chuck is our everyman. Chuck represents the national ethos of the U.S.—he has achieved the American Dream. The opportunity for prosperity and upward mobility in America is unlimited so long as it's propelled by hard work. Our society has few barriers. Anyone can achieve what Chuck, his father, and his father's father have accomplished. Let's face it—we all want to have rich, successful, and fulfilling personal and professional lives. Wanting to be rich is fine, but launching a startup to simply make a lot of money is soul-sucking, and you'll quickly lose interest. Success for most of us is measured by smiles and good feelings, not merely collecting money and possessions. Get into something that makes you want to jump out of bed in the morning. Nothing will fill your heart with pride faster and evoke good feelings that last longer than helping create jobs.

And it won't always be a sunny picnic—we all make mistakes, but the smartest among us avoid all but the most unavoidable missteps in business because we do what utterly escapes the average person—we ask for advice from experts who are already doing what we aspire to accomplish. The number of right decisions a business owner has to make is not large, but the number of mistakes must not be many. Asking for interest-free credit terms and liberal returns policies with suppliers and using meticulous care in the extension of credit to buyers will go far to prevent derailing your success.

It's so crucial to be open-minded and flexible. Too many films, television shows, sites, and influencers glamorize the business shark and idolize false prophets in those who are tough and aggressive. The consequences of leaving corpses and enemies along the journey are drastic—and often lethal. There is always risk in making decisions, but the rewards for making good decisions are enormous. Being open to reinvention will assure continued operations for years into the future—perhaps leaving a dynasty that continues long after you've left this earth. If information is in short supply, then you haven't asked enough experts. The sharpest operators are looking within and without for clues on the future—examining their own sector and competitors but also looking at other industries for clues.

As we come to the conclusion of this journey together, I caution you to be fiercely protective of your time—avoid unnecessary meetings, conversations, and even people who either don't value your time or aren't in line with your personal and career goals. Any relationship that is the wrong fit becomes an anchor pulling down everything. Be sure to send the elevator down occasionally by helping others, but do so in discrete bites of time that are well-managed so as not to hijack your life before you realize it's been passing by.

It is wise to curate tips and advice from multiple sources—to a point. Family and friends will weigh in on everything you're doing, and it is wonderful to be supported. That said, it's best to solicit input and advice from experts on the subject. You wouldn't ask a dry cleaner for advice on which motor oil you should use in your car—but you would solicit their input on what cleaning and conditioning products to use for the genuine leather car seats. Look at any successful person—they rely on the advice of others—but if you truly want to become better at any skill in business, you'll need to speak with actual experts. While we all want to feel the love, support, and validation of our family and those who are extremely close to us, it is common to receive specious advice from non-businesspeople when talking shop in social situations and at the dinner table. Find out who you want to learn from, and prepare a list of questions that provoke deep thought and produce great answers. And don't be someone who only talks about themselves, rambles, and asks meaningless questions—preparing to be mentored is hard work, and you must always prepare for discussions with others, even more so with high-achievers. Their time is priceless. For every 100 wholesalers whom you ask for advice, a handful will gladly give it with no strings attached.

Wholesale distribution is bigger today than it has ever been in the past. You now have all the tools you need to start your very own wholesale distribution business—and to be the success you've always wanted to be. A business in wholesale trade can give you the financial independence you've been dreaming of while you help other people, and with varied, exciting work dealing with interesting factories, other wholesale distributors, and successful retailers, what could be better? You can do it. I'm so certain of it that I'd like you to email me at borntodeal@gmail.com with your personal success story. I want to hear it, and maybe you'll see it in the next edition of this book—by that time, you'll be an old hand at all of this!

You can do it—you really can. But don't just take my word for it—engage in some spirited business scuttlebutt with the owners of other wholesale distribution companies to gain greater understanding, confidence, and inspiration. Anyone can do this, and so can you. May the odds be ever in your favor.

# Wholesale Distribution Resources

They say you can never be rich enough or thin enough. While that's arguable, I firmly believe you can never have enough resources. Therefore, I'm giving you a wealth of sources to check into, check out, and harness for your own personal information blitz.

These sources are tidbits—ideas to get you started on your research. They are by no means the only sources out there, and they should not be taken as the ultimate answer. I have done our research, but businesses tend to move, change, fold, and expand. As I have repeatedly stressed, do your homework. Get out there and start investigating!

## Government Agencies

*U.S. Small Business Administration*
409 3rd Street, SW
Washington, District of Columbia 20416
https://www.sba.gov
(800) 827-5722

## National, State, and Regional Associations

Scan the QR code below to view the most current list of U.S. industry trade groups.

**Wikipedia's List of Industry Trade Groups in the United States**

Here are some additional resources that you may find helpful. Please email me at borntodeal@gmail.com if you would like to recommend a resource for our next edition of this book.

*Alabama Wholesale Distributors Association*
600 Vestavia Parkway, Suite 220
Birmingham, Alabama 35216
(205) 823-8544

*Alabama Grocers Association*
300 Vestavia Parkway, Suite 3500
Birmingham, Alabama 35216
http://alabamawholesale.org
(205) 823-5498

*Arkansas Convenience Store Distributors*
P.O. Box 7601
Pine Bluff, Arkansas 71611
(870) 534-8565

*California Distributors Association*
1215 K Street, Suite 1500
Sacramento, California 95814
https://californiadistributorsassociation.com
(916) 446-7843

*Colorado Small Business Development Center*
1600 Broadway, Suite 2500
Denver, Colorado 80202
https://www.coloradosbdc.org
(303) 892-3840

*Colorado Wyoming Petroleum Marketers Association and*
*Convenience Store Association*
1410 Grant Street, Suite B-103
Denver, Colorado 80203
https://www.cwpma.org
(303) 422-7805

*Convenience Distribution Association*
11250 Roger Bacon Drive, Suite 8
Reston, Virginia 20190
https://www.cdaweb.net
(703) 208-3358

*Florida Association of Wholesale Distributors*
1844 North Lake Brentwood Road
Avon, Florida 33825
https://fawd.org
(850) 443-3663

*Global Market Development Center*
1275 Lake Plaza Drive
Colorado Springs, Colorado 80906
https://www.gmdc.org
(719) 576-4260

*Idaho Petroleum Marketers and Convenience Store Association*
P.O. Box 984
Boise, Idaho 83701
https://www.wpma.com/idaho
(208) 345-6632

*Idaho Wholesale Marketers Association*
P.O. Box 953
Boise, ID 83701
(208) 342-8900

*Illinois Association of Wholesale Distributors*
601 West Monroe Street
Springfield, Illinois 62704
http://www.iawd.net
(217) 725-2187

*Indiana Wholesale Distributors Association*
2346 S. Lyndhurst Drive, Suite D101
Indianapolis, Indiana 46241
http://iwdanet.org
(317) 610-5997

*Industrial Supply Association*
3435 Concord Road, Unit 21889
York, Pennsylvania 17402
https://www.isapartners.org
(866) 460-2360

*Kentucky Wholesale Distributors Association*
7014 Hughes Avenue
Crestwood, Kentucky 40014
https://www.kwda.net
(502) 223-5322

*Louisiana Association of Wholesalers*
3043 Old Forge Drive, Suite A
Baton Rouge, Louisiana 70808
https://www.louisianawholesalers.org
(225) 767-7640

*Maine Grocers and Food Producers Association*
  P.O. Box 5234
  Augusta, Maine 04332
  https://www.mgfpa.org
  (207) 622-4461

*Michigan Distributors and Vendors Association*
  120 North Washington Square, Suite 110B
  Lansing, Michigan 48933
  https://mdva.org
  (517) 372-2323

*National Association of Wholesaler-Distributors*
  1325 G Street, NW, Suite 1000
  Washington, District of Columbia 20005
  https://www.naw.org
  (202) 872-0885

*Nebraska Grocery Industry Association*
  5935 South 56th Street, Suite B
  Lincoln, Nebraska 68516
  https://www.nebgrocery.com
  (402) 423-5533

*New Jersey Wholesale Marketers Association*
  160 West State Street
  Trenton, New Jersey 08608
  (609) 396-8838

*North Alabama International Trade Association*
  P.O. Box 2457
  Huntsville, Alabama 35804
  https://naita.org
  (256) 532-3505

*North Carolina Beer and Wine Wholesalers Association*
  210 North Person Street
  Raleigh, North Carolina 27601
  https://ncbeerwine.com
  (919) 828-1161

*North Carolina Wholesalers Association*
 4907 Augusta Avenue
 Richmond, Virginia 23230
 (804) 353-2322

*Ohio Wholesale Marketers Association*
 88 East Broad Street, Suite 1240
 Columbus, Ohio 43215
 (614) 224-3435

*Oklahoma Wholesale Marketers Association*
 P.O. Box 32457
 Edmond, Oklahoma 73003
 http://www.owmanet.org
 (405) 880-1939

*Pennsylvania Food Merchants Association*
 P.O. Box 870
 Camp Hill, Pennsylvania 17001
 https://www.pfma.org
 (717) 731-0600

*Southern Association of Wholesale Distributors*
 3459 Lawrenceville Suwanee Road, Suite C
 Suwanee, Georgia 30024
 https://the-southern.org
 (770) 932-3263

*Tennessee Grocers and Convenience Store Association*
 1838 Elm Hill Pike, Suite 136
 Nashville, Tennessee 37210
 http://www.tngrocer.org
 (615) 889-0136

*Texas Food and Fuel Association*
 401 West 15th Street, Suite 510
 Austin, Texas 78701
 https://www.tffa.com
 (512) 476-9547

*Vermont Retail and Grocers Association*
    963 Paine Turnpike North
    Berlin, Vermont 05602
    https://vtrga.org
    (802) 839-1928

*Virginia Beer Wholesalers Association*
    17 East Cary Street
    Richmond, Virginia 23219
    https://vbwa.org
    (804) 783-2655

*Virginia Wholesalers & Distributors Association*
    4907 Augusta Avenue, Suite B
    Richmond, Virginia 23230
    (804) 254-9170

*West Virginia Wholesalers Association*
    2006 Kanawha Boulevard East
    Charleston, West Virginia 25311
    https://www.wvwholesalers.org
    (304) 205-5496

## Legal Assistance

*American Bar Association*
    321 North Clark Street
    Chicago, Illinois 60654
    http://www.findlegalhelp.org
    (800) 285-2221

## Angel Capital

*Angel Capital Association*
    10977 Granada Lane, Suite 103
    Overland Park, Kansas 66211
    https://www.angelcapitalassociation.org
    (913) 894-4700

# Business Lobbyists

*U.S. Chamber of Commerce*
   1615 H Street, NW
   Washington, District of Columbia 20062
   https://www.uschamber.com
   (202) 659-6000

# Export Assistance

*International Trade Administration—U.S. Department of Commerce*
   1401 Constitution Avenue, NW
   Washington, District of Columbia 20230
   https://www.trade.gov
   (202) 482-3809

# Market Research and Publications

*Sumner Communications*
   6 Research Drive, Suite 420
   Shelton, Connecticut 06484
   http://www.sumnercom.com
   (800) 999-8281

*IBISWorld*
   The Trump Building
   40 Wall Street, 15th Floor
   New York, New York 10005
   https://www.ibisworld.com
   (800) 330-3772

*Modern Distribution Management*
   6309 Monarch Park Place, Suite 203
   Niwot, Colorado 80503
   https://www.mdm.com
   (888) 742-5060

*Multichannel Merchant*
>    761 Main Avenue, 2nd Floor
>    Norwalk, Connecticut 06851
>    https://multichannelmerchant.com
>    (954) 389-1442

*Industrial Distribution*
>    199 East Badger Road, Suite 100
>    Madison, Wisconsin 53713
>    https://www.inddist.com
>    (608) 692-2304

# Acknowledgments

would like to extend my most sincere gratitude to Matt Wagner, my longtime literary agent; Jen Dorsey, the editorial director for Entrepreneur Press, for giving me this opportunity; Ben Akrish, the technical editor for this book and my mentee, who has consistently kept me honest and on course; and my employees for helping me become a man.

—C.M.S.

# About the Author

Christopher Matthew Spencer is a Burbank, California-based businessperson, author, and public speaker. He owns wholesale, retail, hospitality, real estate, and publishing companies. Experienced in the field of consulting, he has worked for and advised businesses of different sizes, from startups to companies listed in the Fortune 100. Christopher Matthew is an eight-year veteran of the U.S. Navy. He volunteers at least 10 percent of his time and income to nonprofit causes and takes immense pride in helping entrepreneurs to achieve their dreams and score big in business.

Index

CPSIA information can be obtained
at www.ICGtesting.com
Printed in the USA
JSHW010212080221
11465JS00002B/2